You Cannot Die

YOU CANNOT DIE

IAN CURRIE

The Incredible Findings of a Century of Research on Death

A Patrick Crean Book

Somerville House Publishing
Toronto

The Author has used the work of many investigators in arriving at the conclusions which he expresses in this book. But he does not intend to imply that those whose work he cites would necessarily agree with those conclusions, or with his interpretation of the phenomena which they report. For both of these, he alone is responsible.

In many cases, individuals who reported their experiences to researchers asked to be identified by their initials or first names only, in order to avoid the disruption of their personal lives. Their identities, however, are a matter of formal record and can be obtained by qualified researchers.

Canadian Cataloguing in Publication Data

Currie, Ian, 1936-1992
You cannot die

ISBN 0-921051-98-0 (bound) ISBN 0-921051-90-5 (pbk.)

1. Spiritualism. 2. Death. 3. Future Life.
4. Reincarnation. I. Title.

BF1261.2.C87 1993 133.9'01'3 C93-093455-5

Design by Gordon Robertson

A Patrick Crean Book

Published by Somerville House Publishing,
a division of Somerville House Books Limited:
3080 Yonge Street, Suite 5000, Toronto, Ontario M4N 3N1

Somerville House Publishing acknowledges the financial assistance of the Ontario Publishing Centre, the Ontario Arts Council and the Ontario Development Corporation.

Printed in Canada

for all those who fear death

Heartfelt thanks are due to Betty Robinson, my wife Margaret, my son Chris, and Allan Stormont, Carolyn Brunton, and Carolyn Tanner of Jonathan-James Books for their unstinting aid and support. And for the warm and sustaining friendship of the following people, my gratitude is deeper than I will ever be able to express: Shirley Arbuthnot, Kay Bachman, Kenny Benko, Michael and Barbara Cowan, Beverley Janus, Monica Oliver, Dolores Nord, Danny Gerrard, Jackie Goodman, Frederic Sweet, Steve Iron, David and Margaret Sherman, and Kie and Lynn Delgaty. The generous help of Patricia Fysh and Marjorie Horsley of the University of Toronto's Robarts Library was absolutely indispensable.

CONTENTS

FOREWORD TO THE NEW EDITION

Even in the spiritually sophisticated 1990s, those who freely accept their immortality are a relatively small and select group. Skeptics still laugh hard and scornfully at the idea of life after death, repudiating the unseen world with arrogant disdain. And for every skeptic there are a score of agnostics who shrug their shoulders, choosing not to concern themselves with what they consider to be a remote and otherworldly notion. "Who knows?" they ask dismissively, "Guess I'll find out when my time comes."

In the West especially, orthodox religion and materialistic science have conspired to render immortality a dead issue. Ever since the Church banished the doctrine of reincarnation in the Sixth Century, Christians have been taught that eternity starts at birth—a ludicrous proposition since only the beginningless can be endless. This flawed teaching rendered materialism more attractive as a code by which to live, clearing the way for science to win converts to its blinkered vision, a vision sanctioning no reality outside that which can be seen, touched, heard, smelled, measured, weighed, bought and sold.

This is the legacy we have inherited. While more and more people are now piercing the smokescreen of the centuries to regain the expansive cosmology that so-called primitive peoples have long taken for granted, most educated adults are still constrained by severely hampered perception. Scarcely a thought is given either to the prospect of human origins arising long before birth or to the vast, open-ended future that may succeed the death of the body. To live in such confinement is to be conscious only of the railings at the edge of a precipice even as a magnificent panorama unfolds to the farthest horizon. By failing to appreciate the greater world, these people unknowingly disown their cosmic identity and implicitly deny their unbodily source, their natural home. In shunning their spiritual heritage, they renounce their very reason for being.

If there is one message that rings loud and clear in this landmark book it is the assertion that the living and the dead are one and the same, that the soul is eternal and pursues its quest for knowledge and enlightenment through both material and immaterial worlds. This quest is facilitated by reincarnation, a process allowing the soul to cycle in and out of flesh and blood in the cause of learning and refinement.

To be conscious of one's deathless state is to live an entirely different life here and now, to walk an earthly path *knowing* that the trail stretches across eternity. To realize, in Ian Currie's memorable phrase, that *You Cannot Die* is to know that every thought, word and deed is laden with meaning, purpose and consequence unfettered by time and space. Circumstances and relationships are seen, not merely as passing phenomena, but as significant, willed events with anterior causes and future effects. The eventual cessation of physical life is regarded, not with fear and dread, but as a homecoming, a welcome reprieve from terrestrial toil and suffering, an opportunity for renewal. Such insight invests every living moment with staggering potential.

Souls descend to Earth much like explorers venturing into unfamiliar and difficult terrain. A soul inhabiting a body may be likened to a deep-sea diver who steps into a heavy suit for protection from atmospheric conditions on the ocean floor. Or the incarnating soul can be compared to a mountaineer equipping himself to climb a rockface at high altitude with crampons, goggles, and an oxygen mask. The soul's mission is always the same: to search for knowledge, to learn from experience and, in maturity, to help others do likewise. At the close of each exploration, it is the animating spirit within the bodily envelope that survives physical death. This is the "you" that cannot die.

You Cannot Die was first published in 1978 before metaphysics enjoyed an entrenched renaissance in the West, before the coining of that unfortunate sobriquet "New Age," and before Shirley MacLaine unfurled tales of her past lives and companions in spirit. Refreshingly in advance of the bandwagon, this volume maintains a steady sobriety, earnestly presenting and amplifying the facts without succumbing to speculation. Credible, diverse witnesses offer testimony that, rather than leaning upon credulity, appeals to the rational mind. Ultimately, the reader comes to know rather than to believe.

A Canadian professor of sociology who won ten scholarships and fellowships during a distinguished academic career, Ian Currie was drawn to study the evidence for survival by a compelling desire to fathom the unfathomable. His exhaustive inquiry led through the catacombs of a century of research, through personal accounts and medical studies of deathbed visions, hauntings and apparitions, out-of-body experiences, mediumship, reincarnation, and other related subjects.

The burgeoning casebooks of paranormal phenomena pointed consistently to the persistence of life after death. Currie, however, invited and tested other explanations, among them hallucinations, self-delusion, delirium, and cerebral anoxia or oxygen deprivation. The longer he probed the evidence, the more convinced he became that the inhabiting soul is simply a tenant of the body for as long as that body exists. He concluded that the essential self is a ghost enlivening not only a fleshly husk but also a wispy "astral" body which may peel away, temporarily from the physical form. At death, this wraithlike identity separates permanently to pursue its existence elsewhere. Medical and scientific orthodoxy, of course, scoff at such a proposition. For this reason Currie described awareness of the intrinsic human condition as "one of the best-documented secrets of modern times."

On first publication, *You Cannot Die* found eager audiences in Canada, the United States, Great Britain and the countries of the British Commonwealth. Translations appeared in Italy, Sweden, Norway, Holland and Germany where the book raced to second place on the national best seller list. Ian Currie was suddenly in demand as readers worldwide sought explanations for a welter of uncanny experiences ranging from hauntings to past-life memories. Journalists called upon him as an expert witness on the paranormal. Lectures and interviews followed in rapid succession.

Unwilling to remain an objective authority, Currie soon embarked on a series of personal explorations into the mysteries of life after death. He set out to validate at close quarters the very occurrences which had commanded his attention as a writer. Supremely enthusiastic, he was armed only with courage, curiosity, and the theoretical knowledge gleaned from his research.

With the help of Toronto psychiatrist Dr. Joel Whitton, he examined under hypnosis a succession of his previous incarnations experienced in such space-time locales as ancient Egypt, the Central America of one thousand years ago, and Seventeenth Century Europe. In partnership with medium Carole Davis, he became a "ghostbuster," answering the distress calls of people living in haunted homes and confronting nuisance entities before despatching them to the next dimension. In so doing, he was acting upon a statement from *You Cannot Die:* "The dead are not terrifying, nor are they incomprehensible. They can be understood, communicated with, and freed." Currie also practised past-life therapy, hypnotically regressing clients into earlier existences so that they might glean helpful insights into challenges posed by the current incarnation. In all, he conducted more than 4,000 regressions.

Ian Currie was both a passionate adventurer and a vigorous communicator of the supernatural. On television, he would animatedly describe his exploits, relating helter-skelter how he convinced an apparition to abandon its earthly haunts or, perhaps, how he soothed the anguish of a hypnotised subject whose past-life personality was overwhelmed with remorse for an act of cruelty.

Currie's mission, however, was relatively short-lived. On July 5th, 1992 he drifted from a hospital bed into the "undiscover'd country" which had so fascinated him as a parapsychologist. The man who convinced a host of readers and clients that, to quote Chuang Tzu, "Birth is not a beginning; death is not an end," passed away following surgical complications from a perforated colon. He was 56 years of age. One imagines that he is now savouring justification for his life's work, chuckling sardonically at what he had called the "gigantic mistake" of the scientific establishment's view of death. No doubt he is able to recall his declarative *You Cannot Die* with not a little satisfaction.

Ian Currie left behind preparatory material for two more books, a history of the occult and an exposition of his work in past-life regression. We must be content, however, with this sole contribution to the literature of metaphysical discovery. James Thurber wrote: "All men should strive to learn before they die what they are running from, and to, and why." This book provides the perfect framework of understanding for that vital quest.

Joe Fisher
West Garafraxa, Ontario
December 21st, 1992

INTRODUCTION

THE INCREDIBLE DELUSION

> Birth is not a beginning; death is not an end.
>
> – *Chuang Tsu*

> Were an Asiatic to ask me for a definition of Europe, I should be forced to answer him: It is that part of the world which is haunted by the incredible delusion that man was created out of nothing, and that his present birth is his first entrance into life.
>
> – *Schopenhauer*

FEW PEOPLE are aware that death, man's most ancient, mysterious, and relentless adversary, has been studied systematically over the past century by research scientists working in a variety of fields. Even fewer are aware that the harvest of this effort has been a host of fascinating discoveries which lead to four inescapable conclusions:

- Human beings do survive physical death.
- They continue to exist after death at varying levels of awareness and creativity, in a realm that embodied human beings cannot normally perceive.
- This realm is periodically left when the individual takes on a new body, at which time all memory of it, and of former lives, is erased.

- Successive re-embodiments do not occur at random, but appear to be linked by a mysterious and fascinating law of causation.

These conclusions are stupendous. Their implications are awesome. And they are solidly based on scientific research.

Of all of the mysteries investigated by science, eight of the most fascinating have provided the evidence for these extraordinary statements. They are the phenomena of:

- apparitions
- hauntings
- out-of-the-body experiences
- deathbed visions
- resuscitation experiences
- possession experiences
- reincarnation claims
- mediumistic communications

We are the 2,000th human generation to be haunted by the most fundamental of all of the questions that man can ask himself: "Why am I here? Why do I exist? Where did I come from, and what will become of me?"

We will be the last generation, though, not to know the answer.

CHAPTER ONE

MESSENGERS FROM THE LAND OF THE DEAD: APPARITIONS

The undiscover'd country from whose bourn
No traveller returns
– *Shakespeare (on death)*

My God, what are you doing here? Please go back where you belong.
– *a friend of the author addressing the apparition of her father thirteen years after his death*

WITHIN MAN'S physical body dwells his astral body—the *true* "self" which will survive physical death. During one's lifetime, this astral self can emerge from the living, healthy body and appear to others; it can also appear at the time of the body's death, or months, years, or even centuries *after* death. When the astral body is visible to others, it is known as an apparition. There are thus three kinds of apparitions: those of the living, the dying, and the dead.

Apparitions of the living

Mrs. L.: We were building our summer cottage. Olle, one of the neighbor's boys, went away on holiday just when the foundation was laid, and the house went up during his absence. One evening at dusk … it was still light, [and] I saw [a] man … striding obliquely over the rise up toward the house, dressed in light blue pajamas and [looking] just like Olle. The figure walked *right through the spruce trees* and up to the house, where he stopped, and with hands on hips, studied the house—and then disappeared into nothing.

After a few weeks Olle strolled up just the way the figure in pajamas had, but now he avoided the spruces. He looked up at the house completely terrified and burst out, "But I've seen this before!"

Olle: The L. family had just started leveling and grading for the foundation when I went away, so I had no way of knowing how the house was going to look when it was finished. One night I dreamed I was walking along the path that led up … to the L.'s [cottage site]. In the dream, when I reached the cottage I saw it absolutely clearly … I … saw Mrs. L. standing on the steps as if welcoming me.

Later, when I came back from the trip, I walked over to the L.'s to chat. I was terrified when I caught sight of the cottage; it looked exactly as I'd seen it in the dream, and Mrs. L. sat on the steps. She asked me if I'd worn a pair of light blue pajamas the night I had the dream, and in fact I did. The time corresponded, too.[1]

Apparitions of the dying

When I was about fifteen, I [visited] Dr. G. [in England] and … formed a friendship with [his] cousin, a boy of 17 [named Bertie]. We became inseparable…. One night Dr. G. was sent for to see [Bertie], who had been taken suddenly very ill with inflammation of the lungs, and the poor boy died the next night. They did not tell me how ill he was, so I was quite unaware of his danger…. The night he died, [I was] alone in the drawing-room … reading by firelight … when … Bertie … walked in. I jumped

> up to get him an arm-chair near the fire, as he looked cold, and he had no greatcoat on, and as it was snowing, I began to scold him for coming out without his wraps. He did not speak but put up his hand to his chest and shook his head, which I mistook to mean his cold was on his chest, and that he had lost his voice, to which he was subject. So I reproached him again for his imprudence.... [He] walked across the room to the opposite side of the fireplace, and sat down ... I purposely did not ask him any questions on account of his apparent inability to talk, and I myself went on speaking in order to give him time to regain [his] breath, which, on account of his delicate chest, often occurred.... There was nothing in his appearance that struck me as different from usual, except his paleness and silence.... Dr. G. came in and asked me to whom I was speaking. I said, "There's that tiresome boy without his coat, and such a bad cold he can't speak; lend him a coat and send him home."[2]

But Bertie was already dead. He had been for half an hour. Yet though his body was lying in a house several blocks away, his appearance as an apparition was so utterly lifelike that his friend spoke to him for five minutes without realizing that he was not alive.

Apparitions of the dead

> One November afternoon I arrived home from school, and passing through the dining room I noticed my grandfather in his sitting room talking to my grandmother (who had been ill). She was sitting on the couch brushing and combing her hair. She was in her nightgown and robe. I entered the room and said hello to them, and told my grandmother it was nice to see her feeling up to being out of bed. After a minute or two of polite conversation, I said I had better go do my homework. My grandmother then said, "Barbara, it would be best if you don't tell anyone I was up and that you spoke with me."

> I went on upstairs and as I entered my own room it suddenly came over me that my grandmother was dead! She had died a month earlier. My school books dropped out of my hands....[3]

Are these totally improbable experiences? So it might seem. But research shows that experiences very like them have happened to an astonishing number of people.

The ghostly grandmother above is one kind of apparition of the dead. Let's now look at another, of a very different kind.

> At about ten o'clock in the evening in the beginning of August 1967, I was driving on route 119 [in Sweden] west from Ryd, about a kilometer before the border of Skane. The evening was star bright, crystal clear, and completely calm. I was at ease, driving about ninety [kilometers (about 55 m.p.h.)], listening to the car radio, when a couple of hundred meters in front of me something shadowed right in the headlights' glare. First I thought it was an animal, but when I came nearer I could clearly see that it was a person, walking along apparently oblivious of the approaching car. I dipped the headlights without result.... My astonishment grew as I neared the man. I had never seen anyone now living with such old-fashioned clothes. Now I came right up close by him and eased the car slowly as far out in the left lane as I could.
>
> He was dressed in a loosely fitting, blouselike, collarless, gray coat of coarse material gathered at the waist with a leather thong. The coat hung down and swung loose below the thong. His trousers were gray and of material similar to the coat, rather sack-like and gathered up under the knees with thongs. These had been wound criss-crossed down his shins and were tied to a pair of moccasin-like soft leather shoes. On his head he wore a dark, round, low-crowned hat. Hung from his left shoulder he carried a hunting bag on his right hip, and on his left side a powder horn. In his left hand he carried a long flintlock rifle with a narrow butt and chin piece. I could see that the man had long

hair and wore a rather massive beard. I hoped he'd turn around, so that I could see his face. However, he took absolutely no notice of me but instead just marched along with light, springy steps. Staring steadily at his head, I rolled up alongside him. But at the very instant he appeared through the side window, he vanished!

I braked hard, lit the back lights and hopped out, thinking he'd fallen down, but the road was deserted and empty and the forest stood dark and silent around me.... I became completely terrified and drove away from there at terrific speed.

At the end of November that same year I drove again on the same road. At the same time in the evening and in the same place I saw the man again. A difference was that this time the road was damp and wet and very dark. So I saw the man even more clearly in the headlights' beam ... he was carrying the rifle in his left hand.... It didn't look as if he'd harm me ... and I felt brave enough to decide to get to the bottom of the mystery. So I put the car in neutral, opened the door a bit, lit the back light, and took out a pocket flashlight just before I slowly rolled up alongside the mysterious apparition. Just then I noticed that the man had a shadow! (I hadn't noticed it the first time.)

As I suspected, he disappeared in exactly the same way he had the first time. In a second, I was out of the car on the road, which stretched along just as silent as the time before. Not the slightest sound of footsteps or rustling in the woods. No one huddled down in the ditch by the roadside, no footprints anywhere. I investigated the surroundings of this second occurrence; it was absolutely still and the sky was clear and bright, but there was no moon. The road had no lighting, no buildings in the neighborhood, no other travelers passing by.... No bushes, trees, or other vegetation, no milk-collecting platform, signboard, or anything similar was around, behind which someone out to trick me could have hidden. My windscreen was clean.

After the second experience, I drove to a farm, knocked and asked to use the telephone. But this was just a pretext to ask if

> any eccentric was known in the neighborhood, someone who habitually went out walking with a flintlock. The people at the farm reacted visibly to my question but gave no definite answer. An old woman in the room who was hard of hearing didn't catch my question. When it was repeated for her she burst out, "Good heavens, he's seen the old man!" Then they said it was late and I had to go; I got the impression that they didn't want to talk about it, but did want to get rid of me as quickly as possible.[4]

Clothing of the type described was common in this part of Sweden from the seventeenth century until far into the nineteenth, and a road had existed in the place the man was seen for a very long time. The man is a haunting ghost, tied to a place rather than to people. judging by his garb, he has probably been dead for more than a century. But what is he *doing* there, with his flintlock and his game bag? We *will* be able to answer that question—later. Is he "rare"? Not really. We'll also be meeting some exorcists soon, men and women who deal with such entities on a regular basis, removing them from the dwellings of people like us, people with physical bodies, because they have made them uninhabitable. A weird way to spend your time? Perhaps—but some of them have more work than they can handle.

Contact—with the dead

What barrier could possibly be greater, more total, more absolute, than that between the living and the dead? For with death comes the complete destruction of the physical body. Yet contact with the dead is not rare. It is, in fact, commonplace. In 1973, University of Chicago sociologist Andrew Greeley asked a representative sample of 1,467 Americans a very blunt question: "Have you ever felt that you were really in touch with someone who had died?" The reply was astounding. *Twenty-seven percent said that they had!*[5] A representative sample of the people of only one other country have been asked that question—Iceland. The results are just as interesting—thirty-one percent said yes![6]

Dr. Robert Kastenbaum, a psychologist at Wayne State University in Detroit, asked one hundred and forty people whether they had ever had an experience of contact with the dead. A resounding forty-five percent said that they had.[7] Dr. W.D. Rees, a British physician, talked to three hundred widows and widowers in Wales. Forty-seven percent admitted that they had had experiences—often occurring repeatedly over a period of years—which had convinced them that their dead spouses had been in contact with them.[8] Two other studies of widowed spouses have uncovered identical findings. Dr. Earl Dunn talked to Canadian widows,[9] Dr. P. Marris to British ones.[10] A full fifty percent of each group reported contact experiences with the dead spouse. Far from expecting such contacts, many worried that they might be "going crazy," and fearing ridicule, had kept completely silent about their dead visitors.

Some of the dead had been "felt." Others actually spoke. But in the most dramatic cases, they were seen.

> My husband died in August, 1970. The following Christmas I spent with my married daughter.... On ... Dec. 27th ... we were all playing Monopoly and at that time I was not even thinking of my husband. I looked up from my game and my husband was sitting on the settee opposite. This I could not believe. I covered my eyes with my hands and looked again; he was still there. I then ... counted the people present and there were six of us, not five. I must have looked very distressed, everyone looked up from the game and enquired what was wrong. I was a little incoherent and wept, and my husband got up from the settee, crossed the room ... and went out, turning at the last moment, putting his head back inside the door and smiling at me. He appeared as in life ... wearing his charcoal colored trousers and an open necked white shirt. I was overcome with grief and went to bed at once.[11]

The dramatic power of this contact is quite characteristic of such experiences. Here is another case:

> At 3:15 a.m. on Xmas morning [my wife] died … I brought her body home … where it lay until … I buried her in the grave she herself had chosen…. For some six weeks after her death I remained quite certain that [she] still lived and that we would meet again. Then doubts concerning survival after death began to assert themselves, as had often been the case with me in past years. Gradually I reached a state of disquieting uncertainty, when I could only … hope, and finally I lost even that…. A week or two later the event which I now relate took place….
>
> Shortly before sundown I was walking in the wood at the rear of [my] house with my wife's sister…. We had been looking at the seedling trees which my wife had planted before she was taken ill. I remarked on how gratified she would have been to see how well they were doing. Her sister replied: "I'm quite sure that she does know, and that she often comes to see them." I said nothing, for I did not wish to shake a faith which I had ceased to share. We returned to the garden which lies to the front of the house, my sister-in-law turning east to shut up the chickens, and I to the west, for the purpose of closing the shutters over the French windows of the drawing-room. As I made my way along the path in front of the house, I was not thinking of my wife but of a neighbour to whom I had sent some valuable books and, as I walked, I was picturing his pleasure on opening the parcel. As I reached the rose garden, on which the drawing-room windows open, I came instinctively to an immediate halt, for standing on the lawn beyond the rose garden and less than thirty yards from me was my wife. She stood looking straight at me as though she had been expecting me. Her face and figure were as distinct and as clear-cut as in life. She wore no hat and the slight evening breeze did not ruffle her hair or disturb the folds of her dress. She was clad in a perfectly fitting soft grey gown which reflected the shadows thrown on it by the pergola behind her…. She looked

> in perfect health but what struck me most was the expression with which she regarded me. Steadily, without change of aspect, she gazed intently at me without suggestion of either joy or sorrow, but with a puzzled look of remonstrance as though she were surprised and disappointed with me over something which I was doing and from which she wished me to desist. Translated into words her expression would well have been rendered by: "How stupid of you!" ... The vision lasted a full minute at least ... although I believe that I smiled and that my face reflected my joy at seeing her, I made no attempt to speak or to approach her. With her eyes still meeting mine, she faded from my sight—not suddenly but quite gradually.[12]

People do not take such experiences lightly. They are intensely vivid experiences, unforgettable, shocking, even terrifying. And they have happened to literally millions of people. They have been repeatedly studied, in the 1890s, 1930s, 1940s, and 1970s. They are a human universal, a recurring theme in the literature and folklore of all societies, and all ages. There's a reason for that. *They're real.*

What are apparitions like?

Most apparitions are so completely lifelike that they are typically mistaken for real persons. In February, 1950, Mrs. Jessie Glasgow moved into an apartment with her husband and six-year-old daughter, Susan. A few days later Susan saw a woman standing in the living room of the apartment. Slight of build and short in stature, she was wearing a long black dress and a black veil pulled well down over her forehead. Susan went into the kitchen to tell her mother about their puzzling visitor, and her mother, believing Susan's story to be a fantasy, said lightly, "Ask her if she'd like a cup of tea." Susan returned to the living room, where the woman, who had been facing away from her, was now turned toward her. "Would you like a cup of tea?" Susan asked her. The woman, whose face Susan described as kindly, smiled at her but did not reply. Susan returned to the kitchen to report that the lady would not answer her. When the two returned to the living room, their mysterious visitor had vanished. (An embodied person could neither have entered nor left the living room without being seen through the open kitchen door.) Their apartment was in a building which had at one time been a convent school, staffed by nuns. The lady, dressed in a nun's habit, and absolutely lifelike in her appearance, had been an apparition.[13]

In fact, the amazingly "real" quality of most apparitions approaches the uncanny:

> As a nine-and-a-half-year-old, one of my more pleasant household "chores" was to take the baby up to bed at six p.m., and sing him to sleep.... The baby having duly fallen asleep, I levered myself gingerly off the bed, so as not to waken him, and quietly opened the bedroom door, still watching the baby to make sure he didn't "disturb." As I turned my head, I was gazing directly at the window on top of the stairs, along the landing from me. Sitting on the landing window-sill was a very old man. I was startled into immobility.... He was very old, rheumy-eyed, grey-haired. He wore old, dirty-looking dark trousers, a cream Welsh flannel shirt without a collar, unbuttoned at the neck, an extremely dirty-looking old "weskit" which was food and grease-stained. He had a muffler tied round his neck.... On his head was an old bowler hat, black, and past its best by many a long day. The muffler, by the way, was black, red, and white, the old man was leaning on a walking stick, his two old hands folded one on the other on top of the stick. His mouth was open slightly, and slack, as some old men look, and I'm sure that if he had been a living man, I would have [heard] his breathing quite clearly. As it was, I could only hear street noises from outside. The man's head was slightly inclined towards the window but he was not gazing out through the window. With hindsight, I realise now that he was *listening*, from his window seat ... this apparition lasted about ten seconds ... [and then] vanished as suddenly as a

> light goes out. I can't say I had been "rooted to the spot" ... it was just that I ... stood stock-still with surprise.[14]

Later she saw the apparition again—dressed precisely as before, dirty, rheumy, and food-stained still.

But apparitions—quite apart from the fact that they don't have physical bodies—are *not* "just like people." They often display astounding eccentricities of appearance, movement, and departure, which have given rise to much of the folklore about ghosts.

> My bedroom was on the first floor, the door of this was at the foot of the stairs leading to the next floor. The bathroom and toilet were on my floor at the end of a fairly long corridor amply lighted throughout the night. The time would be about 2:30 a.m. as I went *just as usual* to the toilet. Returning I saw what I was certain in my mind was a middle-aged or elderly female wearing a dressing gown partly over her head and shoulders, crossing the corridor toward the stairs outside my bedroom door. Quite sure that this was a flesh and blood person I wondered briefly why the gown was worn in that way. Visitors ... were very frequent, so I was not surprised to see a stranger, but assumed she was a guest.
>
> I surmised that by the time she would be about three or four steps up the stairs we would just about draw level, and as we did so I turned my head towards her intending to say, "Hello, another Night Rake." "She" stood still, and turned "her" head towards me. The words died in my throat and "she" bent slightly forward as though to continue upwards. I saw with a dreadful shock, not a woman but the shadowy cadaverous face of a man wearing the hooded habit of a monk. *I could see the wall through the phantom*, yet "she" had appeared solid enough from a few yards distant. The fact that the figure turned toward me convinces me that "he" was fully aware of my presence. I was chilled with shock ... dashed into my room.... I was badly scared.[15]

Not content with mere transparency, apparitions often compound our consternation by gliding along above the ground in open defiance of the law of gravity, entering and exiting through solid doors and walls, and fading away before our very eyes:

> Some years ago, a friend and I were returning from an outlying village. It was a mild clear night with half-moon. Coming through an avenue of trees, we approached a large open field with houses on the opposite side of the road. *Appearing to float across that field,* just above ground level, was the figure of a woman with arms slightly outstretched. She was completely colorless, with the exception of her long fair hair which streamed behind her. We both stopped dead and watched. To our utter bewilderment, she disappeared straight through the wall of the convent school opposite. A man cycling towards us dismounted and enquired, "Did you see that?" We replied we certainly had. He left us saying, "That's the third time—I don't like it, I don't like it!" "She" was gliding roughly one and a half feet above ground level.[16]

In 1943 Mrs. Gill was living in a large and very old house in Middlesex, a house which provided her with a midnight experience which she will never forget:

> During the war I had a bed in an indoor shelter in my hall; and in September 1943 I was resting about midnight and awaiting my call for 1 a.m. duty in the wardens' post outside my drive gates *when a woman in a morning dress of the Victorian age "floated" through the closed door of my music room, which faced me, and went through the closed front door.* Ten days later a friend who had heard my story produced a head-and-shoulders photograph of the woman I had seen. She was a Mrs. Drake who had been mistress of my house more than seventy years before.[17]

Equally disconcerting are sudden or gradual disappearances, in complete defiance of everyday laws of optics:

> One summer evening, when I was twenty … I went for a … drive … with a friend.… we stopped … near J. Farm.… It was quite light. We sat quietly, just enjoying the evening. Looking up the road I saw an old lady walking slowly down, with a shawl round her shoulders, skirt to her feet. She was leaning heavily on a stick. I thought she looked worn out, and wondered why she had come so far from the houses. She crossed right in front of the car … I turned my head, to look at her. She saw me, for the first time. A look of anger came on her face. *She vanished like a bubble bursting.*[18]

The dead can do such things because they now occupy their astral bodies—which may become invisible, defy gravity, and pass through physical matter. As we will later see, the living have astral bodies too.

Messengers from the land of the dead

According to Shakespeare, the land of the dead is one from whose domain no traveler returns. But with all due respect, the great bard was wrong—and spectacularly so. The dead *do* return. And because they are, in fact, so much like us, their reasons for coming back can, with a little effort, be understood.

Death compacts

The British Society for Psychical Research was founded in 1882. In the past century, it has collected in its files thousands of cases of apparitions of the dead. Of these, about one in twenty involves "death-compacts."[19] The motive behind such agreements is an understandable one—to find out if we survive death. Two people may arrange that, if the one who dies first finds himself still alive after the death of his body, he will attempt to appear to the other. As the S.P.R. statistics show, *quite a number of these agreements have been fulfilled.* Here is a typical example of such a compact:

> I awoke … and saw a brother who had been dead more than five years standing at the foot of my bed. He stood still, gazing at me earnestly.… I said, "Oh Arthur!" and jumped up to go to him, when he vanished.… My brother … had said he would appear after death if possible.[20]

And he did. So have a lot of other people, including a school friend of Lord Brougham, an English peer.

Brougham was traveling in Sweden with friends. Tired and chilled, they stopped at an inn for the night, where Brougham luxuriated in a hot bath before going to bed. And while in the tub, he had what can only be described as a remarkable experience. When at university, he and a friend, identified only as "G.," often speculated on the question of whether the dead survived, and whether, if they did, they could ever appear to the living. "We actually committed the folly," he says, "of drawing up an agreement, written in our blood, to the effect that whichever of us died first should appear to the other." After graduation, G. took a Civil Service job in India; the years passed, and Brougham had almost forgotten G.'s existence.

> While lying in the tub and enjoying the comfort of the heat, after the … freezing I had undergone, I turned my head round, looking toward the chair on which I had deposited my clothes, as I was about to get out of the bath. *On the chair sat G., looking calmly at me.* How I got out of the bath I know not, but on recovering my senses I found myself sprawling on the floor. The apparition … of G. had disappeared. The vision produced such a shock that I had no inclination to talk about it … it … was too vivid to be … forgotten; and so strongly was I affected … that I wrote down the whole story, with the date, 19th December.… Soon after my return to Edinburgh, there arrived a letter from India, announcing G.'s death, and stating that he had died on the 19th of December.[21]

Mrs. Arthur Bellamy of Bristol, England, made a similar agreement while still a schoolgirl with a friend, Miss W. Years later, Mrs.

Bellamy, who had not seen or heard anything of her former schoolfriend for many years, learned that she had died. Remembering their agreement, and becoming nervous, she confided in her husband, who had never seen a photograph of his wife's friend, nor heard any description of her.

> A night or two afterwards ... I ... awoke, and saw a lady sitting by the side of the bed where my wife was sleeping soundly. At once I sat up ... and gazed so intently that even now I can recall her ... features ... I remember that I was much struck, as I looked intently at her, with the careful arrangement of her coiffure, every single hair being most carefully brushed down.

After some minutes, the lady disappeared. When his wife awoke, Mr. Bellamy described their mysterious visitor.

> I described her, ... all of which exactly tallied with my wife's recollection of Miss W. Finally I asked, "Was there any special point to strike one in her appearance?" "Yes," my wife promptly replied: "We girls used to tease her at school for devoting so much time to the arrangement of her hair."[22]

"I'm dead!"

Contact between the living and the dead can be more spontaneous than the fulfillment of a death compact by an apparition. When momentous events happen to people, they usually feel like telling somebody about it. Imagine that you are now dead. What's the first thing you would want to do? Tell those who are closest to you, of course. And in fact, precisely this motive is apparent in many apparition cases. Here are a few typical examples of such "visits" by the newly-dead.

Second Lieutenant Leslie Poynter was killed on October 25th, 1918. That evening at nine o'clock, his sister, miles away in England, had just settled herself in bed when she saw him enter her room. He bent over and kissed her, a kiss which she "did not feel," and then stood up and looked at her, smiling. "I've never seen anyone look so intensely happy in my life," she said. "This is one of the things that makes me know there's a second life or he would not have looked like that."[23] As she watched, he faded away. Two weeks later a War Office telegram informed the family of his death on that date.

The absolute realism of such experiences often makes witnesses believe that the "appearer" is still alive and paying an unexpected visit. Flight-Lieutenant Ronald Sokell, for example, served in the British forces in the Second World War. On the night of November 24th, 1944, his mother was at home in bed, asleep; his father, a Unitarian minister, was away on a preaching engagement.

> There was brilliant moonlight and at 2 a.m. she woke to see her son, in his RAF uniform, standing by her bed. He appeared to be physically solid. "Hullo, Ron," she said, but he did not answer, although he looked down at his mother and appeared quite calm ("maybe a little puzzled that his daddy wasn't with me"). Mrs. Sokell did not feel fear or alarm and fell asleep. Two hours later she woke again and the figure of her son was still there. Although she addressed him, he did not reply.[24]

Two days later the Sokells received a telegram. Their son was missing on a bombing mission, and Mrs. Sokell had seen him on the night of the flight from which he did not come back. "I knew," she said, "that he would never return."

Sometimes, in fact, the apparitional visitor does more than simply indicate his death—he may "demonstrate" it. In another case of a strange visitation, a Mrs. Paquet wakened feeling depressed and sought solace in a cup of tea, but she was not to drink it in tranquility:

> I turned around [and saw] my brother Edmund [standing] only a few feet away ... with his back toward me ... [he] was in the act

> of falling forward—away from me—seemingly impelled by two loops … of rope drawing against his legs. [In] a moment, [he disappeared] over a low railing or bulwark … I dropped the tea, clasped my hands to my face, and exclaimed, "My God! Ed is drowned!"[25]

What she saw had in fact happened. Six hours earlier her brother had drowned, just as he had shown her.

The above three apparitions were silent. Some, however, make their motives perfectly clear by speaking.

> On the night of June 11, 1923, in Indianapolis, Mrs. Gladys Watson … was awakened from a deep sleep by someone quietly but insistently calling her name. As she roused and sat up, she was astonished to see her paternal grandfather, to whom she was devoted, leaning toward her. He looked perfectly real and lifelike. There was a pleasant smile on his face. "Don't be frightened," he reassured her in a warm, affectionate voice. "It's only me. I've just died." Mrs. Watson found tears starting in her eyes and she instinctively reached across the bed to rouse her sleeping husband. "This is how they'll bury me," her grandfather said, indicating the dark suit and black bow tie he was wearing. He added: "I just wanted to tell you I've been waiting to go ever since mother was taken." Gladys Watson could see that her grandfather looked as solid as though he were physically present in the room. And she heard his voice not with an inner ear but as though he were actually speaking to her.[26]

Mrs. Watson shook her husband again, but the apparition had vanished before he awakened. He told her that she had simply been dreaming, and that her grandfather was alive and well with her parents in Wilmington. Because she was so upset he decided to prove it by phoning them—only to learn that his wife's grandfather had died at home a few minutes before.

Loving concern and confusion

The apparitional visitors we have been discussing appear because they want to make contact with specific people for obvious purposes: to fulfil a death compact, or to communicate the fact of their own deaths. There are two other common motives for the appearance of non-haunting apparitions: a loving concern for particular living persons, and a temporary confusion on the part of the recently-dead over their new "state." (Should this confusion become prolonged—and it can—they could become "haunting" apparitions.)

The confusion experienced by apparitions of the dead may be cheerful and unwitting or dazed and uncomprehending, but in either case, it indicates a failure to grasp that death has taken place. Thus, although resuscitation experiences suggest that those who die realize it, there are obviously some cases in which people don't immediately understand what has happened to them.

In June of 1935 Mr. T.M. Healey was a fifteen-year-old schoolboy living with his parents in Middleton, a suburb of Leeds, England.

> Riding home from school on my bicycle on 16 or 17 June 1935, I was traveling along Dewsbury Road, Leeds, and coming to a busy crossroads called Hunslet Hall Road. I saw my grandfather, James … Healey, approaching me and walking in the opposite direction. As we passed each other at a distance of six or eight feet I waved to him and shouted, "Hello, Grandad." I was quite used to seeing him at approximately this place, perhaps two or three times a week, because he regularly went to a shop nearby to buy his tobacco. His appearance was distinguished by a luxuriant walrus moustache and the fact that he always carried a walking stick. In his usual manner Grandad lifted his stick and waved back at me, calling, "Hello, Morton." I rode on, and Grandad walked on without stopping towards his home. I did not look round; even if I had wanted to, the traffic was too busy.
>
> A few minutes after I arrived home I casually mentioned to my mother and my step-father, "I saw Grandad on my way

home." There was a long silence as my parents looked at each other, and then my step-father said, "You had better tell him," and he left the room. My mother then told me that my grandfather had died three days earlier.[27]

The following experience occurred in 1975.

Across the road from me lived a brother and sister called Peggy and Bill Smith. They were very devoted to each other, having lived together for nearly fifty years, since the death of their parents. Both were in their seventies. I was a great friend of both of them, as they were young in heart. I had been away for several weeks at my [parents'] home in Suffolk.... On coming back to Greenwich, I did not go out for three or four days....

Then one day I decided to go to the library and had to pass the Smiths' house. It was bitterly cold and snowing, and to my surprise I saw ... Bill Smith standing in the garden wearing a light-colored summer shirt. He looked very ill. I stopped to speak to him, telling him, gently, that he really ought not to be out in such cold weather without a warm coat, etc. He never answered but looked straight through me, and after a short monologue on my part, I decided I'd better go. (Privately, I thought he'd gone a bit senile.) I looked back after some fifty yards, and he was still there, staring after me. When I got home, I remarked to my husband that I'd seen Bill, how ill he looked, and that he didn't seem to know I was there....

Three days later I went to a female coffee morning—about ten people were there, including Peggy Smith, Bill's sister. The conversation turned to holidays, and someone mentioned a hotel in Scotland that catered specially for older people—and I remarked impulsively to Peggy, "Why, that sounds just the place for you and Bill! No stairs, etc." There was a ghastly silence! I rambled on, wondering if I'd made some sort of faux pas ... then someone had the sense to say, "Bill died six weeks ago, suddenly, when you were away...." I said, "But I was only talking to him

> three days ago...." Then to my embarrassment, Peggy Smith broke down in uncontrollable weeping, and I offered to take her home, which I did. I made feeble excuses to her—but—I *had* seen and spoken to her brother, several weeks after he was dead, although I had *no* previous knowledge of his death whatsoever. It was an incident none of my friends ever forgot![28]

"Loving concern" for the living is expressed by apparitions in a variety of ways, ranging from a social visit that is almost casual in quality to intervention if the life of a living person is threatened. The following two experiences are typical of visits by the dead of the casual, almost "social" kind.

> Our eight-year-old daughter died in 1967 and about two weeks after she died, as I sat down after my lunch, I distinctly saw her in the chair opposite, just as we always sat at this time. I was conscious of my brain questioning what my eyes saw ... but was overjoyed to see my daughter.... I'm sure I'd have always doubted my own eyes, but for the fact that Rosemary spoke so clearly. She said in a matter-of-fact way, "My foot is better," and swung her foot towards me. This was something that had worried her during her long illness in hospital, but she had so much else to contend with that we never told the doctor about it. Although she was sitting facing me, I realized that it was the affected foot she swung. I had forgotten about it in the grief of her death.[29]

In another case, a husband and wife both saw the apparition of a dead relative:

> Nearly twelve years ago my mother died. My son was then eleven years of age. A month after she died I went upstairs to fetch something. The landing light was on and my son's bedroom door was open and he was asleep. As I passed the door I saw my mother standing at the foot of the bed. She looked so normal

> that in that instant I forgot that she was dead and turned to laugh at her (we always said she spent more time looking at her grandson than talking to us when she came to stay) ... my amusement quickly turned to amazement, whereupon she put her finger to her lips and gently shook her head as much as to say, "Don't make a sound. He would wake and be frightened." As I watched she smiled a happy smile and disappeared. She had looked quite solid but as she went it was from the feet upwards.... I did not mention this to my husband for some weeks, expecting he would think me fanciful. When I did he said, "Oh yes, I saw her several times, but like you thought it was better kept to myself."[30]

Many appearances of the dead seem to be motivated by a very simple, and very human, concern: "Don't grieve for me because I'm fine, and I still love and feel close to you:"

> My mother died in December 1945 ... I saw [her] ghost ... the following May. I had done a day's teaching, which had given me a rest from grief. I had come home, and gone into a rather dark passage to leave my outdoor things. Suddenly I saw my mother. She was about three feet away from me. The sun never shone into the passage, but she was radiant as if in full sunlight. She looked quite solid and clear in outline. She looked very young, about twenty. I particularly noticed her rich, high colour. Her hair was arranged in two full puffs above her forehead. She was so clear that I could see the texture of her jacket and skirt. She was wearing a cinnamon brown woollen jacket of a twill weave and rather soft material, a skirt with a small black and white check, also woollen, and a dark blue and green shot silk blouse. The clothes were of the style of the 1890s.
>
> I felt myself surrounded by her love and sympathy. It was not the sympathy she had given me in my adult sorrows, but the sympathy shown to my childish griefs. I do not know how long I stood there. Suddenly she had gone. Later, I told my sister. She

> said, "Yes, yes," but did not believe me. But when I described her clothes, she said, "Yes, you've seen her, Mary. She had those clothes when she was in college."[31]

The concern expressed may be entirely in keeping with the former relationship between the dead and the living. A dead grandfather visited his granddaughters, with results which went well beyond his intentions:

> I was … eleven years old. We lived in my grandmother's house in Slough, along with many other relatives, due to the housing shortage. I shared a large double bed with my sister Janet, who was then six years old. She had been asleep for some time, but I was awake because there were visitors downstairs and the noise was considerable. It was a bright, frosty moonlit evening and very light still in our room. Suddenly I realized I felt squashed and turned over to push Janet back to her side of the bed. My grandfather was lying in between us, on his back but with his head turned, looking at Janet. I asked him what was the matter, thinking it most strange that he should be in our bed at all. He turned his face towards me, when I spoke, and I put my hand out and started stroking his beard. (He always allowed me to brush it for him as a special treat.) He answered quietly, saying not to jump around too much in case I woke Janet, and that he was only making sure we were all right. It was only then that I remembered that he had died the previous June, and the fear and horror I felt then can be imagined and I started screaming for my mother. The grown-ups passed it off as a bad dream, but I was able to tell them a lot of their conversation of the evening, that had drifted up to me, as I lay awake.[32]

And finally we come to the most dramatic examples of loving concern expressed by the dead for the living, cases in which the dead intervene *to protect the lives* of the living. In the fall of 1949, Elaine Worrel and her husband Hal were living in an apartment on the top floor of an old house in Oskaloosa, Iowa. In another apartment on that floor lived Patricia Burns, a young woman recently widowed. Their relationship was limited to a polite exchange of greetings when they passed in the hall. One Saturday Elaine had gone down the hall to have a bath. While searching in the dark bathroom for the light switch, she smelled pipe smoke. Suddenly a tall young man was standing beside her. His eyes were grey. He had black, curly hair and a horseshoe-shaped scar on his left cheekbone. In one hand he held a briar pipe. An unaccountable feeling of urgency rose in her, and she felt mysteriously compelled to follow him up the hall toward Patricia's apartment, where he suddenly vanished. Although it was not at all characteristic of her to be so boldly intrusive, she felt that she must enter the apartment. Opening the door, she found a lightswitch. There on the bed lay Patricia, bright red blood flowing from slashed wrists. Staunching the bleeding, Elaine called her husband, who soon arrived with a doctor. Patricia later thanked Elaine for saving her life. Despondent, overwhelmed by grief, she had impulsively determined to join her husband. But he, as it turned out, had had other ideas. When Patricia showed Elaine a picture of her husband, Raymond, she immediately recognized the mysterious man with the pipe, who had so unaccountably vanished.[33]

This is not a unique case. In a number of others, the same motive—to save the lives of the living—can clearly be seen. Consider what happened to Betty Gray, who now lives in southeast London.

> On 20 January 1943 I was a thirteen-year-old schoolgirl attending Catford Central School. My father had been seriously ill in hospital for some months. My mother went to work and I left for school at 8:30 a.m. At 12:45 it was lunchtime at school. The lower floor had some reinforced classrooms acting as shelters, and the hall on the ground floor was full of children eating lunch. We heard a distant air-raid warning so some of us made our way down to the shelters. There were children in the playground, and as we reached the ground floor we heard them call

out that two planes were flying round low over the roof tops. Then someone shouted, "They're Jerries" [Germans], so we ran for the nearest reinforced classroom. I was just inside the doorway when a bomb hit the school, demolishing two-thirds of the building.

For some seconds it was silent (or I went deaf). Then there were deafening screams, as it was pitch black and our mouths were full of grit and dust. We just stood petrified, screaming. Suddenly, to my left, I saw a ray of light and my father stood there, and I said, "Oh Dad, help us." He just smiled and beckoned, so I called out, "Come on, it's my Dad—this way." We went towards the light and found a space in the debris out into the playground.

About two hours later, arriving home, I was surprised to find mother there because she normally didn't get home until five. She said, "A policeman came to the works to tell me Dad died this morning at 8 o'clock."[34]

Phantom animals

We have looked at evidence that people have apparitional bodies which can sometimes appear, after death, to the living. If people have apparitional bodies, why can't animals have them, too? The answer is that they can, and do. Quite a few people have seen apparitions of animals, and here we find a very interesting parallel with human apparitions: there are haunting animal ghosts who frequent a particular place, and there are non-haunting ones which appear, after death, to people to whom they were close.

In the following case, a dead cat was seen by four different people, appearing so lifelike that its body was finally dug up to make sure it was really dead. Smoky was a pure-bred blue Persian of quite distinctive appearance. After being severely bitten by a dog, she had died.

My sister and I were at breakfast ... I was sitting with my back to the window, which was on my sister's left. Suddenly I saw her

> looking absolutely scared, and gazing out of the window. I said, "What is the matter?" and she said, "There's Smoky, walking across the grass!" We both rushed to the window and saw Smoky, looking very ill, her coat rough, ... walking lamely across the grass in front of the window, three or four yards from it. My sister called her, and as she took no notice, she ran out after her, calling her. I remained at the window, and saw the cat turn down a path leading to the end of the garden. My sister ran after her, calling her, but to her surprise, Smoky did not turn or take any notice, and she lost sight of her among the shrubs. About ten minutes afterwards, my sister and a friend living with us saw Smoky again going through a hedge in front of the window.... She was next seen about half an hour afterwards by the servant, in the kitchen passage. She ran to get her some milk and followed her with it, but the cat walked away.... Of course we thought there had been some mistake about her death.... The gardener was so indignant at the suspicion that he had not buried the cat, that he went to the grave ... and dug up the body of Smoky.[35]

This was a haunting—by a cat, who had returned from the grave not to see her former masters (indeed, she *ran away* when pursued by the narrator's sister), but simply to frequent her familiar surroundings.

But animals also return from the grave to see loved ones, just as human beings do:

> Thirteen years ago, I was in the Army, stationed in Germany, and coming home on leave by ship, and train, usually meant arriving home somewhere during the early hours of the morning. My parents knew on which day I was arriving, and left the back door open. This meant going through a dark passage between the two houses.... I had made good friends with the next-door neighbor's dog "Bobby," a large black mongrel. Before I went in the Army, we had grown very fond of each other, and an outsider would have thought he was my dog—I would take

him for walks every day without fail. I volunteered for the Army to be a Regular Soldier, but my attachment to the dog was so great, that I almost didn't "join up." Nevertheless, I did, but don't mind admitting I suffered quite a lot of emotional upset over the dog.

On the night in question, I arrived home at about 2 a.m., and sure enough, as soon as I opened the side gate, "Bobby," who normally slept in a kennel outside the house, bounded up to me, and made a terrific fuss of me, nuzzling and licking my face. I stayed with him for some ten minutes or so, and then went indoors. There is no question in my mind, to this day, that I played with "Bobby" for that short time. I knew and loved him so well, that there couldn't possibly be any mistake about his identity. As he left me, he disappeared out of sight into my neighbor's large dahlia bed, and that was the last I saw of him.

The following morning after an enjoyable reunion with my family, I made my usual visit to my neighbor, the dog's owner, who was a very great friend of ours. I told him about meeting Bobby the previous night, and remarked quite casually that he was out of his kennel (he was normally kept chained in). My neighbour was thunderstruck, and said, "Bobby died three months ago, and is buried in the middle of the dahlias."[36]

Are they just hallucinations?

I have given many talks on apparitions of the dead. Almost invariably, someone in the audience will get to his feet, and usually looking either frightened or indignant will say, "Yeah, I've heard about all this stuff. It's just hallucinations!"

It would be comfortingly easy to explain such experiences as hallucinations, or the figments of an overworked imagination. But this would be dishonest, for there are serious flaws in the hallucination theory. What are they?

The normality of the witnesses

To begin with, seeing apparitions of the dead turns out to be an extremely "democratic" phenomenon. If these experiences happened only to occultists or spiritualists, they could be readily dismissed. Instead, the vast majority of those who see apparitions are perfectly ordinary people. In fact, about the only thing they seem to have in common is their normality, and it is *rare* for a witness to state that he has had more than one or two such experiences in his entire lifetime.[37] Furthermore, the great majority of witnesses are in a state of normal health, physically and emotionally. But how about their state of mind just before the experience? Hardly any report anything in any way unusual in the way of shock, stress, or elation; virtually all were in a perfectly ordinary frame of mind. But surely they were *expecting* something peculiar to happen? Again, no. The experience was totally unexpected, occurred in familiar surroundings,[38] and "burst in" on them while they were going about their daily business.[39] *And there are so many of them*—one in every four people has had an experience which convinced him that he was in contact with someone who was dead![40]

Collective experiences

Hallucinations are purely subjective—they are seen only by the hallucinator. *But many apparitions of the dead have been seen collectively, which means that they cannot be hallucinations.* The number of people involved in these shared, and therefore non-hallucinatory experiences, ranges from two to as many as nine. Let's consider an example at each end of that spectrum.

On Christmas Eve, a young English couple with a busy day ahead of them decided to go to bed early. They were settled in bed by 9:30, with the light still on, as the baby was expected to wake up for a feeding. The wife wrote:

> I [was] just pulling myself into a half-sitting posture against the

> pillows, thinking of nothing but the arrangements for the following day, when to my great astonishment I saw a gentleman standing at the foot of the bed, dressed as a naval officer, and with a cap on his head having a projecting peak.... He was leaning upon his arms which rested on the foot-rail of the bedstead.

The lady was astounded by the sudden appearance of this mysterious visitor, as the doors of the house, including their bedroom door, were locked, and there had been no sound of footsteps, no doors had opened, nothing had happened to alert them to the fact that they were about to receive an unexpected social call in their bedroom.

> I was too astonished to be afraid, but simply wondered who it could be; and instantly touching my husband's shoulder (whose face was turned from me), I said, "Willie, who is this?" My husband turned, and for a second or two lay looking in intense astonishment at the intruder; then lifting himself a little, he shouted, "What on earth are you doing here, sir?"
>
> Meanwhile the [man], slowly drawing himself into an upright position, now said in a commanding, yet reproachful voice, "Willie! Willie!" I looked at my husband and saw that his face was white.... As I turned towards him he sprang out of bed as though to attack the man, but stood by the bedside as if afraid ... while the figure calmly and slowly moved towards the wall. As it passed the lamp, a deep shadow fell upon the room as of a ... person shutting out the light from us by his body, *and he disappeared ... into the wall.*
>
> My husband ... very agitated ... turning to me said, "I mean to look all over this house, and see where he is gone." I was by this time exceedingly agitated too, but remembering that the door was locked, and that the mysterious visitor had not gone towards it at all, remarked, "He has not gone out by the door!" But without pausing, my husband *unlocked the door,* hastened out of the room, and was soon searching the whole house.... He

> came back looking very white and miserable. Sitting upon the bedside, he put his arm about me and said, "Do you know what we have seen?... It was my father!" *My husband's father had been dead fourteen years.*[41]

A man who has been dead for fourteen years doesn't have a physical body. And yet there he was, solidly visible, even speaking, with an "admonishing" tone in his voice. Was he "warning" his son about something? As it happened, the son *was* in great financial difficulties. He had been about to take the advice of a man who, he later admitted, would have led him to ruin, perhaps even prison. But, he said, his father's appearance caused him to reconsider and prevented him from becoming involved with this man.

A story like this might seem entirely fanciful were it not for the most significant point about it—it was collective! Both persons saw the same figure and both heard it speak the same words. *It cannot have been a hallucination.*

In June of 1931 a man named Samuel Bull died of cancer in his cottage on Oxford Street in the town of Ramsbury, England. His widow and a grandson, James Bull, continued to live in the cottage. Soon after her husband's death, Mrs. Bull became too ill to leave her bed and in August, 1931, a married daughter, her husband and five children moved into the cottage as well in order to look after Mrs. Bull. There were thus nine people in residence. During February of 1932 Mr. Bull, by now dead seven months, began to appear in the cottage. On the first occasion, he ascended the stairs to the second floor, and went *through* a door into the room in which he had died. All nine members of the family saw the apparition repeatedly, both separately and as a group. Its visits were frequent, continuing from February until a last appearance on April 9th. The apparition appeared solid, walked rather than glided, was dressed as Mr. Bull would normally have been dressed after work, and was visible for as long as half an hour at a time. It invariably took up a position by the widow's bedside, sometimes placing its hand on her forehead. Mrs. Bull described the hand as feeling "firm but cold."

These post-mortem appearances by the dead man were a great shock to the family, whose initial reaction was terrified screaming. The apparition's main concern appeared to be the condition of his widow, who was, in fact, dying.

Nine people, to my knowledge, constitutes the record for a collective sighting of an apparition. As the family grew more accustomed to the figure of the dead man, their initial terror abated to a state of awe, but they still, understandably, found these ghostly visits harrowing. Mrs. Edwards, the married daughter, admitted to an investigator from the Society for Psychical Research that Mr. Bull's appearances "took a great deal out of them."[42]

Successive experiences

As the above case indicates, and as we will see later when we look at hauntings in detail, haunting apparitions may be seen by half a dozen or more different people over a period of years. Since people who live in haunted premises are often extremely reluctant to talk about them, successive visitors to, and occupants of, the premises often see the *same apparition with no prior knowledge of its existence.* It is usually mistaken, at first, for a real person. Furthermore, in quite a number of cases the apparition is recognized as a former resident of the dwelling, now dead. In many other cases where the apparition is not recognized by the present occupants, it has been identified as a deceased former resident through interviews with former tenants and the examination of photographs and portraits. *Such apparitions obviously cannot be hallucinations.*

Objective phenomena

As we will see later, the appearance of a haunting apparition often involves tangible physical phenomena such as the movement and breakage of objects, and sounds, most commonly footsteps, which have been recorded on tape. These occurrences cannot, therefore, be dismissed as hallucinatory.

Animal reactions to apparitions

If apparitions of the dead were purely private hallucinations on the part of deluded witnesses, animals present during the experience would not react to them. But animals often do react to apparitions —quite often with fear.[43] In fact, in a number of apparition cases, animals appear to have seen the apparition before the human beings present noticed it.[44] Experiences such as the following clearly cannot be hallucinations.

In this instance, an apparition was seen by two people over a two-year period, as well as by their dog. The figure was first seen in October of 1967, soon after they had moved into the house, and looked just like a normal person. It was a man of middle height, wearing glasses and always the same clothing. "He" always approached the house from the entrance gate to the grounds some three hundred yards away, proceeding along the drive, past the kitchen windows, and to the coach house where he would suddenly vanish. His walk was unsteady. One witness wrote: "Our dog used to bark and follow him, then would suddenly stop, always at the entrance to the coach house, looking around very surprised at having lost the visitor." The apparition was also seen some four times in the house, on one occasion coming out of the bathroom, naked to the waist and carrying a towel over his arm. While being watched, it would suddenly vanish. The apparition was finally successfully identified:

> When [I] described the figure to a resident in the district ... [I] discovered the description fitted that of the son of the previous owner of the house. This young man, [I] was told, often used to come home drunk—hence the unsteady walk—and when he was in this condition he slept in the coach house. Eventually he committed suicide.[45]

An apparition identified as that of a dead person who formerly lived in the house, seen repeatedly by two persons, and repeatedly seen and followed by their dog, cannot be a hallucination.

Veridical apparitions

"Veridical" or "truth-telling" apparitions convey correct information about the "appearer." They often indicate that he is dead, and may even give other details, later confirmed, such as the condition of the body, the clothing worn by the deceased at the time of death, and even information about how he died. Such apparitions obviously cannot be hallucinations.

Reciprocal apparitions of the living

In these cases, a living person undergoes an out-of-the-body experience and visits someone he knows, usually by "thinking" of that person. While doing so, he is seen by that person and then vanishes, or fades away. He then finds himself back in his body. Here is a typical example.

A New York physician was travelling from Jacksonville to Palatka, Florida. During the night he had an out-of-the-body experience and, while in this state, he thought of a friend who was more than a thousand miles away. He then found himself, in a body form which resembled his own, standing in a room, observing this friend from behind. The friend turned round, saw him, said: "What in the world are you doing here? I thought you were in Florida,"[46] and moved towards the doctor, who, although hearing these words distinctly, found himself unable to answer. He then found himself back with his physical body, which he re-entered. Shortly thereafter he received a letter from this friend, describing the incident exactly as he had experienced it.

Hornell Hart, a professor at Duke University, carried out a fascinating piece of research with such apparitions. Gathering all the published accounts of such cases, he noted the basic features of their appearance and behavior, as reported by those who saw them. He did the same for apparitions of the dead, and compared these two types of apparitions by means of a careful statistical analysis. In doing so, he discovered something extremely interesting: *there were no significant differences between them. Apparitions of the living and the dead were the same.*[47] This brings us to a very simple, and very important, conclusion: Because reciprocal apparitions of living people cannot be hallucinations, and are the same, in appearance and behavior, as apparitions of the dead, apparitions of the dead cannot be hallucinations either.

The above evidence shows that serious investigators have uncovered seven real flaws in the hallucination theory—seven reasons why apparitions *must be something other than hallucinations.*

CHAPTER TWO

THE DEAD AMONG THE LIVING: HAUNTINGS

> Dead! Who the hell are you to tell me I'm dead! You don't know me, and I don't want to know you! Now get out of my house! Get out! They took my body! They carried it away and buried it! I want my body! I want my body!
>
> – *a haunting ghost speaks through the entranced medium Sybil Leek*

SOME "hauntings" are fraudulent, the work of publicity-seekers or practical jokers; some are the result of over-worked imaginations; and some are caused by paranormal powers of living persons and have nothing to do with the dead. But genuine hauntings are caused by dead human beings who have not made the kind of transition into death often described by those who have died and been resuscitated. For a variety of reasons which we will explore, they are "stuck" right here with the living, without the benefit of physical bodies. Many of the dead find this so frustrating that they become extremely disruptive and can render a dwelling uninhabitable for living persons.

Genuine hauntings need not involve an apparition, though they often do. They can, however, involve all of the human senses—seeing, hearing, feeling, and smelling—except taste. Most commonly, they involve sounds. Sometimes objects will be moved in hauntings, and human beings will be "touched," and occasionally particular odors for which there is no normal cause will be associated with some of these events.

What's it like to live in a haunted dwelling? Let's consider three typical hauntings: the first involved only sounds; the others, actual apparitions.

The haunted vicarage

An urbane and witty English cleric calmly endured his haunted premises for a year, keeping a detailed record of the strange occurrences in the house during his stay. It was his first parish appointment as an Anglican clergyman and a large country house had been offered him. He and his wife arrived on a Friday afternoon in February.

> The vicarage we were to occupy was a square, spacious building, surrounded by lawns and shrubberies.... The house was ... a short distance from the village, and separated by a road from two or three cottages, which were the nearest dwellings. Our rooms were large ... everything was in good repair, and we congratulated ourselves.[1]

By Saturday night, the cleric and his wife had two or three rooms ready. Thoroughly exhausted, they locked up and went to bed. Only three living persons were within those four walls—the young couple, and a local woman whom they had hired. But as it turned out there was a fourth occupant—a dead one. Everyone had been deeply asleep for hours when they were suddenly awakened by an extremely loud noise.

> The sound was so palpable ... so peremptory ... pealed on our half-awakened senses with so prolonged a crash, that ... its

> reality [could not] be doubted.... It struck me then and afterwards, as being like the crash of iron bars falling suddenly to the ground. Certainly there was a sharp metallic ring about it. Moreover, it was prolonged, and instead of coming from some fixed point it seemed to traverse the house like a succession of rattling echoes treading hard on one another's heels....
>
> I may as well say at once that my acquaintance with it was not limited to the experience of that one early Sunday morning.[2]

This sound occurred many times during their year in the house. But it occurred, invariably, at one specific time only: 2 a.m. on Sunday morning.

After that first noise, the vicar hurriedly dressed and searched the entire house, but could find no clues as to what had happened. The next morning the couple learned that the local woman had also been awakened by the sound, but she wasn't quite as surprised by it as they were. All she would say was that she had heard of such things happening in the house before. She refused to discuss it further, although she did say that she would sleep at her own house from then on.

That evening, the vicar and his wife decided to search the house before going to bed.

> We ... set off together, and, passing out of our sitting-room, found ourselves in the square entrance hall, the door of which opened into the garden. Scarcely were we there before we heard a noise which made us pause and listen. The sound came from the long passage upstairs into which all the bedrooms opened, and was simply *the sound of human footsteps walking slowly but firmly along the passage.* There was no mistake about it. Bold, distinct, and strong, each footfall reached our ears. At once ... I dashed upstairs, three steps at a time, and in a moment was on the landing and in full view of the passage. But there was nothing to be seen ... we entered and searched the bedrooms. But our search was fruitless. If anybody had been there he had contrived by some way inexplicable to us to make his escape.[3]

But the vicar was not to be so easily discouraged. He searched the entire house from top to bottom and found nothing. He even unlocked the back door and looked outside.

> From this ... I was rather hastily recalled by my wife, who announced that the inexplicable footsteps were again in motion; and though on my return they had ceased, yet once more that night they did us the favour of letting us hear them before we went to bed. Now at this point I am bound in honesty to say that ... my wife and I, in discussing the matter, did hint at the possibility of our having fallen in with "a haunted house."[4]

For the next couple of weeks, nothing much happened except for the occasional sounding of the same footsteps.

> However, in due time we were favored with a new development. ... There was ... a range of attics at the top of the house ... and we converted them into storerooms.... They were reached by a small staircase opening off the main passage upstairs; and having deposited in them everything that we wished to put out of the way we secured the staircase door.
>
> We had gone to bed one night as usual, and were about ... asleep, when all at once there commenced a tumult overhead, which very soon made us as wide-awake as we had ever been in our lives. The noise ... seemed to be the result of the tossing about over the attic floors of all the boxes, cases, and bundles stored there. It was loud, boisterous, and persistent. There was a bump, and a rattle, and a roll, and a crash ... an investigation discovered nothing. All was quiet. Everything was apparently undisturbed and as much in order as it ever had been.[5]

Nor was this all. The ghostly inhabitant also provided some "supplementary entertainments:"

> From time to time a succession of distinctly audible knocks

> would greet our ears. These knocks varied in their type. At one time they were hurried, eager, impatient; at another, slow and hesitating. But, however, in one style or another we were treated to them,... on the average, four nights a week.... They were not very alarming, ... and after a little familiarity ... they were not particularly disturbing.
>
> One feature about them, however, deserves to be noticed. Sometimes, while lying awake, an involuntary listener to their tattoo, I was provoked to the use of a little sarcasm ... I would ... address the ... agent and bid it "be quiet, and not disturb ... people in their beds," or I would challenge it, if it had any request to make or any complaint to lay, "to come out and do it in a ... straightforward way."... These remonstrances were not well received. *They always led to louder, more hurried, and more passionate knocking.*[6]

Notice that when the "raps" were addressed, they responded "passionately." Something—or rather, *someone,* wanted to communicate. Had the vicar brought in a trance psychic, a most interesting conversation might then have taken place—with a ghost. The vicar might even have been able to "release" it, had he known enough. But we'll talk about that later.

The haunting, then, consisted of four kinds of noises: rappings, footsteps, attic noises, and the great 2 a.m. "crash"—in varying sequences. Visitors to the house also heard the same sounds. The vicar finally brought the matter up with a woman who lived across the road. He learned that previous occupants of the house had been troubled by the same noises, and the house was regarded locally as "haunted."

And finally, there was the behavior of the vicar's dogs:

> I have always been something of a dog-fancier, and I had at that time two Skye terriers of pure breed, excellent house-dogs, ... ready for any fun, with no delicacy as to letting their sweet voices be heard, if they saw good reason for speaking out. Once ... they

> did speak out to good purpose. The winter was a rough one, times were not good, and there were several robberies of houses in the neighborhood. An attempt was made on the vicarage. My trusty dogs, however, gave prompt alarm. I was roused by their fierce barking, reached a window in time to see more than one dark figure on the lawn below … [He drove the burglars off with a few pistol shots.] I mention this incident simply to contrast the behavior of the dogs on that occasion with their conduct in the presence of the mysterious noises. Against these they never once [barked] … when at such times, in [searching] … the house, I came where they were, *I always found them cowering in a state of pitiable terror.*[7]

This isn't unusual. It often happens in hauntings. And it has even been experimentally investigated. Dr. Robert Morris, a psychologist, reports that a researcher investigated a supposedly haunted house in Kentucky with the help of *four* animals—a dog, a cat, a rat, and a rattlesnake. The haunting phenomena seemed to focus on one room in the house, where tragic events had occurred. When placed in another room in the house, the animals behaved quite normally, but when placed in the haunted room, they reacted strongly. The dog snarled and refused to stay in the room at all. The cat hissed, and, leaping from the investigator's arms, spat at an unoccupied and apparently innocent chair in the room. Although the rat did not react unusually when brought into the room, the rattlesnake did—it immediately assumed an attack posture facing the same chair which had upset the cat![8]

The haunted lawyer

The next case involves haunting by an apparition, which was seen repeatedly by everyone who lived in the house. While still children, Mary Vatas-Simpson and her brother Walter repeatedly saw it. Later, in an account written as an adult, Mary described her first encounters with the apparition.

> We lived in a very ancient house.... The staircase was narrow ... with frequent landings, from which we loved to lean down to see what was going on below.... One day when I was leaning over at one of our posts of observation, I saw a frail old lady come slowly up the stairs and enter the drawing-room. It surprised me greatly.... There was a whispered conversation between me and my brother Walter, who was sitting astride ... the upper banisters, and we resolved to go and see who the intruder was. We went quietly down to the drawing-room ... and ... found nobody there ... as I went up the stairs again I gave a cry of astonishment because I saw the old lady pass on the landing where I had been.[9]

A few days later she and another brother, Garry, were playing their favorite game, which involved reversing two chairs and placing a rug over them to form a kind of tent. She suddenly threw the rug into the air...

> The first thing I saw was the old lady, dressed the same as before, a very worn black garment, a velvet cape on her shoulders, and a big bonnet on her head.[10]

Thinking that the lady wished to see her father, a lawyer, she went after her to redirect her, but the lady disappeared. After that they saw her often, and assumed, for a long time, that although mysterious, she was nonetheless "real."

Their father also had a rather dramatic meeting with this same lady, a meeting which was vividly recorded in his wife's diary. She says that her husband had refused to take reports on the "lady," whom she had also seen, seriously. She wrote: "Last night [he] received a great shock, for he saw the phantom himself." He had been ill, and a lot of work had accumulated on his desk. Deciding to devote the evening to it, he asked not to be disturbed, and retired to his study.

> Suddenly I heard a noise in the direction of the study, I heard the door open and … my husband furiously denouncing the servants for allowing a stranger to enter his study. Who had contravened his orders? He was told nobody had, and he said: "Don't deny it. Where is the woman? When did she come? What does she want? I receive nobody at night. Let her come tomorrow if it pleases her. Now show her the door."
>
> All this was said as if the intruder were still in the house, and with the intention of making her hear. Meanwhile the servants were protesting that they had not shown in anybody, and had seen nobody go up or down stairs. Suddenly my husband's face changed. He said no more and stood motionless. He seemed … struck with … confusion. Then he pulled himself together … saying that in the morning he would find out who had taken the liberty of showing a woman into his study. And if the woman came again he would ask her.
>
> He said these words to hide his thoughts, for he spoke very differently when we were alone. He told me that when he was looking among his papers for a very important document, and was much preoccupied, he had happened to raise his eyes, and had seen a frail little old lady on the threshold. Though she came at an inconvenient time he did not fail in courtesy, but got up and asked her to come in. Seeing that she did not move or speak, and only kept looking at him, he advanced to repeat the invitation. But the lady remained silent and immobile, and seemed to regard him with a sad expression. Thinking that she was out of breath from mounting the stairs, my husband waited some time, but since no reply came he came forward, the lady imitating him with a gliding movement. The room being large, there was always some distance between them, and my husband took several steps toward her. At last he walked resolutely forward,

> decided to probe the mystery of the silence. But then he saw her no more. She had disappeared! …
>
> He said his study was brightly lighted.… He had never thought he was face to face with a phantom.… He described [her] in these terms: … an old lady, small and frail, very pale, dressed in dark garments, with a large bonnet on her head, tied under the chin, and [her] hands always crossed. She had come forward with a … gliding motion.[11]

A ghost—a very real ghost. But what was she doing there, in her quaint, old-fashioned clothing, moving about the house as if she "lived" there? *She does live there*, just as she used to when she had a flesh and blood body.

The haunted widow

In October of 1929, Mrs. Clarice Deane spent the weekend in Cleveland, Ohio, at the home of a Mrs. Mills, whom she had hired to care for her daughter. Mrs. Deane knew almost nothing about the Mills family—only that Mrs. Mills was a widow with a young son. That night Mrs. Deane had an experience which she will never forget.

> Whilst undressing for bed on my first evening I heard a sound at the bedroom door as if the knob were being turned and on opening it saw a good-looking young girl, normally dressed, standing there.… I said, "Hello, who are you?" to which she replied, "I'm Lottie and this is my room," but when I said, "Won't you come in?" she just smiled and entirely disappeared.
>
> Strangely, I did not feel at all nervous and slept quite soundly that night. In the morning I said to Mrs. Mills, "Who's Lottie?" She replied, "Lottie was my pet name for my daughter Charlotte who died a few years ago, but how did you know about her?"
>
> So I told her of the visit to my bedroom the night before. She

> showed me a photograph of Charlotte, who looked just as I had "seen" her.[12]

Mrs. Deane had suspected nothing unusual until the girl disappeared as she watched. She appeared completely solid, and in her late teens or early twenties. Mrs. Mills was "very upset" about the incident and refused to discuss it, as people in haunted houses often do.

The incidents described in these three cases are typical of hauntings. Unlike other types of apparitions, the haunting dead do not try to "appear" to living human beings with whom they have emotional ties. Rather, they are tied to particular dwellings where they once lived; they are linked, not to a person, but to a place.

Would *you* live in a "haunted house"? You might—if the ghost weren't too troublesome. In fact, some ghosts are exceedingly well-mannered, to the point that they may inspire feelings of affectionate concern on the part of the living. Others, however, are so troublesome that the premises become almost impossible to live in.

In 1942 Danton Walker, a journalist, bought an old eighteenth-century house in Rockland County, New York. Walker soon realized that he had an invisible guest, a guest whose activities became so disruptive that Walker was finally forced to abandon the house, which had been beautifully restored at considerable expense.

His problems began one afternoon in 1944, with violent knocking on the front door. When he opened it, no one was there. It soon became clear that the "knocker," who might issue his summons at any hour of the day or night, was invisible, for no one was ever there, even when the door was opened immediately. Heavy footsteps in empty parts of the house became commonplace. Loud thumping sounds, as if someone had fallen violently, were heard from empty rooms. Household objects were inexplicably moved and damaged; pewter pitchers fell near guests, almost as if thrown. Paralyzing sensations of "cold" that bore no relation to drafts or thermal conditions in the room were felt by Mr. Walker and his guests. Once, seized by such a chill when he was ill and had gone to bed early, Mr. Walker unthinkingly shouted, "Oh, for God's sake, let me alone!"

The "chill" immediately ceased. A weekend guest, an entirely down-to-earth friend who regarded "ghosts" as nothing but nonsense, insisted on sleeping in the house despite Walker's warning that he was likely to spend an uneasy night. Scoffing at such notions, he went peacefully to bed, but he was not peaceful for long. His bedside light blinked on and off repeatedly, although all other lights in the house behaved normally. He was awakened from a deep sleep by a violent slap in the face, although no one was in the room. Leaping upright in bed, he saw a shirt he had hung across a chair waving back and forth. This was too much for the skeptical guest, who spent the rest of the night in another house Walker had built nearby. By this time, Walker says,

> I myself had not spent a night alone in the main house in four years. It got so that I just couldn't take it. In fact, I built the studio specifically to get away from staying there. When people have kidded me about my "haunted house," my reply is, would I have spent so much time and money restoring the house, and then built another house to spend the night in, if there had not been some valid reason?[13]

The ghost, when contacted through a trance psychic, turned out to be a Revolutionary War soldier who had been agonizingly tortured and had later died nearby. He was "helped" by methods we'll consider later, and the haunting phenomena ceased.

Just how common are hauntings?

It would be reasonable to suppose that such bizarre phenomena are extremely rare, but there's a good deal of evidence to suggest that they're not. There are, to begin with, plenty of reasons for concealing the fact that you're living in a haunted house. If you are, you'll probably want to move. And what could be worse for real-estate values than an active ghost? It's interesting to note, in that regard, that in

European law, hauntings have been recognized for centuries as adequate grounds for breaking a lease! In fact, the belief that houses can be haunted is so ancient and so widespread that

> … in every language there are words to describe it: *spuken* in German, *haunting* in English, *spiritate* or *infestate* in Italian, *hanter* in French, without counting numerous local terms.[14]

There are other reasons for concealing a haunting that are even more obvious: a desire to avoid personal embarrassment for oneself and one's family, and a desire not to be thought insane! I have talked to a few owners of haunted premises, who confided in me only after they had heard me discussing such matters openly. "Now you're going to think I'm crazy," they would say, "but…." Others begin: "Now the wife and I are completely normal. We've got a snowmobile, a boat, two cars…." And when we talk to those from whom the haunted seek help, such as clergymen willing to perform exorcisms, we begin to get an idea of just how common hauntings are. Canon J.D. Pearce-Higgins, for example, is a London clergyman with a scholarly as well as a compassionate interest in ghosts. Once the public learned that he would exorcise houses of their ghosts, he found himself inundated with requests for help. Writing in 1973, he said:

> All I can say is that … during the past few years some hundred or so houses have been cleared of their unwanted visitors.… Some of these cases received a good deal of publicity and … [now] I cannot deal with even all the ghosts in Southwark let alone other parts of England![15]

Hauntings—by the living

Typical haunting phenomena—rappings, bangings, and objects moving about under their own power—may sometimes occur *only* in the presence of a young person between ten and twenty years of age, in most cases a girl. If that person leaves the premises to go to school or to work, or moves to a different dwelling, the phenomena accompany her. And, according to W.G. Roll, who has studied these mysterious events, there are some recurrent personality factors involved: "In all cases there is evidence of tension, mostly anger, which cannot find ordinary ways of expression." Unlike hauntings by the dead, which can go on for decades or even centuries, hauntings by the living are brief, lasting only a few days, weeks, or months. But, however brief, they are extremely bizarre and dramatic, to the point that—as the following case will show—observers can scarcely believe their eyes.

In the "Sauchie" case, the phenomena centered around an eleven-year-old Irish girl, Virginia Campbell, who had been sent to live with her older brother in Sauchie, Scotland. Within a short time, Virginia's mother left to take work elsewhere, and Virginia was deprived of those to whom she was close. Starting on November 22nd, 1960, and continuing intermittently until March, 1961, some extraordinary phenomena began to occur. They consisted of paranormal noises and the paranormal movement of objects, and they always ceased completely when Virginia went to sleep. Knocking would sound from objects in Virginia's vicinity, varying from gentle tappings to violently agitated and very loud raps. Harsh, rasping, sawing noises also occurred—some of these were recorded. A sideboard once floated five inches away from the wall, and then floated back. A large linen chest floated off the floor and moved eighteen inches; the lid opened and shut of its own accord several times. At school, a desk behind Virginia was seen to float an inch off the floor and then settle down again. While Virginia was standing beside her teacher's desk, a blackboard pointer began to vibrate vigorously, as did the desk. The pointer floated off the desk onto the floor, and the desk, at which the astounded teacher was sitting, floated off the floor and came to rest in another position. An apple was seen to float out of a fruit bowl under its own power, as did a shaving brush, which took off and flew round the bathroom under the gaze of astounded observers. In all of these incidents, there is no question of trickery through wires, levers, hidden threads, and sleight-of-hand, because the objects and surroundings were immediately investigated, on the spot, by responsible observers. Since the house involved had been lived in since 1952, and nothing at all unusual had occurred until Virginia's arrival in 1960, it is obvious that she was the "source."

> The psychological reasons for the [phenomena] ... seem ... obvious. Virginia was feeling "deprived." On several occasions she went into hysterical uninhibited semi-trance states when she complained bitterly of missing her friend Anna and her dog. Clearly she needed attention, and love, and the paranormal disturbances both registered her disapproval of her parents' action and also provided a means whereby she became the centre of the attention and love which she craved. When she had been fussed over and "made her point" the self-therapeutic performance came to an end, having achieved what Virginia herself subconsciously needed but could not consciously admit.[16]

A similar pattern can be discerned in other cases of this type. It seems obvious that the phenomena are paranormally generated by the living "agent"—how, we have no idea.

Hauntings—by the dead

But sometimes haunting phenomena of the Sauchie type show such obvious evidence of intelligence that they can more reasonably be connected with an invisible entity than with a mysterious "force" generated by a living person. Sir William Barrett, a distinguished professor of physics, investigated mysterious rappings and knockings at Derrygonnelly in Ireland. The sounds were associated with a twenty-year-old girl named Margaret. Barrett asked Margaret's father, a farmer in the district, whether the "rapper" would answer questions by giving a certain number of raps. He was told that it would. Barrett writes:

> This it did in my presence.... I mentally asked it, no word being spoken, to knock a certain number of times and it did so. To avoid any error or delusion on my part, I put my hands in the side pockets of my overcoat and asked it to knock the number of fingers I had open. It correctly did so. Then, with a different number of fingers open each time, the experiment was repeated four times in succession, and four times I obtained absolutely the correct number of raps ... coincidence is here practically out of the question, and the interesting fact remains that some telepathic rapport between the unseen agent and ourselves appears to exist.[17]

When haunting phenomena are associated with apparitions of dead people who once lived in the house, and the apparitions are seen repeatedly by many different people over a period of years, there is obviously no doubt that the dead are responsible. Alfred Axtell, of 17 Woodstock Road, Oxford, England, has played host to Mr. Walklett, the deceased former owner of his house, for almost thirty years. A couple of weeks after moving in, Mr. Axtell came face to face with the dead man:

> On the staircase ... I saw distinctly an apparition in the form of Mr. Walklett ... [which then] vanished. I might say that I was well acquainted with ... Mr. Walklett. I ascribed this happening as being probably due to some form of imagination.... I dismissed the matter from my mind ... and did not mention it to anyone.[18]

A few weeks later an elderly woman who lived with the Axtells was extremely frightened by the sudden appearance of a "man" on the same staircase. Mr. Walklett's appearance was quite distinctive, and Mr. Axtell had no trouble identifying him from the woman's description. He asked her to say nothing of her experience, and to try to forget it. Several months later, the same apparition was seen by the Axtells' six-year-old son and by Mrs. Axtell. All of these sightings took place within eighteen months of Mr. Walklett's death, after which he apparently reduced his visibility, but continued to inhabit the premises. Twenty-eight years later he was seen again by Mr. Axtell's stepson, who had never been told about the apparition. Mr. Axtell writes:

> One night, my stepson was in the drawing-room on the first floor with me.... On this particular occasion he went out ... and a few minutes afterwards opened the drawing-room door and called me out. My stepson was ashen grey and very much upset. I took him downstairs, and when he had regained his composure, I said to him, "You saw something—tell me exactly what it was." His description tallied with that of Mr. Walklett, as being a stoutish man five feet seven in height with a long flowing beard of a lightish colour ... the apparition appeared on the landing. [19]

Here is the stepson's story:

> During my mother's lifetime it was my custom to go to 17 Woodstock Road almost every Saturday evening in winter time. My stepfather and I always had a smoke on the landing, as mother disliked it in the drawing-room. On the night when I had my strange experience my stepfather had just left me to finish my smoke, and had returned to the drawing-room. I suddenly heard a shuffling sound, but did not look up for a moment, thinking that he had returned for something. When I did, to my surprise, I saw what appeared to be an ordinary old man in a dressing-gown, walking across the floor. It was all so natural that I was on the point of asking him what he wanted—I was not alarmed at all—*when to my horror he continued his walk until he passed right through a closed door which had not been opened for years, and had*

> *a coatrack screwed right across it ... I thought I was going out of my mind.*[20]

In another similarly dramatic case, the Morton family of Cheltenham, a small city in the West of England, lived with the much more active ghost of a former resident for eight years. During this period the ghost was seen repeatedly by thirteen different people, and heard by about twenty. The ghost was identified as Imogene Swinhoe, the wife of the house's first owner, who had died an alcoholic's death four years before the Mortons moved in. Rose, one of the Morton daughters, kept a detailed diary on its appearances. She describes her first encounter:

> I had gone up to my room, but was not yet in bed, when I heard someone at the door, and went to it, thinking it might be my mother. On opening the door ... I saw the figure of a tall lady, dressed in black, standing at the head of the stairs. After a few moments, she descended the stairs.... [She was] dressed in black of a soft woollen material.... The face was hidden in a handkerchief held in the right hand.... I saw the upper part of the left side of the forehead, and a little of the hair below. Her left hand was nearly hidden by her sleeve and [the] fold of her dress. As she held it down a portion of a widow's cuff was visible on both wrists, so that the whole impression was that of a lady in widow's [dress]. There was no cap on the head but a general effect of blackness suggested a bonnet, with long veil or hood.[21]

On a number of occasions, Rose followed the ghost down the stairs and into the drawing-room, where it would sometimes linger, usually standing on the right-hand side of the bow window. It would then go down the hall to the garden door, where it would always disappear. Rose often attempted to touch the figure, but was never successful: "It was not that there was nothing there to touch, but that she always seemed to be *beyond* me, and if followed into a corner, simply disappeared." She spoke to the figure on several occasions, but, although it would stop and seem *about* to speak, all she ever received from it was a slight gasp.

> I went into the drawing-room … and sat down on a couch close to the bow window. A few minutes after, as I sat reading, I saw the figure come in at the open door, cross the room and take up a position close behind the couch where I was.… She stood behind the couch for about half an hour, and then as usual walked to the door. I went after her … and saw her pass along the hall, until she came to the garden door, where she disappeared. I spoke to her as she passed the foot of the stairs, but she did not answer, although as before she stopped and seemed as though about to speak.[22]

Typical haunting sounds were associated with the ghost: a characteristic footstep, heavy thuds and bumping sounds, and the sound of door handles turning. For the first four years of its appearance, it was entirely solid and lifelike, being mistaken, at first, for a real person. After that it grew less distinct in outline, although never transparent, and finally ceased to appear at all, although its footsteps continued to be heard a while longer. Finally even these were heard no more, and the haunting ceased. Before it did, however, Rose Morton carried out an experiment which is unique in the history of ghost research. She glued fine string across the staircase, after everyone else was in bed, and kept watch. Her patience was rewarded. On two occasions, *she saw the ghost pass through the string without disturbing it.*

The dead among the living: haunting motives

Most of the dead don't seem to end up as haunting ghosts. Can we understand the motives of those who do? Indeed we can. They can be inferred from the behavior of *some* ghosts, and, in exorcisms, actually *discussed* with others—in some of the strangest conversations that have ever been recorded. Both methods seem to yield a very similar set of motives. Let's consider first how ghostly behavior suggests reasons for hauntings.

Instant hauntings

Sometimes a dead person announces his death, not by appearing as an apparition, but by creating an extremely brief "haunting." The noises and the movement of objects that are typical of hauntings may occur for a few moments after a death. In typical examples, a mirror inexplicably shatters, furniture moves of its own accord, paintings fall off the walls, and mysterious sounds are heard: the "slamming" of a door, when the door in fact doesn't move, inexplicable "footsteps," the sound of a heavy object rolling on the floor when there is nothing to be seen. Here is a recent example from Sweden:

> Evening in the country. Father, mother, brother, and I in the kitchen. Kille lay in his basket, he was the world's worst watchdog: he loved people, good and bad alike, and never barked.
>
> "Someone's coming," said my brother, listening to sounds from the gravel path. We all heard steps—they rounded the corner of the house and approached the kitchen door. Kille started, growling deep down in his stomach. Someone knocked on the door. In the country a person always knocks on the outer door first, then opens and walks in and knocks on the inner door, so no one bothered about opening. The knocking came again. "Go open the door," said father. Kille raised a thick ruff around his neck—the hair stood straight up. Mother walked over to open the inner door; then Kille rose up cautiously, his body stiff as a board and his hair on end. Just as she opened the outer door, Kille flew like lightning out of his box, barking loudly, and rushed into the wood-storage room and disappeared under the stove there. Outside there was *nothing.* How well I remember the open door and the darkness outside, and that mysterious nothing which was there as if it were someone. Father

> and my brother went outside ... to see if a tramp was there, but found nothing. The next day one of mother's relatives came and told us that one of our close relatives had died. Later when I reminded mother of what happened, she only answered curtly, "Yes, that was the evening Mans Nilsson died."[23]

In addition to the strong reaction of the dog, this case has another interesting feature, the two sounds involved, for *footsteps* and *knocking* are probably the most common haunting noises. Why some of the newly dead "haunt" briefly, while others appear as apparitions and still others do not manifest at all, is something we simply do not know.

Unkept promises by the living

Some haunting phenomena cease when a promise which has been made to a dead person, but not kept, is carried out. In one such case, pieces of wood began to float and fly about of their own volition in an English carpenter's shop in the little village of Swanland. Regardless of who was in the shop or absent from it, this went on continuously for six weeks, and was witnessed by all who worked there, as well as by dozens of curious visitors. One of the carpenters, a Mr. Bristow, described what life in a "haunted" carpentry shop was like:

> The pieces of wood cut by us and fallen on the ground worked their way into the corners of the shop, from where they raised themselves to the ceiling in some *mysterious and invisible manner*. None of the workmen, none of the visitors, who flocked there in great numbers during the six weeks of these manifestations, ever saw a single piece in the act of rising. And yet the pieces of wood, in spite of our vigilance, quickly found their way up in order to fall on us from a place where nothing existed a moment before. By degrees we got used to the thing, and the movements of the pieces of wood, which seemed alive and in some cases even intelligent, no longer surprised us.[24]

One person in particular was impressed with these events, a man named John Gray. His brother, who had died owing money to creditors, had had a son who had been an apprentice in the carpentry shop, but who had died of tuberculosis. Local gossip held that John Gray had promised his dying nephew to pay his brother's debts. But he had not. When the haunting began, Gray became extremely afraid, and after six weeks, paid the debts, which amounted to one hundred pounds. *As soon as he did, the phenomena immediately stopped.*

Unfinished business by the dead

This is a theme which comes through clearly as a haunting motive during "conversations" between psychics and ghosts. It is also suggested by some apparitional cases, such as the following one. On Sunday, the 20th of September, 1953, George Jonas, caretaker of the Yorkshire Museum in York, England, was on duty there following an evening meeting. After he and his wife locked the front door, they went into the basement kitchen. To their surprise, they heard footsteps overhead. When Mr. Jonas went up to investigate he encountered an elderly man coming out of the museum director's office.

> I thought he was an odd looking chap, because he was wearing a frock coat, drainpipe trousers and had fluffy side whiskers. He had very little hair and walked with a slight stoop. I decided he must be an eccentric professor. As I neared the top of the stairs, he seemed to change his mind, turn, and walk back into the office. When I got to the door, he seemed to change his mind again and turned quickly to come out. I stood on one side to let him pass and said, "Excuse me, Sir, are you looking for Mr. Willmott?" [the museum's director]. He did not answer but just shuffled past me and began to go down the stairs towards the library. Being only a few feet from him, I saw his face clearly.... He looked agitated, had a frown on his face, and kept muttering, "I must find it; I must find it."
>
> It was queer, but I did not think about ghosts for one minute.

> He looked just as real as you or me. But I did not want him roaming around so late at night, and anyway I wanted to lock up and catch my bus. As I followed him down the stairs, I noticed that he was wearing what seemed to be elastic-sided boots, and I remember thinking how old-fashioned the big black buttons looked on the back of his coat.
>
> Still muttering, he went into the library. It was in darkness and I switched on the lights as I followed him in a few yards behind. He was standing between two tall book racks.... He seemed anxious to find something. I thought to myself, this has gone far enough. So, thinking he was deaf, I stretched my right hand out to touch him on the shoulder. But as my hand drew near his coat he vanished.[25]

A month later Mr. Jonas saw the same apparition again. It descended the stairs from the first floor, crossed the hall, and walked *through* a closed door.

Long dead, and obviously unaware of the passage of time (as many ghosts are), the old man continued to search for something he had urgently wanted to find—before he died.

Transfixed by death

The behavior of some ghosts clearly shows that they have been so traumatized by their deaths that they are completely "fixed" at that point in time, and re-live their deaths over and over again. In August of 1904, three sisters were walking across the fields near an old Elizabethan manor house. It was a sunny afternoon, and the last thing they expected to encounter was a strange man by an oak tree. The youngest sister recalled:

> Walking closer, I saw that it was a man, hanging ... from [the] oak tree.... He was [wearing] a loose blouse [and] heavy ... boots. His head hung forward, and the arms dropped forward too.... I saw the shadow of the [fence] railings *through* him.[26]

When she got within fifteen yards of the "hanging man," he suddenly vanished. Hung long ago from that old oak tree, and transfixed by his death agony, he had been "hanging"—ever since.

In July, 1965, two Australian tourists came to stay in an old farmhouse in the English village of Waresley. One of the women, Mrs. Herbert, had been strongly psychic all her life. During her first night at the farm:

> I quickly fell asleep as I usually do, and I think I had been asleep for some time when I was awakened by a little boy kneeling at the side of my bed and looking at me with a pleading look. I can still see his face, so thin and drawn and he gave me the impression that had he stood up he would have been tall and bony. His hair was fair and straight and falling to one side.
>
> I sat up in bed, and although he did not speak, I could feel he was asking me to call his mummy, and I tried to call, "Mummy." The strange thing was that I knew Mrs. Ross [her companion] was sleeping in the next room, but I also knew that was where he wanted me to call his mother from. I could feel his hands clawing at my arm—almost hurting it. I can remember the sensation vividly. This seemed to go on for a long, long time, and I was very distressed but not afraid.
>
> Eventually I called "Mummy!" rather loudly, and at that moment he disappeared.[27]

When Miss Margaret Minney, who had lived at the farm all her life, was told about this experience, she recognized the little boy as her brother Johnnie, who had died an agonizing death from meningitis *forty-five years earlier.* When he first fell ill he would scream with pain and call constantly for "Mummy." During the later stages of his illness he had been *unable to speak.* This poor little boy, who died in 1921, has been in the house ever since, still transfixed in his death agony, still trying in vain to call for his mother!

Joan Grant, a talented psychic who has worked with the troubled dead, has given us an even more vivid example of this after-death state. On a summer holiday, she was staying at the Palace Hotel in Brussels. Exhausted, she decided to go to bed early.

> I had a long, hot bath. But instead of feeling relaxed I was becoming increasingly tense. In bed I tried to read, but after about half an hour, finding I was unable to concentrate, I switched off the light. I was still very wide awake when suddenly a young man rushed out of the bathroom; and before I had time either to move or speak he flung himself out of the window.
>
> I dived under the bedclothes, so that I should not hear the dreadful thud of his body hitting the paving-stones. After a couple of minutes I forced myself to sit up and listen. But I heard nothing: no agonised groans ... no shrieks.... So no one could have seen him fall.... I must shout for someone to help him [her room overlooked an interior service courtyard].
>
> Clutching the handrail I peered down ... but there was no corpse there. And where the corpse should have been, a waiter was carrying a crate of bottles. This was the first time I had found myself alone in a room which was being haunted by a suicide. If I prayed hard enough someone would come to look after him and then I should stop being so terrified. I prayed until the sweat ran down my forehead: and then got back into bed and tried to sleep.
>
> But I still had my eyes open when the same dreadful sequence was repeated. This time I made myself listen, but I heard nothing; so I was unable to learn whether he had lingered screaming or died instantly.
>
> Praying hadn't helped the poor man, so freeing him from the despair in which he was trapped was a job that I was expected to do. My heart was pounding so hard that it was difficult to think clearly. I had freed many newly dead people ... but I had been able to do so because I had managed not to be affected by their fear. I could feel his panic soaking into me like ink into blotting-paper. I should have to feel what he was feeling before I could get close enough to him to be of any real help ... but then his fear

> might be stronger than my dwindling courage [and] my body might follow his on that horrifying plunge.
>
> At least I could guard against this danger by pulling the chest of drawers across the window, so that whatever happened I could not fall out. When this barrier was in place I felt a little braver, but could only just hold back the waves of fear which I knew would get much more insistent when I attained the necessary degree of identification.
>
> I know that I shared that man's fall. As he leaned over the balustrade he suddenly tried to regain his balance … but it was too late. He tried to thrust out his arms to break his fall … he seemed to fall so slowly … so slowly.… Then he realised that he would be terribly injured, and tried to pull back his arms so as to land on his head. He felt no pain … only a grinding thud … and then he was back in the bathroom again and running towards the window again … over and over again.
>
> I found myself standing with my hands stretched upwards, saying aloud, "Your fear has entered me and you are free … your fear has entered me and you are free." The fear, both his and mine, began to release itself in a flood of tears.[28]

The next morning she learned from the hotel manager that the previous occupant of her room had thrown himself from the window five days earlier.

Where shall I go?

According to exorcist John Pearce-Higgins, most haunting ghosts continue to inhabit their familiar surroundings because they don't know what else to do. Many do not realize that they are dead and seem to be "frozen" in time, confused, unaware that decades may have passed since their deaths. It seems clear that many haunting *noises* are efforts on the part of ghosts to call for help, to call attention to themselves, for they apparently are fully aware of what is happening around them, but, without bodies, are unable to participate in any way—a situation which they find perplexing and frustrating, especially as they appear perfectly solid and normal to themselves, dressed in familiar clothing. A minority do realize that they are dead but don't know where else to go. The behavior of many haunting apparitions seems to support this explanation. Here are two who behave exactly as if they are still "living" in the house.

> I was living with my mother in a ground-floor flat in Sussex Gardens.... This flat was shaped like a ... letter L and there was a step in the long part of the corridor just before reaching the main bedroom.... I often saw an old lady with a stick pausing before she negotiated this step, presumably on her way back to the bedroom from the loo round the corner.... I did not tell my mother about her, because I did not want to upset her.... One night, I can't think why, I spent the night in this room and had a terrible time, scared stiff of something that appeared to resent my presence. I was too frightened to sleep. I can't think now why I was not in my own room round the corner—perhaps we had guests—but next day I told mother that I wouldn't sleep there again. She said, "I wonder if it was the old lady." She had kept quiet about her for fear of worrying me.[29]

Here was an old lady with a stick, painfully making her way from her bedroom to the bathroom and back again, resenting the new tenants, unable or unwilling to realize what has happened to her—that she is dead.

Here is another similar case:

> It ... became apparent ... that we had a gentleman resident who used to glide in and out of rooms ... at any time of the day and night. At first my wife and I used just to say, "Ooh," as he glided through; but for a long time we never saw his face.... One night ... I was ... by the fire reading ... I became aware of [him] sitting opposite to me. There was no feeling of fear. Just the usual recog-

> nition of a normal person. He ... sat there, normal, placid, and unsmiling. He was tall; near six feet; dark hair brushed back and parted to the side.... He had dark eyes, a pale, sallow complexion; he wore a navy blue serge suit, with a white shirt and dark tie ... this was the fellow who used to glide through the house at any old time, and he still did it until we left.[30]

This fellow seems, and is, a perfectly normal person—*except that he's dead!*

Three exorcists talk to the dead

Hans Holzer is a psychical researcher who uses a trance medium to talk to, and release, haunting ghosts. John Pearce-Higgins, the Anglican churchman who has specialized in exorcising haunted dwellings, also works through trance psychics. Psychical researcher Hewat McKenzie collaborated with Eileen Garrett, one of the best-known trance mediums of this century. Their conversations with ghosts are among the strangest and most fascinating dialogues ever to be recorded. From them, we can understand directly what motivates a haunting ghost.

In order to exorcise, or release, a haunting ghost, a trance psychic and a colleague are required. Haunting ghosts find fully entranced psychics irresistible, and, entering their bodies, speak through them. This process has some rather startling side effects. The voice coming from the mouth of the medium does not sound like hers; it may be strongly masculine, or a feminine voice of a very different quality. In addition, an even more startling phenomenon can accompany the process: the facial features of the psychic may change substantially until she appears to have another face—that of the ghost. In conversing with the ghost through the psychic, the colleague must persuade it that it is dead and no longer belongs in its earthly surroundings. Conversations with haunting ghosts have revealed several basic motives for hauntings, which recur again and again.

Deranged by the trauma of death

In these cases the ghost is so obsessed by the events and emotions of his death that he is "transfixed," and cannot perceive the world which awaits him beyond death. He may even be so affected that he is, although conscious, "in darkness," as in the following case which involves a haunted apartment on New York's Fifth Avenue. The ghost was released by Hans Holzer, working with the trance medium Ethel Meyers. The proceedings were taped from beginning to end (it took seventeen sessions over a five-month period to deal with this ghost). With their help, we are about to meet a ghost.

> With bated breath, we awaited the arrival of whatever personality might be the "ghost" referred to. We expected some violence and … we got it. This is quite normal with such cases, especially at the first contact. It appears that a "disturbed personality" continuously relives his or her "passing condition," or cause of death, and it is this last agony that so frequently makes ghostly visitations matters of horror. If emotional anxiety is the cause of death, or was present at death, then the … entity will keep reliving that final agony, much like a phonograph needle stuck in the last groove of a record. But here is what happened on that first occasion.

Sitting of July 11th, 1953, at 226 Fifth Avenue

The medium, now possessed by unknown entity, has difficulty in speaking. Entity breaks into mad laughter full of hatred.

> **Entity:** … they're coming … Where is Mignon? WHERE IS SHE?
> **Question:** We wish to help you. Who is Mignon?
> **Entity:** She should be here … where is she … you've got her, Where is she! Where is the baby!
> **Question:** What baby?
> **Entity:** What did they do with her?

Question: We're your friends.
Entity: (in tears) Oh, an enemy … an enemy …
Question: What is your name?
Entity: Guychone … Guychone … (expresses pain at the neck; hands feeling around are apparently puzzled by finding a woman's body.)
Question: You are using someone else's body. (Entity clutches throat.) Does it hurt you there?
Entity: Not any more … it's whole again … I can't see. All is so different, all is very strange … nothing is the same.

I asked him how he died. This excited him immediately.

Entity: (hysterical) I didn't do it … I tell you I didn't do it, no … Mignon, Mignon … where is she? They took the baby … she put me away … they took her … [Why did she put you away?] So no one could find me. [Where?] I stay there [upstairs] all the time.
Question: Do you find it difficult to use this body?
Entity: WHAT?? WHAT?? I'm HERE … I'm here … This is my house … what are YOU doing here?
Question: Tell me about the little room upstairs.
Entity: (crying) Can I go … away … from the room?

At this point, the entity left, and the medium's *control* [a discarnate who works with this particular medium], Albert, took over her body.

Albert: This individual … suffered violence.… He was a Confederate [soldier in the American Civil War].
Question: What was his name?
Albert: It is not as he says. That is an assumed name, that he likes to take. He is not as yet willing to give full particulars.…
Question: What about Mignon and the baby?
Albert: Well, they of course are a long time *on this side* [dead],

> but he never knew that, what became of them. They were separated cruelly.
> **Question:** How did he die?
> **Albert:** By violence. [Was he hanged?] Yes. [In the little room?] Yes. [Was it suicide or murder?] He says it was murder.[31]

The séance ended. The medium stood up and began swinging forward and back like a suspended body. She said that she felt very stiff from "hanging" and was surprised to find that her body was intact, as her abdomen had been cut open. The medium was experiencing the dead man's memories of his death by hanging and of an abdominal wound he received before death at the hands of those who murdered him. She continued to feel pain in her throat and stomach for some time. Holzer noticed that, while "Guychone" was speaking through her "a luminescent white and greenish glow [covered] the medium, creating the impression of an older man without hair, with high cheekbones and thin arms."

"Guychone" followed Mrs. Meyers home after this first seance.

> [He] twice appeared to her at night in a kind of "whitish halo," with an expression of frantic appeal in his eyes. Upon her admonition to be patient until the sitting, the apparition … vanished.[32]

The next sitting took place on July 14th, and proved to be equally dramatic. Like most haunting ghosts, Guychone was entirely unaware of the passage of time since his death.

> **Question:** Do you know what year this is?
> **Guychone:** 1873.
> **Question:** No, it is 1953. Eighty years have gone by. You are no longer alive. Do you understand?
> **Guychone:** Eighty years? EIGHTY YEARS? I'm not a hundred and ten years?
> **Question:** No, you are not. You're forever young. Mignon is on

your side, too. We have come to help you understand yourself. What happened in 1873?

Guychone: Nobody's goddamn business ... mine ... mine!

Question: All right, keep your secret then, but don't you want to see Mignon? Don't you want justice done? (mad, bitter laughter).... The fact you are here and are able to speak, doesn't that prove that there is hope for you? What happened in 1873? Remember the house on Fifth Avenue, the room upstairs, the horse ... ?

Guychone: Riding, riding ... find her ... they took her away.

Question: Who took her away?

Guychone: YOU! (Threatens to strike interrogator.)

Question: No, we're your friends. Where can we find a record of your Army service? Is it true you were on a dangerous mission?

Guychone: Yes.

Question: In what capacity?

Guychone: That is my affair! I do not divulge my secrets. I am a gentleman, and my secrets die with me.

Question: Give us your rank.

Guychone: I was a Colonel.

Question: In what regiment?

Guychone: Two hundred and sixth.

Question: Were you infantry or cavalry?

Guychone: Cavalry.

Question: In the War Between the States?

Guychone: Yes.

Question: Where did you make your home before you came to New York?

Guychone: Charleston ... Elm Street.

Question: What is your family name, Colonel?

Guychone: (crying) As a gentleman, I am not yet ready to give you that information ... it's no use, I won't name it.

Question: You make it hard for us, but we will abide by your wishes.

Guychone: (relieved) I am very much obliged to you ... for

> giving me the information that it is EIGHTY YEARS. Eighty years!
> **Question:** Is there anything you want us to do for you? Any unfinished business?
> **Guychone:** Eighty years makes a difference ... I am a broken man ... God bless you ... Mignon ... it is so dark, so dark.[33]

Holzer proceeded to explain to Guychone that he was communicating temporarily through a woman's body, and how the hatred he felt for those who killed him had kept him in the house on Fifth Avenue and prevented him from making a normal transition to a post-mortem existence.

> The transcript cannot fully convey the tense situation existing between a violent, hate-inspired ... personality fresh from [long] darkness, and an interrogator trying calmly to bring light into a disturbed mind. Toward the end of the session, Guychone ... began to realize that much time had passed since his personal tragedy.... Actually, the method of "liberating" a "ghost" is no different from that used by a psychiatrist to free a flesh-and-blood person from obsessions or other personality disturbances. Both deal with the mind.[34]

It is a typical progression in exorcisms that the entity's consciousness is raised by the exorcist to the point that he can perceive dead loved ones. Typically, these take him in hand and lead him to a normal post-mortem existence. By July 28th, this was happening to Guychone. He said, "I want to say my mother is here, I saw her, she says God bless you. I understand more now. Thank you."

Uncompleted tasks

There are many kinds of "unfinished business" that can bind a ghost to a given place. Three examples of this type of haunting will reveal the range of circumstances that can keep a spirit "earthbound."

The first case, which was described earlier, involves the haunting of Danton Walker's house in Rockland County, New York. The ghost, a Polish immigrant, had served with American troops during the American Revolution. He was carrying secret military plans when captured by the British, who beat and tortured him savagely during interrogation. As a result, he became partially deranged and died a number of years later, still obsessed by the military information which he had been carrying and had hidden, before his capture, on what is now Mr. Walker's estate. His "unfinished business" was the safety of these hidden plans, with which he was still obsessed. A Park Avenue psychiatrist, identified only as "Dr. L.," conducted the exorcism of Danton Walker's house with the help of the trance medium Eileen Garrett.

Dr. L.: We are friends, and you may speak with us. Let us help you in any way we can. We are friends.
Entity: Mhh–mhh–mhh– (inarticulate sounds of sobbing and pain).
Dr. L.: Speak with us. Speak with us. Can we help you? (More crying from the entity) You will be able to speak with us. Now you are quieter. You will be able to talk to us. (The entity crawls along the floor to Mr. Walker, seems to have eyes only for him, and remains at Walker's knee throughout the interrogation. The crying becomes softer.) Do you understand English?
Entity: Friend … friend … friend. Mercy … mercy … mercy … (The English has a marked Polish accent, the voice is rough, uncouth … emotional.) I know … I know … I know … (pointing at Mr. Walker) [His attraction to Walker turns out to be the result of Walker's resemblance to a beloved brother of the entity.]
Dr. L.: When did you know him before?
Entity: Stones … stones … Don't let them take me!
Dr. L.: No, we won't let them take you.
Entity: (More crying) Talk …
Mr. Walker: You want to talk to me? Yes, I'll talk to you.
Entity: Can't talk …
Mr. Walker: Can't talk? It is hard for you to talk?

Entity: (Nods) Yes.

Dr. L.: You want water? Food? Water?

Entity: (Shakes head) Talk! Talk! (To Mr. Walker) Friend? You?

Mr. Walker: Yes, friends. We're all friends.

Entity: (Points to his head, then to his tongue.) Stones … no?

Dr. L.: No stones. You will not be stoned.

Entity: No beatin'?

Dr. L.: No, you won't be stoned, you won't be beaten.

Entity: Don't go!

Mr. Walker: No, we are staying right here.

Entity: Can't talk …

Mr. Walker: You can talk. We are all friends.

Dr. L.: It is difficult with this illness that you have, but you can talk. Your friend there is Mr. Walker. And what is your name?

Entity: He calls me. I have to get out. I cannot go any further. In God's name I cannot go any further. (Touches Mr. Walker)

Mr. Walker: I will protect you. (At the word "protect" the entity sits up, profoundly struck by it.) What do you fear?

Entity: Stones …

Mr. Walker: Stones thrown at you?

Dr. L.: That will not happen again.

Entity: Friends! Wild men … you know …

Mr. Walker: Indians?

Entity: No.

Dr. L.: White man?

Entity: Mh … teeth gone (shows graphically how his teeth were kicked in).

Mr. Walker: Teeth gone.

Dr. L.: They knocked your teeth out?

Entity: See? I can't … Protect me!

Mr. Walker: Yes, yes. We will protect you. No more beatings, no more stones.

Dr. L.: You live here? This is your house?

Entity: (violent gesture, loud voice) No, oh no! I hide here.

Mr. Walker: In the woods?

Entity: Cannot leave here.

Dr. L.: Whom do you hide from?

Entity: Big, big, strong … big, big, strong …

Dr. L.: Is he the one that beat you?

Entity: (Shouts) All … I know … I know… I know …

Dr. L.: You know the names?

Entity: (Hands on Mr. Walker's shoulders) Know the plans …

Dr. L.: They tried to find the plans, to make you tell, but you did not tell? And your head hurts?

Entity: (Just nods to this) Ah … ah …

Dr. L.: And you've been kicked, and beaten and stoned. (The entity nods violently.)

Mr. Walker: Where are the plans?

Entity: I hid them … far, far …

Mr. Walker: Where did you hide the plans? We are friends, you can tell us.

Entity: Give me map. (The entity is handed note pad and pen, which he uses in the stiff manner of a quill.)

Entity: In your measure … [I] hid … (drawing)

Mr. Walker: Where the wagon house lies?

Entity: A house … not in the house … timber house … log…

Mr. Walker: Log house?

Entity: (Nods) Plans … log house … under … under… stones … fifteen … log … fifteen stones … door … plans—for whole shifting of …

Mr. Walker: Of ammunitions?

Entity: No … men and ammunitions … I have plans for French … plans I have to deliver to log house … right where sun strikes window …

Dr. L.: Fifteen stones from the door?

Entity: Where sun strikes the window … Fifteen stones … under … in log house … There I have put away … plans … (agitated) Not take again!

Mr. Walker: No, no, we will not let them take you again. We will protect you from the English.

> **Entity:** (Obviously touched) No one ever say—no one ever say—I will protect you …
> **Mr. Walker:** Yes, we will protect you. You are protected now for always.[35]

From that day, the haunting phenomena ceased.

Another case involving much less dramatic "unfinished business" concerned the family of a "no-nonsense" retired British Navy admiral. His two sons began to complain to him that "someone" was in the room where they slept at night. They heard sounds, and in the morning would find that their shoes had been moved. The mother confessed that she had heard footsteps. Then one day as the Admiral was having a glass of scotch and soda, it moved away from him of its own accord and crashed to the floor. When, a day or two later, something similar happened with a jug he was using, he realized that something was very wrong. He was advised to seek help from a medium, and Eileen Garrett took the case. It turned out that the mother's brother was responsible. He had died two years previously, mentally ill, and in this state, had made a will which gave his estate to a distant cousin, leaving his much-loved wife with nothing. After death, realizing what he had done, he became desperately anxious to right the situation, trying to gain their attention somehow with noises and the movement of objects. The situation he had created was corrected, and the haunting ceased. [36]

Another haunting of this type was exorcised by John Pearce-Higgins with the help of psychic Ena Twigg. The haunting was in a vicarage where footsteps were often heard and a terrible atmosphere of depression, which affected the family occupying it, prevailed. This was a rather rare case in which the previous vicar, a sad, middle-aged bachelor who was responsible for the haunting, *knew* that he was dead. He said that he was tied to the place from a terrible sense that he had wasted his life. He was told that he didn't belong any longer in his earthly surroundings, to which he replied, "But I don't know where to go." He then broke down and sobbed, thanked them for helping him, and said that he was "freed". The haunting ceased.[37]

It is obvious from these three examples that almost any kind of "unfinished business" can tie a ghost to his earthly surroundings; it need only be something that the ghost considers of great importance.

Concern over events following death

In one haunting of this type, the ghost responsible was a wealthy mother who had died disinheriting her daughter, with whom she was on poor terms. (She disapproved strongly of her daughter's husband.) She caused rather dramatic phenomena: paintings fell from the walls, coat-hangers sailed up onto the roof, footsteps sounded throughout the house. Worse, the daughter, who was quite psychic herself, on several occasions seemed to be "taken over" by her mother, once attacked her husband with a hammer while in this state, and cursed him in a way quite foreign to her nature. These events began to jeopardize the marriage. Realizing what was happening, they called in a medium. The mother took over the medium's body. She was enraged that they were contesting her will, which had left all her money to a charity. On a second occasion she came again, greatly chastened, and, while in the body of the medium, went to her daughter and asked her forgiveness. Thereafter, all the haunting phenomena ceased.[38]

Eileen Garrett handled a number of cases in which the cause of the haunting was the deceased's feelings about actions of the living. In one, a widow and her daughter began hearing strange rappings and other mysterious disturbances in their home. With Eileen in trance, the exorcist, Hewat McKenzie, learned that the woman's dead husband was the cause. He had died two years previously, and had left some money for the care of his beloved daughter. But the unscrupulous lawyer who had handled the estate had seduced the widow and the two of them had squandered most of the money. The haunting was his way of protesting against all this. He felt that he simply could not permit his precious child to live under such outrageous conditions. He revealed that he had drawn energy for the haunting from his daughter. In this case it seems that there was little the exorcist could do; if ghosts choose not to cooperate in ending a haunting, it is difficult to force them to.[39]

A final example of this type of haunting occurred in a Sussex farmhouse, where two boys lived with their stepfather. A veritable storm of haunting phenomena had occurred: noises, household objects moving and breaking of their own accord, bedclothes pulled off people while they slept. The farmer complained bitterly about the ghosts, but got more than he bargained for when Mrs. Garrett went into a trance. His former wife, the mother of the two boys, came through and revealed that it had been her money which enabled him to buy his farm in the first place. During the last year and a half of her life she had been virtually paralyzed by a stroke. A woman had been brought in to help care for her, and a relationship had developed between her and the farmer. They had tried, apparently unsuccessfully, to guide her paralyzed hand into signing a document which would leave the farmer all her property. She had succeeded in leaving a considerable sum of money to her two boys, but was desperately worried that the unscrupulous stepfather would manage to get it away from them. The haunting had been her attempt to draw attention to this situation. McKenzie contacted some relatives of the boys whom she had named, and under their supervision, and with the agreement of the chastened stepfather, the boys' inheritance was placed under legal protection. (Interestingly, the haunting spirit of the boys' mother also claimed that she derived the energy she needed to perform the haunting from her two sons.)[40]

Thus, in all of these cases, a strongly held conviction on the part of the dead that their desires are being thwarted by the living, plus an embodied human being from whom "energy" can be drawn, brings about a haunting.

Feelings before death

Obsessively powerful emotions such as anguish and guilt, held by the ghost before death, can bind him in his familiar surroundings and produce a prolonged haunting after death. John Pearce-Higgins describes his experience of such a haunting:

> On receiving an urgent call from a newly and happily married young bride, who was aware of dangerous suicidal influences around her, I went next day. The lady's clairvoyant sister, who had spent two nights in the flat, had seen the apparition of a distressed girl wringing her hands in despair and saying, "He let me down, what shall I do, shall I take an overdose, or cut my wrists?" (It appears she did the latter.)[41]

After an exorcism service, the "atmosphere" immediately cleared. In this case the unknown girl's pre-suicidal anguish kept her bound to the flat after death, so absorbed in her own pain that she did not even realize she was dead.

Another similarly caused haunting took place in an old eighteenth-century house in Stamford Hill, Connecticut. The owners, Bob and Dorothy Cowan, were not afraid of the ghost and did not find it particularly obtrusive. But they were extremely curious to know who the ghost was and what it wanted, so they got in touch with Hans Holzer, who went to the house with Ethel Meyers. This rather complex case turned out to involve two ghosts—a young woman whose name was Lucy (she was also called Laurie) and her grandfather, whose first name was Samuel. Lucy had wanted to marry a young man named Benjamin, but her grandfather had opposed it, as there were religious differences which he considered important. In a frenzy of rage, the grandfather had evidently struck the young man over the head with a stick and dumped his body down the well. Lucy never forgave him the murder, nor could he forgive himself. Bound by grievance and by guilt, the two had remained in the house ever since. Their story was revealed through the entranced psychic.

> "There is [a] young woman ... Laurie ... very pretty face, but so sad ... she's looking at you, Hans. [With her is] a youngish man

with brown hair, curly, wearing a white blouse … and over it a tan waistcoat.…" I asked what he wanted and why he was here. This seemed to agitate the medium somewhat.

"Bottom of the well," she mumbled, "bottom of the well.…"

"Somebody had a stick over his shoulder," the medium said now, "older man wearing dark trousers, heavy stockings. His hair is gray and kind of longish; he's got that stick." I asked her to find out why …

"Who is down in the well? Him who I drove into the well, him.…" Ethel was now fully entranced and the old man seemed to be speaking through her.

"What is your name?" I asked.

"She was agrievin'," the voice replied, "she were grievin' I did that."

"What is your name?"

"Ain't no business to you."

"They're all here … accusin' me … I see her always by the well."

"Did someone die in this well?" Outside, barely twenty yards away, was the well, now cold and silent in the night air.

"Him who I mistook. I find peace, I find him, I put him together again."

"What year was that?"

"No matter to you now … I do not forgive myself … I wronged, I wronged … I see always her face … "

"Are you in this house now?" I asked.

"Where else can I be and talk with thee?" the ghost shot back.

"This isn't your house any more," I said quietly.

"Oh, yes it is," the ghost replied firmly. "The young man [Bob Cowan, the present owner] stays here only to look upon me and mock me. It will not be other than mine. I care only for that flesh that I could put again on the bone and I will restore him [the murdered man] to the bloom of life and the rich love of her who suffered through my own misdemeanor."

At this point the ghost realized that he was not in his own

> body, and as I explained the procedure to him, he gradually became calmer. At first, he thought he was in his own body and could use it to restore to life the one he had slain. I kept asking who he was. Finally, in a soft whisper, came the reply, "Samuel." [Events now take an extremely dramatic turn: the murdered man and the wronged granddaughter appear to him.]
>
> "*Oh, he is here, the man I wronged.*" He seemed greatly agitated with fear now. The big clock started to strike. The ghost somehow felt it meant him. "The judgement, the judgement … Laurie … *they smile at me. I have killed. He has taken my hand! He whom I have hurt.*" Suddenly, he was gone, and after a brief interval, an entirely different personality inhabited Ethel's body. It was Laurie.
>
> "Please forgive him," she pleaded, "I have forgiven him." The voice was sweet and girlish.
>
> "Who is Samuel?"
>
> "My grandfather."
>
> "What year were you born?"
>
> Hesitatingly, the voice said, "Seventeen-fifty-six."
>
> "What year is this now?"
>
> "Seventeen-seventy-four."[42]

Thus ended the haunting. The procedure "raised" the consciousness of the two ghosts so that they could see the young man who, taking his murderer by the hand, led them both away to a new existence.

Am I dead?

Some ghosts do not realize that they are dead, and simply continue with their former existences, operating partially in the material environment, it seems, and partially in a kind of "dream" world generated by their own minds. John Pearce-Higgins describes such a haunting:

> We cleared, after several visits, an ex-vicarage in the Midlands … haunted by two Tudor monks from [a] local Priory [monastery],

> which had been dissolved [in the sixteenth century]. They were clearly a bad lot, one had made an Irish maid-servant pregnant; and the other had taken away and killed her baby. The girl herself through the medium also spoke to us, pitifully saying, "Mistress Longhurst will not let me go out any more." Apparently Mistress Longhurst was her employer, and the house had been used as a guest house by the Priory. The girl had been locked in an attic and finally poisoned after her baby had been despatched. She was still looking for her baby, unaware of its death and of the passage of time. *The monks also had continued to perform their daily offices and although the Priory had been dissolved in A.D. 1536, still imagined themselves to be carrying out the daily monastic routine in field and church.* I had a most interesting time trying to persuade them that they were dead, which they found it hard to believe since they expected to sleep until the last trump [the day of judgement] and then, in virtue of their vows [that is, because they were monks], to go straight to paradise or heaven. They could not understand at all where they were.[43]

Eileen Garrett encountered a case of this type involving a haunting in a fisherman's cottage in the Severn valley in the West of England. The youngest boy in the family was particularly aware of this ghost, who seemed attracted to him. He described the ghost to the others as a dark, swarthy man, rough and rather threatening in demeanor. The others, it turned out, were well aware of this ghost, but considered him harmless. But the ghost often frightened the boy by snatching off his bedclothes. When Eileen Garrett arrived on the scene, she made direct contact with the ghost. He turned out to be a distant relative who had lived in this same house generations before. He said that he still liked the place, and liked to return to it at those times when the fishing was at its best.

> He was not a pleasant person, and he told a gruesome, tragic story with a gusto that revealed how definitely he was still living in, and enjoying, the passionate past. He and a brother had

> smuggled as well as fished together, and at one point in his talk he offered to conduct the group to the local church where they had hidden the laces, wines and other contraband goods that they were able to smuggle over from the Continent, and also to reveal the path that they had used coming up from the sea....
>
> He recounted that eventually he and his brother quarreled, and that he had shot and killed his brother—an act for which he evidently had neither regret nor penitence; he continued that he had had to keep the dead body in the house for several days before he could dispose of it without endangering his own safety.... He reported how the family had at one time owned immense areas of land and considerable wealth, and how everything had been gambled away; money, land, horses, women, anything and everything had been risked on the fall of the cards or the dice—risked and lost....
>
> When the alien "one" was asked why he came here, he said truculently that this was his place and he liked it. He did not know who these present occupants of the house were, and he resented their presence in no uncertain terms. When he was asked why he had been troubling the youngest son of the family, he declared that he hadn't meant to frighten him, but that he liked the lad and wanted to attract his notice.[44]

This man spoke through the medium in a boasting and boisterous manner. Loving himself and the life he had led during his bodily existence, he continued to cling to it in death, as unaware of what had really happened to him as he was of the passing of the years.

Hauntings do happen. They are more common than we think, and many of them are caused by the dead. We should not let that fact paralyze us with fear, for the dead are not terrifying, nor are they incomprehensible. They can be understood, communicated with, and freed.

CHAPTER THREE

THE GHOST WITHIN: OUT-OF-THE-BODY EXPERIENCES

Because it is sometimes so unbelievable, the truth escapes becoming known.

– *Heraclitus (circa 500 B.C.)*

The experience was utterly real. It had a quality of absolute objectivity.[1]

– *Carl Jung describes his out-of-the-body experience.*

IT'S BEEN A LONG, somewhat tiring day. After settling between cool, comfortable sheets, you close your eyes and let your mind drift into a soothing, cottony world of images, floating toward the borderland of sleep. The slow breathing at your side tells you that your spouse has already preceded you. Suddenly, you have the sensation of falling into blackness, followed by a gentle rocking motion. You feel as if you are floating slowly upwards. Although your eyes were closed moments before, they now seem to be open, and, to your astonishment, the bedroom wall is moving slowly past as you rise towards the ceiling. Incredulous, you look down and see your spouse calmly asleep in bed. Beside her—is someone else. It can't be you, because you're up here—and yet it is! There on the pillow, calmly asleep, is that face that has looked at you from the mirror all these years. My God, it's you! A surge of panic courses through you, and your sight dims as, with lightning speed, you are drawn to your body, slamming back into it with a shock. That's what usually happens if you get scared. If you don't, you may just continue on your way, as did one courageous friend of mine, rising *through* the plaster, drifting upwards into the darkness of the attic, proceeding through the roof and out into the night, where he floated down the moonlit street. This is an *out-of-the-body experience* (OBE); they are not as rare as you might suppose, and they tell us a great deal about the world beyond death.

Some extraordinary claims concerning the dead will be made and documented in this book: that they are sometimes visible; that they haunt places that have emotional significance for them; that they can communicate after death through mediums; that they are seen at deathbeds and during resuscitation experiences; that they report on their lives beyond death; that they constitute the essential self which reincarnates, and that, under certain conditions, they may "possess" the living.

In effect, these claims argue that we are all—in essence—"ghosts." And, through personal experiences with our own bodies, many of us have become aware that this is true, that there are really "two" of us—the fleshly and the other. This awareness is one of the best-documented secrets of modern times.

The statements made above about the "dead" are certainly controversial, but let us make another which is at least their equal: as we will see in this chapter, *the living can do all of these things too*—in out-of-the-body experiences.

It seems a reasonable enough assumption, particularly in an age of science, that consciousness depends upon a body and a brain. How, then, can anyone have an experience in which consciousness and the body separate? Let us look at four examples of out-of-the-body experiences, which should more than begin to make this claim credible.

Four out-of-the-body experiences

The Virginia psychiatrist

Dr. George C. Ritchie now lives in Charlottesville, Virginia, but in 1943 he was a nineteen-year-old private in the United States army. In December of that year, he was admitted to the base hospital at Camp Barkley, Texas, suffering from what medical records of his case describe as "acute naso-pharyngitis." His condition grew worse, and was rediagnosed as "severe lobar pneumonia." Early on the morning of December 20, Private George Ritchie died. The attending physician, Dr. Donald Francy, said later in a notarized statement that Ritchie gave no evidence of having any respiration or heartbeat. Concluding that Ritchie had died, Dr. Francy gave orders to the ward attendant to prepare the body for the morgue. However, nine minutes later, the attendant thought he detected slight chest movements in the dead man and summoned Dr. Francy. "[I administered] adrenalin into the heart," he said, "and Private Ritchie began to evidence increase in respiration and developed perceptible pulse."

What had happened to Ritchie while he was dead? Speaking of these experiences, Ritchie says:

> I don't understand it any more than I ask you to. All I can do is describe the events as they happened. They were the clearest and most profound events of my whole life. My experience rekindled my dying religious faith and permanently erased any fear of death.

During the height of his medical crisis, Ritchie suddenly became aware that he no longer felt sick. He felt, instead, joyous, buoyant, as light as a feather. Then he realized that he was standing beside his hospital bed looking down at a grey-faced form.

> [I noticed that] someone was still lying on the bed I had just left. I stepped closer in the dim light, [and] then drew back. He was

> dead. The slack jaw, the grey skin, were awful. Then I saw the ring [he was wearing]. On his left hand was the Phi Gamma Delta fraternity ring I had worn for five years. [The man lying on the bed] was me!

Astounded, Ritchie realized that there were two of him—one, obviously dead, lying on the bed; the other, a completely conscious observer. He thought, "This is death—this is what we human beings call death."

Understandably, Ritchie was upset—in fact, he was very badly frightened. He walked from the room, and an orderly carrying a tray of instruments, who did not appear to see him, *walked right through him.* In a blind panic now, he decided to do what many terrified people have tried to do—head for home! Reaching an exit door, he tried in vain to open it, only to discover that his hand kept going through it. He walked *through the closed door* and found himself traveling through the air at terrific speed. He came to an unknown town. Alarmed and baffled, he saw a lone pedestrian and approached him to ask where he was, but the pedestrian didn't seem to see him either. Ritchie says he tried to touch this man to get his attention, but much to his bewilderment, his hands seemed to pass right through the man. This shook him greatly, and he decided that if he could not be seen by anyone, then there was not much point in traveling to his home. (Some time later, after he was revived from death, he happened to visit this town, to which he had never been before in the flesh, and recognized it as the one he had been in during his experience. Interestingly, it was on a direct route, as the crow flies, from Camp Barkley to his home. It seems he had been going home after all!) He decided to try to get back to his body. No sooner had this thought entered his mind than he found himself again flying through the night. Arriving at the hospital, he had some difficulty finding the room where his body lay, its face covered by a sheet. He sat down rather disconsolately on the edge of the bed. Ritchie says that at that moment he sensed a presence beside him.

> The hospital room began to fill with light until it was flooded, ... illuminated, by the most total compassion I have ever felt.

From out of this blinding light, this presence Ritchie had sensed emerged as a luminous, majestic, loving and compelling figure.

> [His presence] was so comforting, so joyous and all-satisfying, that I wanted to lose myself forever in the wonder of it.

The walls of the hospital room seemed to drop away and Ritchie felt he was being transported into another world. He says:

> I saw a city—but a city, if such a thing is conceivable, constructed out of light. At that time I had not, incidentally, read anything on the subject of life after death. But here was a city in which the walls, houses, streets, seemed to give off light, while moving among them were beings of pure light. This was only a moment's vision. The next instant the walls of the hospital room closed around me.

But the shining being, whose loving presence Dr. Ritchie says he felt he never wished to leave, was still with him. Then the dazzling light faded, and he seemed to fall asleep, awakening back in his body.

Talking about this experience later, he said he had no idea why he had died and then come back to his body. "All I know is that when I woke up in that hospital bed I was not a happy man—I was not glad to be back—I yearned to be where I had been when I was dead." Retta Irvine, the nurse who was present at the bedside during Ritchie's apparent death, stated that when Ritchie opened his eyes, "He told me he knew he had been dead and that he had had an experience that would change his life."[2]

The French gentleman

The two incidents described below happened to a Frenchman named

Hymans. They were investigated and published by Charles Richet, Professor of Physiology at the University of Paris and a winner of the Nobel Prize in medicine, in collaboration with a colleague, Dr. Eugene Osty. Hymans, in a written account which he gave to Richet in June of 1928, says:

> The first time … was while [I was sitting] in a dentist's chair. Under anaesthesia, I had the [experience] of awakening and of finding myself floating in the upper part of the room, from where, with great astonishment, I watched the dentist working on my body … the anaesthetist at his side. I saw my inanimate body as distinctly as any other object in the room.… The second time I was in a hotel in London. I awoke in the morning feeling unwell (I have a weak heart) and shortly thereafter I fainted. Greatly to my astonishment, I found myself in the upper part of the room, from where, with fear, I beheld my body inanimate in the bed with its eyes closed. I tried without success to re-enter my body and concluded that I had died … [but] I had not lost either memory or self-consciousness. I could see my inanimate body like a separate object: I was able to look at my face. I was, however, unable to leave the room; I felt myself … chained, immobilized in the corner where I was. After an hour or two I heard a knock at the locked door several times, without being able to answer. Soon after, the hotel porter appeared on the fire escape. I saw him get into the room, look anxiously at my face, and open the door. The hotel manager and others then entered. A physician came in. I saw him shake his head after listening to my heart, and then insert a spoon between my lips. I then lost consciousness and awoke in the bed.[3]

All of these events were later confirmed by the other participants.

The English traveler

Mrs. M. was away from home on a trip, staying at a hotel. While asleep, she was almost asphyxiated by a defective gas-jet which had developed a leak. She felt herself, much to her astonishment, leave her body. Highly puzzled, she thought of her home, and immediately found herself there, standing in her husband's bedroom. She saw another man, a friend and neighbor, who was asleep in the same room as her husband, which rather surprised her. What surprised her more was her observation that, leaning against the head of the bed, was a thick club made from a branch with some bark still attached to it, and the fact that the room was in a state of disorder. She stroked her husband's face to try to awaken him, but was unable to make any impression on him. Then she thought, "I must get back to my body!" No sooner had this occurred to her than she found herself again in the hotel room with her body. She then lost consciousness and regained it back in her body, to find a doctor beside her. He told her he had given her up for dead. When she described her experience to him, he was interested enough to check her story. All of its details were verified. It turned out that her husband's friend had come to spend the evening at their house. During his visit, a rat had run across the floor, and they had hunted it with a club from the woodpile which still had bark adhering to it. They upset furniture chasing the rat, causing much disorder in the room. The friend stayed the night, the club being left within reach by the bed in case the rat returned.[4]

The Scottish professor

Auckland Geddes, a doctor and a professor of anatomy at the University of Edinburgh, described the following experience in an address given in 1937 to the Royal Medical Society in Edinburgh. He stated at the time that he was withholding the name of the narrator for professional reasons; it is now generally believed that he was reporting his own experience. In his account, he says:

> On Saturday, 9th November, a few minutes after midnight, I began to feel very ill and by two o'clock was definitely suffering from acute gastro-enteritis, which kept me vomiting … until about eight o'clock. By ten o'clock, I had developed all the symp-

toms of very acute poisoning: intense gastro-intestinal pain, diarrhoea, pulse and respiration quite impossible to count. I wanted to ring for assistance, but found I could not, and so quite placidly gave up the attempt. I realized I was very ill.... Thereafter at no time did my consciousness appear to me to be in any way dimmed, but I suddenly realized that my consciousness was separating from another consciousness which was also me. These, for purposes of description, we could call A and B consciousnesses, and throughout what follows [my awareness was attached] to the A consciousness. The B consciousness I recognized as belonging to my body, and as my physical condition grew worse ... I realized that the B consciousness ... was beginning ... to disintegrate, while the A consciousness, which was now me, seemed to be altogether outside my body, which it could see. Gradually I realized that I could see, not only my body and the bed on which I was [lying], but everything in the whole house and garden and then I realized that I was seeing, not only "things" at my home, but in London and Scotland, in fact [seeing things] wherever my attention was directed.... Although I had no body I had what appeared to be perfect two-eyed vision, and [I felt as if I were] visible.... I saw "A" enter my bedroom.... She got a terrible shock [when she saw the condition of my body] and I saw her hurry to the telephone. I saw my doctor leave his patients and come very quickly and heard him say ... "He is nearly gone." I heard him quite clearly speaking to me on the bed, but I was not in touch with the body [that lay there] and I could not answer him. I was really cross when he took a syringe and rapidly injected my body with something which I afterward learned was camphor. As my heart began to beat more strongly, I was drawn back [to my body], and I was intensely annoyed, because I was so interested [in my new state]. I came back into my body, and once back, all the clarity of vision [I had experienced] disappeared, and I was just possessed of a glimmer of consciousness which was suffused with pain ... this ... experience has shown no tendency to fade as a dream would ... but for medical treatment of a prompt and vigorous kind, I [would have been] dead.[5]

The "soul" in action

Although the experiences just described may seem extraordinary, they actually have a long historical tradition behind them, having been reported throughout history and throughout the world. In recent years, many hundreds of cases have been extensively studied. This research has revealed that the experience has certain basic characteristics. What, then, are we dealing with?

Often people who have these experiences see themselves as being in another body, and typically this other body resembles the physical body rather closely in shape, size, and general outward appearance, except that it is usually perceived as transparent, and is almost always experienced as being much lighter and less substantial than the physical form. It is typically incapable of manipulating matter, but capable of passing through it. Since many of these people are actually conscious of emerging from their physical bodies, and of later re-entering them, they conclude that this "other" body is normally located within the physical one, but is sometimes capable of leaving it and even of traveling a considerable distance. *It seems obvious that such experiences are the basis for the traditional and universally-held idea that human beings possess a soul.* They convince the people who have them that everyone possesses a kind of secondary body, which can separate itself temporarily from the physical body during life, and permanently from it at death. In fact people who have died and been resuscitated often describe this experience. OBEs sometimes involve highly pleasurable and vividly clear states of consciousness which seem so superior to in-the-body consciousness that there is a lack of interest in returning to the body, and some "re-entrants" express anger and disappointment at finding themselves back in their physical forms. A typical after-effect of an OBE is a loss of the fear of death.

But surely they're only dreams!

People who have not had such experiences often assume that they must be vivid dreams, but the "dream" explanation has some embarrassingly serious weaknesses:

1. People who have had out-of-the-body experiences dream just like everyone else, and they refuse to accept the idea that the experience was a dream—for them, it was very different from a dream.
   a) In dreams, we do not see our own bodies objectively from outside them, while this is characteristic of OBEs.
   b) In OBEs, surroundings are seen as they are in normal consciousness.
   c) Dreamers, upon awakening, realize that they have been dreaming. But no such realization accompanies the end of an OBE. The firm conviction that the experience was real, rather than a dream, holds not only while the experience is occurring, but when it is thought about later. For instance, William Gerhardt, who had such an experience and wrote about it, stated that even if the whole world told him that his OBE was a dream, nothing would ever be able to convince him of that.[6]

2. What is seen and what happens during OBEs is in many cases verified by others who are present with the apparently sleeping, unconscious or dead body.

3. Many report that their perception of their surroundings is more vivid, more real, and more unquestionably convincing than the perception that accompanies normal consciousness. As the famous psychiatrist Jung said in describing one of his OBEs, "The experience was utterly real. It had a quality of absolute objectivity."

The historical evidence for OBEs

Historical evidence clearly shows that these experiences represent a very firmly rooted and enduring human ability, having been reported throughout recorded history and in all societies, quite often by people who were outstanding individuals.

The first OBEs occurred long before written languages were available to record them, but the literature of the ancient world contains many accounts of such experiences. The sixth-century B.C. philosopher Hermotimus of Clazomenae was apparently capable of inducing OBEs at will, and used this ability to investigate the nature of after-death states. The Greek biographer, Plutarch, wrote of one Aridaeus of Asia Minor who in 79 A.D. was knocked unconscious and had an OBE in which he met and spoke with the dead, including an uncle, who greeted him warmly and reassured him that he was not yet dead, as his soul was still tied to his body. In the fifth century A.D. Augustine, Bishop of Hippo, in Numidia, North Africa, wrote of the experiences of Curma, a senator, who, seriously ill, was comatose for several days. Upon his return to consciousness, he reported that he had been out of his body and conversed with the dead, who, as in the case of Aridaeus, assured him that he was still alive. The Roman philosopher Apuleius described similar experiences. Many famous historical figures have written about their own OBEs, or those of people close to them, among them St. Augustine, Aristotle, Plato, Goethe, and Shelley.[7]

The universal nature of the OBE becomes especially clear when we look at the vocabulary of foreign languages. A term for the "double" or externalized form in which the OBE takes place exists in most languages of the world, obviously reflecting the experiences of its people.

> The Hebrews called it the *ruach*. In Egypt it was known as the *ka*, an exact replica of the physical body, but less dense. The Greeks knew it as the *eidolon*, the Romans as the *larva*, while in Tibet it is still referred to as the *bardo* body. In Germany, it was

> the *Jüdel* or *Doppelgänger* and in Norway the *fylgja*. The Ancient Britons gave it various names: *fetch*, *waft*, *task*, and *fye*. In China the *thankhi* left the body during sleep and was seen by others. The ancient Hindus spoke of the second body ... as the *Pranamayakosha*. The Buddhists called the double the *rupa*.... Stories [of out-of-the-body experiences] have come to us from primitive societies everywhere—from Australian aborigines, from North and South American Indians, from Zululand, Siberia, New Zealand, Tahiti, and elsewhere. The pattern is similar throughout.[8]

The great majority of people in the modern world, who don't believe in such things, are extremely startled when they have these experiences, but, interestingly enough, they describe them in terms very similar to those used by people brought up in societies which do believe in them. In short, the experience itself is so universal that it is not influenced by belief.

Have all God's chillun got wings?

Just how widespread are such experiences today? This question is not at all easy to answer. Since most of the people who have the experience have never heard of it, they are likely to regard it as unique, probably abnormal, and for obvious reasons, better kept to oneself. But there is a good deal of evidence that OBEs are less rare than might be supposed. For instance, quite a number of modern authors have written accounts of their own OBEs. Among them are Wordsworth, Emily Brontë, George Eliot, Alfred Tennyson, D.H. Lawrence, Virginia Woolf, John Buchan, Arthur Koestler, and Ernest Hemingway.[9]

More convincing evidence has been obtained by the sociologist Hornell Hart. In 1952 Hart asked 155 students at Duke University in North Carolina the following question: "Have you ever actually seen your physical body from a viewpoint outside that body, like standing beside the bed and looking at yourself lying in bed, or floating in the air near your body?" Twenty percent said yes. Fourteen years later, in 1966, a British research scientist named Celia Green asked 115 undergraduates at Southampton University a similar question, and in 1967 she put the same question to 350 Oxford undergraduates. Nineteen percent of the Southampton students said yes, while at Oxford 34 percent admitted to having had the experiences.[10]

Most of the people were, naturally, baffled by the experience and were unable to explain it, for not only does our society provide no explanation of such experiences, it doesn't even admit that they exist. Psychologist Francis Banks found that 45 percent of a group of churchgoers whom he questioned had had the experience. Psychiatrist Jule Eisenbud estimates that 25 percent of the population of the United States have projected their consciousness to points separate from their bodies, and in the course of lecturing before various audiences on the subject of OBEs, Robert Monroe and Herbert Greenhouse discovered that between one quarter and one third of their audiences admitted that it had happened to them.[11]

These incredible figures—a low of 19 to a high of 45 percent—indicate that OBEs are probably the best-kept secret of modern times. As the weight of orthodox scientific opinion holds that such experiences are impossible, most people prefer to keep quiet about them.

But do they really happen? Four levels of evidence

To try to answer this question, let's examine the evidence as systematically and thoroughly as possible. We will discuss four types of cases, arranged according to the amount of evidence supporting them.

Those cases on the first level, with the least evidence, are ones in which the person claims to have had an OBE but is alone throughout the experience and remains in the immediate vicinity of his or her body. The leading scholar of OBEs, an English geologist in his eighties named Robert Crookall, has gathered *over one thousand cases* at or above this level of evidence. It must be kept in mind that most of these people had never heard of the experience before, had never discussed it with anyone, had never read about it, and had, in fact, no idea whatever that it could happen. Despite this, these one thousand experiences are virtually identical, a fact which lends them a powerful validity.

Here is one of hundreds of examples of this type of case from Crookall's work:

> [A] Mrs. Prothero reports that she was so cold in bed one night that she covered her head with the bedclothes and, without realizing it, almost suffocated herself. She says, "I found myself out of my body, suspended horizontally above the bed. I looked down on the figure on the bed. I realized what was happening and thought, 'I must get my arms out and get some air.' Then I made a vigorous effort. I slipped back into my body. [The experience] was extremely pleasant and I was not afraid. [It] convinced me that I have a soul as well as a body."[12]

Or, also from Crookall's files, let us take the case of Mrs. D. E. Boorman, who writes:

> I was resting in bed. There was first a stillness. Then there was a swaying of what I thought was my physical body and I rose horizontally above it. "Enough," I cried and stopped a foot from the ceiling. Looking down I saw my physical body lying on the bed. Wishing myself back, I felt what was like a violent push in the chest. It then felt like slipping into a coat and I found myself back in my body.[13]

Because anyone can *say* that they have had an OBE, those experiences of greatest interest to researchers are cases in which the person observes events or situations that he was not in a physical position to see (because he was asleep, unconscious, clinically dead, or physically elsewhere), and these events are later confirmed by others.

Experiences of this type represent the second level of evidence, and many hundreds could be cited. The case already described of the English traveler who correctly observed all of the details of her husband's room while physically unconscious in a hotel room many miles away, is one of this kind.

In her survey of out-of-the-body experiences, Celia Green found a number of cases in which individuals had, during the experience, made observations about persons, events, or physical settings which could not have been visible to them from their physical bodies. She found that in all cases where it was possible to check these observations, they were in fact correct. (For example, one man, during his experience, noticed two pins and a pebble on top of a window ledge. These objects were completely invisible to view from below, but an investigation showed that they were indeed there.)[14]

In cases at the third level of evidence, the individual projects himself to a place distant from his body, *where he is seen in apparitional form by those present.* These cases are rarer than those in the two preceding categories because the astral body does not usually carry from the physical body sufficient physical material to be visible.

Nonetheless, many such cases exist, verified by all concerned. Consider the experience of Mr. Walter E. McBride, a bachelor farmer living a few miles southeast of Indian Springs, Indiana.

> About eight o'clock on the evening of 23rd December, [1935] I went to my bedroom which is on the lower floor of my house ... and retired ... feeling quite normal in every way.... The next thing I knew I was, preposterous as it sounds, floating in the room ... wide awake.... I saw that I was floating upward through the building ... the ceiling and upper floor failed to stop me ... I passed through them with ease.... I realized that I was moving through the air toward the north, and while I was not trying to do so, I seemed to know that I was going to my old home, several miles away [where his father still lived]....
>
> Going to the bedroom (by passing through the walls) I stood at the foot of the bed in which I saw Father reclining. "Father," I

> said to him, "Father!" ... he was watching me, for his eyes were fixed upon me and there seemed to be a look of surprise upon his face. [Mr. McBride stated that he had been concerned about his father during the entire day preceding his experience, as he felt that his father might be ill.] The knowledge came to me as I stood there that he was well.
>
> A moment later I found myself leaving again.... Reaching my bedroom once more ... I saw ... my own body, still lying on the bed where I had left it.... I got up and ... wrote down the time ... and ... what I had just experienced. Two days later, on Christmas Day, I paid Father a visit. Mrs. J.E. Wires, and her son, Earl G. Wires, of Shoals, Indiana, were also there visiting at the same time. Father verified my experience by stating that *he had seen me*, just as I had stood at the foot of his bed.... He too had written down the time of his vision, and it tallied.[15]

This written account was sent to OBE researcher Sylvan Muldoon by Mr. McBride. It was accompanied by a written statement signed by Mrs. Wires and her son attesting that the conversation between Mr. McBride and his father had taken place as described.

Another example of this kind has been provided by Mr. W.P. Herbert, who states that once, while living in England, he projected to the house of a friend of his in Nairobi, Kenya, a house which was entirely unfamiliar to him as he had never been to it. While there, he was visible to his friend's two little daughters.

> While projected there, I could see the house and everything about it.... When the two little girls were observing me their mother called and asked what they were doing. "Looking at Nunkie," was the reply. And they certainly were. They were looking right at me. They could not seem to understand how I got there.... When I later wrote to my friends, I described the house into which I had been projected and how I had seen the little girls; they wrote back that my description of the arrangements of the rooms, the windows, etc., was very accurate. They

> even sent me a photograph to show me the unusual window over the veranda which I described.[16]

At the fourth and highest level of evidence are cases in which, in addition to being seen, the projector is able to accomplish something further in front of witnesses, such as moving an object, awakening a witness by touch, speaking, carrying on a conversation, or discovering some detail of the environment which was unknown to witnesses, but later verified by them. These cases are rarest of all, but a number exist.

Eileen Landau, who regularly has OBEs, joined her husband Lucien in an experiment in September, 1955. Eileen, who slept in a room across the hall from her husband's, was to attempt, while "out," to move a physical object from her room into his. Awakening at dawn, Lucien found Eileen in his room, looking perfectly life-like except for her extreme pallor. As she glided backwards toward her own room, he rose from bed and followed her, at which point he saw *two* Eileens, because the physical one was still lying asleep in bed. The astral Eileen vanished in the vicinity of the sleeping physical one. Returning to his room, Landau found on the floor a toy rubber dog which belonged to her and which had been sitting on the bureau in her room—Eileen reported that she had awakened to find herself out of her body, and, remembering that she was to attempt the experiment, succeeded in lifting the toy dog.

> "I remember taking it through the door, across the landing, to the other room. I did not find the dog heavy, or difficult to hold."[17]

In another case of this fourth type, a woman fell asleep one night thinking of her dead cousin, whose funeral was to take place the following day. As she was unable to attend, a friend had gone in her place. Awakening out of her body, she

> floated out of the room, down the stairs, and through the door. With no consciousness of traveling, she found herself standing …

> in the dining room of her cousin's home eighty-six miles away. She noted the position of the night lamp on the table, the place in the room where her cousin's body lay, and the color of the casket. Then she went into her friend's bedroom and pulled the sleeping woman's arm. Her friend opened her eyes and saw her, and an instant later she was above her physical body, then back in it.

A day later the friend returned and told her that she had been awakened by a tug at her arm, and had then seen her friend, who disappeared a moment later.[18]

The case of Mrs. Katheryn Riggs is one of several published cases which have involved conversations. She writes:

> Some ... years ago, I was a patient at G_____, I_____, and was prepared to undergo a very serious operation. I was flat on my back and could not move—could not help myself in any way. ...
>
> One day another patient was brought in, operated upon, and placed in a ward some distance from me.... Her moans were pitiful and during the night I felt I wanted to go to her and say something to comfort her. *I felt myself leave my body.* I left that body in the bed and went down the ward to her side. I spoke to her for a little while, and then said: "I must leave you now or my body will be cold." I then went up to my own bed and saw my body lying upon it. ...
>
> I told the sister about it later on, and she was very interested and said she would take me to see the other patient when I was able to go.... When she did so ... the woman said: "Oh—... I know you—you are the one who came in here to cheer me up that night after the operation when I was so ill." The sister was so interested in all this, because she knew I had been too ill to move at the time.... It seems so very strange. I hope my letter is of interest to you.[19]

Finally, we have the experience of Oliver Fox, whose girlfriend Elsie discovered, while projected, something about his room that he didn't know himself. The two agreed that, on a particular night, she would attempt a projection to his room, to which she had never been. During the night, Fox awoke:

> Suddenly there appeared a large egg-shaped cloud of intensely brilliant bluish-white light. In the middle [of it] was Elsie, hair loose, and in her nightdress. She seemed perfectly solid as she stood by a chest of drawers near the right side of my bed. Thus she remained, regarding me … and running her fingers along the top and front side of [my] desk.… Rising on one elbow I called her name, and she vanished as suddenly as she had come.…
>
> The following evening we met and I found Elsie very excited and triumphant. "I did come to you!" She greeted me. "I *really* did. I went to sleep, willing that I would, and all at once I was *there!* This morning I knew just how everything was in your room."[20]

Elsie described to Fox everything she could remember, including the relative positions of the door, bed, window, fireplace, wash stand, chest of drawers and dressing table. She gave him a detailed description of a leather-covered desk lined with gilt, and said that she had run her fingers along a projecting ridge on the front of this desk. Fox protested that there was no projecting ridge on the front of his desk, but when he got home he saw that the desk, placed to face the wall, had hinges which he had quite forgotten. These hinges made a continuous projecting gilt ridge, just as Elsie had described. Owing to its position, Elsie had mistaken the back of the desk for the front.

Why do they happen?

The evidence of these last four cases is compelling. Do such extraordinary experiences have any clearly discernible cause, or do they just inexplicably "happen"? An investigation of hundreds of published cases shows a clear pattern: these experiences are of three different kinds—spontaneous, voluntary, or enforced.

Spontaneous experiences

These almost always occur while the person is falling asleep, waking up, or actually asleep. (It is interesting to note here that occultists have long believed that the self regularly leaves the body during sleep, although most persons are unaware of it.) The individual will awaken fully to find himself out of his body. In fact, this type of OBE is the most common. Although we don't understand why, the "self" can separate from the physical body during sleep. Interestingly, an examination of many hundreds of these experiences reveals that once separation has occurred, there are three possibilities: consciousness may be full, partial or nonexistent. If full consciousness is present, then the person has a vivid OBE. In cases of partial consciousness, the person has dim, dream-like memories of the experience, with consciousness fading in and out, and can be certain that the experience occurred only if he was seen externalized by witnesses. If there is no consciousness, then the individual will have no memory whatever of his experience, and only the fact that witnesses saw him "out" indicates that the experience occurred. That consciousness can vary during the experience is clear from the fact that Sylvan Muldoon and many other habitual projectors have become conscious, or intermittently conscious, while out some distance from their bodies, but have no memory of the rest of the journey.

Voluntary experiences

In these cases the person may be a habitual projector whose first experience was spontaneous. A desire to have OBEs at will has led several such people to develop procedures for getting "out," usually involving relaxation techniques while on the verge of sleep. Such methods are described in books by Sylvan Muldoon, Oliver Fox, Yram, and Robert Monroe.[21]

More commonly, the voluntary projector has one or a very small number of OBEs, usually during sleep, apparently in response to a strong desire to see someone about whom he is deeply concerned; he awakens to find the "trip" to that person occurring. Voluntary experiences appear to be the rarest category.

Enforced experiences

These appear to be intermediate in frequency between the common spontaneous experiences, and the rarer voluntary type; they occur in connection with traumas to the physical body which seem to force the self temporarily "out." Many such experiences have been caused by asphyxiation, anaesthesia, illness, unconsciousness from an injury to the body, and the use of psychedelic drugs.

Modern scientists in search of the soul

An extensive historical tradition supports the existence of OBEs, and, in fact, the evidence strongly suggests that probably the only group of people who do not believe in these experiences are those who have had the benefit of a modern education. Now, a small group of scientists, intrigued by the weight of this historical evidence, and by the profusion of contemporary accounts of such experiences, has begun systematic research with individuals who claim that they are able to leave their bodies at will.

This work is being sponsored by the American Society for Psychical Research in New York, the Psychical Research Foundation of Durham, North Carolina, the Division of Parapsychology of the University of Virginia, and the Stanford Research Institute in Menlo Park, California. These researchers, whose work may one day be remembered as among the most significant ever undertaken by scientists, have begun their search for the soul. As is to be expected with a new research venture, some of the experiments which they have designed have yielded negative or inconclusive results. But they have come up with some findings, findings which can only be described as fascinating.

The electroencephalograph

The first OBE experiment with an electroencephalograph, or EEG (a device for recording the electrical activity of the brain), was conducted by Dr. Charles Tart, a University of California psychologist, after one of his friends, a young woman in her early twenties, claimed that, since childhood, she had had OBEs two to four times a week during sleep. She would awaken, she said, to find herself floating near the ceiling, looking down at her sleeping body below. He invited her to reproduce this feat in his laboratory while wired to an electroencephalograph to see what her brain was doing while she was "out." Tart constructed a shelf close to the ceiling of the room in which she was to sleep. Above it he placed an electric clock, and on it a five-digit random number. On the fourth night of the experiment, Miss Z awoke, correctly identified the number (it was 25132), and indicated at what time she had floated up to see it. When her EEG readings for that time period were examined, they were discovered to be unique. Dr. William Dement, one of the world's leading authorities on sleep research, was unable to identify her reading as any known sleeping or waking pattern.[22]

Another habitual projector, Robert Monroe, produced unusual EEG readings in conjunction with his OBEs,[23] and a consistent EEG finding has been a loss of voltage in the subject's EEG reading while he claims to be "out."[24] Something, it seems, is going on.

The dials went wild

Dr. Karlis Osis, Director of Research at the American Society for Psychical Research (ASPR), constructed a box containing an electrical field and instrumentation designed to detect any disturbance of it. He asked Pat Price, a habitual projector, to try to "fly into" the box. On several occasions when he claims to have done so, says Dr. Osis, "the recorder went wild as if something had disturbed the electric field inside the box."[25]

Flashes of light

Alex Tanous, another habitual projector being studied by the ASPR, experiences himself, while out, as giving off light. Could this impression be measured objectively? Obliging researchers set up a totally black darkroom containing a number of light-sensing devices known as photomultipliers, which detect and augment light. From a room in another part of the building, Tanous was asked to project himself into the darkroom. "Simultaneously with my entering the darkroom," says Tanous, "the photomultipliers recorded five or six bursts of [light]."[26] Such a coincidence between subjective and objective impressions is rather remarkable.

Swaying feathers

A further experiment has been carried out by the ASPR, using an enclosure containing a feather suspended on a string. The projector is asked to sit in another room, go out of his body, and take an astral "dive" into the enclosure in an effort to move the feather; any such movement is measured electronically and recorded on graph paper. Alex Tanous, Pat Price, and several other subjects have apparently brought about measurable movement of the feather when projected.[27] Thus, it would not be overly optimistic to say that positive results from instrumentation experiments are beginning to accumulate.

Animal detectors

The apparent sensitivity of animals to paranormal phenomena has often been noted. This sensitivity is now being tested in the scientific search for the soul. Dr. Robert Morris, a psychologist at the Psychical Research Foundation in Durham, North Carolina, has conducted experiments with Stuart "Blue" Harary, using a gerbil, a hamster, a snake, and a cat. The animals were caged and observed to determine their normal behavior pattern in this kind of captivity. They were then observed while Blue, in another room, attempted to project himself into the cage with the animal. The gerbil and the hamster did not react, but the snake and the cat did. According to Morris,

> the snake ... got pretty upset at the time Blue was trying to visit it. It hyperventilated. There was definitely a reaction.

Scott Rogo, a psychical researcher from California who observed this experiment, put it more dramatically:

> When Blue visited the snake in his out-of-the-body state, it stopped its typical manoeuvring around the cage and started literally to attack. It sort of bit at the air, viciously, for about twenty seconds—twenty seconds which were right in the middle of the time Blue, without knowing what was going on in the laboratory, claimed to be out of his body and in the cage with the snake.

The cat, a pet of Blue's given to him by Morris, normally raced back and forth in his cage, but suddenly became completely quiet during the time that Blue claimed he was projected into the cage with the animal. Morris repeated the experiment four more times with identical results; each time, the animal calmed down dramatically whenever Blue claimed to be present with it in the cage. According to Morris, the results, statistically, were "dramatically beyond ... chance." During the time the cat was "alone," it ran around the cage constantly and meowed thirty-seven times. During the time that Blue claimed to be visiting it, however, "the animal stopped running around the cage, did not meow once, and seemed to be attentive to a presence in the enclosure that no human in the room could perceive."[28]

Indoor targets

A question of basic interest to OBE researchers is whether the projector is literally outside his body, or is simply gathering impressions of the "target" area clairvoyantly while he is actually still within it. To try to find the answer, in 1971 Dr. Osis advertised for people who could voluntarily project. Those who lived near the ASPR's New York headquarters were tested there in person; the rest were invited to "fly in" to Dr. Osis's office to identify target objects which he had prepared. Some who did described their journeys in vivid detail:

> A projector from Toronto, Canada, Mrs. Terry Marmoreo, was drawn [at first] to a burning building a block away. Another projector flew into an apartment across the street, attracted by more interesting things than were happening in Dr. Osis's office. In one case, a psychic who admitted she was stimulated more by people than by objects found herself on the first floor of the ASPR building, where several persons were preparing an art exhibit. She accurately described what a young woman was wearing and saw a man carrying a long box to the back yard.
>
> The mode of travel differed from psychic to psychic. Some, like Alex Tanous, merely had to think of the office and they were there in a flash.... Terry Marmoreo was conscious of flying from Toronto and saw ships in New York harbor. When she got to the building, she was momentarily trapped in the hall on the fourth floor. Ann Jensen of Enid, Oklahoma, passed over Louisville, Kentucky, on the way to New York, but had trouble getting through the door of the ASPR building. Paul Neary, who made it from Atlanta, Georgia, to New York in five minutes, floated over Columbus Circle a few blocks away, then glided up the steps of the building.

In order to determine whether his projectors were actually there, rather than merely gathering clairvoyant impressions at a distance, Osis designed targets involving, in some cases, optical illusions which could be seen only from a given point in space. Were the projector using a kind of clairvoyant "x-ray" vision to gather impressions from a distance, he would not see the illusion, only what was actually there. For example, Ingo Swann was asked to project himself to a target which consisted of objects hidden from view in a closed box and visible only through a small opening. Someone who looked through this opening would be able to see the target objects, but only reflected in a mirror. Swann saw the objects reversed, precisely as he would have had he been literally, physically present, looking at the mirror.

Another subject, Elwood Babbitt, was instructed to enter Dr. Osis's office by the door (most projectors find they can as easily enter through the wall or ceiling), and from that angle of vision describe what was on a table.

> He correctly saw the brown-tinted plasticine figure of a smiling girl on the right-hand side of the table. He also saw a very large plant that was at the right rear of the office and a picture hanging on the wall. A small toy chair had been placed behind the girl's back so that it could not be seen from the doorway.

When Babbitt sent Dr. Osis a sketch of what he had seen, it was accurate. The objects he had seen were, in fact, precisely where he had drawn them. *But most interesting of all, the toy chair, which could not be seen from the door, was not sketched.*

Another similar experiment involved a box christened an "optical image device" containing a picture which was actually an optical illusion visible only when the projector looked through a viewing slot. Dr. Osis later described the results as "significant" and "consistent with the OBE hypothesis." But perhaps as significant are two unforeseen incidents which occurred during this experiment. On one occasion projector Alex Tanous complained that he couldn't see the target picture properly because there was too little light in the box. The experimenters investigated and discovered that Tanous was right: a mechanical failure had occurred, darkening the box. And Ingo Swann, after one of his projections, made the same complaint. Investigation this time revealed that the light in the box had gone out!

Projectors often report that they travel in a body which looks like their physical form, but which is invisible to most embodied persons; a number of psychics, however, have claimed to be able to see these OBE bodies. With these claims in mind, Dr. Osis asked psychic Christine Whiting to be present in a target room during the time that some of the projectors were scheduled to appear there. During one of Alex Tanous's scheduled projections, she claimed to see his astral body next to a table with target objects on it which had been prepared for his proposed visit.

> Although she had never met him, she gave an accurate description of his physical appearance and said that he was astrally dressed in brown corduroy trousers and a long-sleeved white cotton shirt with the sleeves rolled up to his elbows.
>
> When I spoke to Alex later, I asked him to describe what he wore during his fly-in episodes but did not tell him how he had appeared to Miss Whiting. He recalled wearing a cotton shirt with sleeves rolled up and brown slacks which [he said] looked like corduroy trousers.

When Christine Whiting met Tanous for the first time some months later, she recognized him as the man she had seen projected into Dr. Osis's office.[29]

Outdoor targets

These experiments are among the most bizarre and astounding yet carried out on OBEs. At the Stanford Research Institute in Menlo Park, California, two physicists, Dr. Russell Targ and his associate Harold Puthoff, have conducted some mind-boggling experiments involving what they call "remote viewing." Reasoning that subjects might be more motivated to project to interesting places such as other countries, rather than to artificial targets like "optical image devices," Targ asked Ingo Swann to choose his own "outdoor" target.

When Swann suggested that he be given only the latitude and longitude of such a target, Targ obtained a pair of geographical coordinates from the geographical division of the Institute, without finding out for himself to which location they applied. He gave the bearings to Swann, who then projected to an island in the Indian Ocean so tiny that it is not on most maps: Kerguelen, where the French maintain a meteorological station. Swann sketched the island, including the general shape and the more prominent landmarks. When this sketch was compared with an actual map of the island, the two were found to be almost identical. In addition, Swann had correctly observed that the few inhabitants of the island spoke French.

Could this incredible feat be duplicated? The same experiment was tried with a second volunteer subject, Pat Price, a former mayor and police commissioner of Burbank, California. Upon being given only the geographical coordinates, Price was able to travel to the same island, where he stated that he heard the inhabitants speaking French. His subsequent sketch of the island was also accurate, and contained even more correct detail than had Swann's.[30]

Characteristics of the OBE

It is important to remember that most people who have had OBEs were previously unaware that such an experience was possible. This makes it all the more fascinating to discover the same features recurring constantly in the hundreds of accounts of OBEs which have been collected.

Reality

The first feature repeatedly mentioned is the *compelling reality* of the experience. Perhaps the best evidence of this reality is the statement by many projectors that they did not realize that anything unusual was occurring until they happened to see their own unconscious bodies. But so vivid are these experiences that even the sight of one's own unconscious body may not be enough to convince the projector that the situation is really "abnormal." The following case, which involves a Wisconsin farmer, will illustrate the point:

> He had hitched his team, one wintry day, and gone into the country after a load of firewood. On his return he was sitting atop the loaded sleigh. A light snow was falling. Without warning, a hunter (who happened to be near the road) discharged his gun at a rabbit. The horses jumped, jerking the sleigh and throwing the driver to the ground, head first.
>
> ... no sooner had he landed upon the ground than he was conscious of standing up, and of seeing another "himself" lying motionless near the road, face down in the snow. He saw the snow falling all about, saw the steam rising from the horses, saw the hunter running toward him. All this was very exact; but his great bemuddlement was that there were *two* of him, for he believed at the time that he was observing all that occurred from another physical body.
>
> As the hunter came near, things seemed to grow dim. The next conscious impression he had was of finding himself upon the ground, with the hunter trying to revive him. What he had seen from his astral body was so real that he could not believe that there were not two physical bodies, and he even went so far as to look for tracks in the snow, at the place where he knew he had been standing.[31]

Marcel Louis Forhan, a habitual projector who wrote a book about his experiences under the pseudonym of Yram, described the experience of getting up in the morning without realizing that his physical body had remained behind on the bed; so ordinary did everything seem to him that it was not until he noticed his body that he realized he had unwittingly projected.[32] So well known are such cases to students of OBEs that they have been called cases that "lack insight," meaning that the subject is at first unaware that he is in an abnormal state.

The following two examples are from Oxford University researcher Celia Green's book, *Out-of-the-Body Experiences.* "In a typical case of this kind," she writes, "the subject may ... continue on his way without realizing that his physical body has sustained an accident and is lying unconscious."[33]

> I got up from the ground where I lay, surprised that I felt no pain or bruising, and moved away. I saw people running and looked around to see why. Then I saw that my body was still laying [sic] in the road and they were running toward that, some of them passed me as I stood there ... [they did not seem to see her]. I was moving about, thinking I was my normal body.... Everything looked normal.[34]
>
> I was seated at the tea-table with my family ... about 5 p.m. on an autumn afternoon. My mother or father suddenly reminded me ... that I should be at my music lesson, so I hurriedly collected my music case and rushed out of the front door and out of the gate on to the wet pavement which was strewn with leaves.
>
> *What I thought:* I must hurry. I must be careful. It would be awful if I slipped on one of those leaves and fell. Vivid picture of my prostrate body on the pavement outside the house, while "I" sped along the road, almost reaching the corner of the block.
>
> *What actually happened as told me later:* My parents watched me leave the house.... They saw me fall, then my mother said, "She's not getting up." My father got out to me and I heard him say to another person who had crossed the road to help me, "I'll take her. I'm her father."[35]

The sight of the person's own body will usually lead to an awareness that an abnormal event is occurring, and to a rapid termination of it caused by the strong emotions of fear and amazement produced by the experience.

> Then I saw on my left a group of white-coated figures [she had been hospitalized], bending over "something" on the floor.

> Suddenly I realized that that "something" was me. And immediately I flashed back into my body with the speed of light.[36]

In fact, in Celia Green's survey of 400 people who claimed to have had OBEs, many commented both on the utter reality of the experience and on the sense of personal completeness involved in it. *None of her subjects* stated that he had felt personally incomplete, insubstantial, or unreal during the experience; all felt completely identified with their normal selves.

> The part of me that was out of my body was the real me, as I knew it, the part that sees, thinks and feels....
>
> My identity and consciousness were exactly the same as usual....
>
> I felt completely me.[37]

The OBE *body*

While out of the body, in what shape or form, if any, does one find oneself? Is the shape of the self a replica of the physical form? Is it some shape other than the recognizably human one? Or does the fundamental human consciousness have any shape at all, or even occupy space? When we examine the vast number of published accounts of OBEs we can answer such questions quite clearly. And it turns out that all of these things may happen—for the human self is protean, and may appear in many forms once free of the physical body—even, as we shall see, fully dressed!

Many projectors have a fully human shape, precisely duplicating the physical body and including either the clothing being worn at the time, or another commonly worn outfit. Here is one projector's experience:

> I looked down at my second self and found myself to be a complete replica of my material self. I touched my clothes, and looked at myself and was astounded to see that I was wearing the

> same black skirt [and] white blouse with small red spots on it [and the] same shoes etc.... I can remember touching myself and feeling the texture of my clothing. This all felt quite solid.[38]

I have already described Eileen Landau's successful attempt to move an object while "out." As she was concluding this experiment, her husband saw her.

> I woke up suddenly, it was dawn, and there was just about enough light coming in through curtains to enable me to read ... [there] stood ... Eileen, facing northwest, and looking straight ahead towards the window. [She] was wearing a night dress, [her] face was extremely pale, almost white. [She] was moving slowly backwards towards the door, but ... was otherwise motionless, [she] was not walking ... I got out of bed and followed. I could then clearly see [her] moving figure, *which was quite opaque and looking like a living person* ... and at the same time the head of [the physical] Eileen, asleep in her bed, the bedclothes rising and falling as she breathed.[39]

Other doubles, while precise replicas of the physical form in all other respects, are transparent. Mr. F. Thompson describes his experience:

> I found myself in my bedroom, fully conscious and ... hovering horizontally over my body! This hovering "body" of mine seemed [to be of] a diaphanous composition, and its form seemed to be a counterpart of my physical self and aligned above it correspondingly.[40]

In other OBEs, the subject's consciousness and sensory awareness are contained not in a duplicate body but in a form which entirely lacks the familiar human shape! Some of the non-human possibilities are illustrated in the following examples:

"I" had no substance or form of any kind, but was aware of an area of control vaguely oval in shape, about 2½ feet in breadth and about a foot in depth.

It was as if I, that is, the part of me that thinks, were contained in a small circle.

I feel like a single eye that is lit up and about 2½ inches in diameter.

I am disembodied, but in a small space which has a definite size and location.

It was not another body; [it was] more like a magnetic or electric field.[41]

The evidence that some projectors may occupy non-human shapes while "out" is not confined to the testimony of projectors themselves. Robert Monroe is a Virginia businessman who has written a book about his numerous OBEs. After making it clear that he most often occupies a shape which appears human to him but is usually invisible to embodied persons, he describes the following experience:

In the early evening, around seven-thirty, I decided to try to visit R.W. in her apartment some eight miles distant ... I had no difficulty [projecting], and found myself immediately in a living room. There was ... R.W. sitting in a chair near a bright light. I moved toward her.... Then I was sure she saw me, but she seemed frightened. I backed away ... but something pulled me back to [my body], and I found myself in my bedroom.

There was a most unusual aftermath. The next day R.W. asked me what I was doing the night before. I asked her why, and she stated, "I was sitting in the living room after supper, reading the paper. Something made me look up, and there on the other side of the room was something hanging and waving in the air." I asked her what it looked like.

"It was like a filmy piece of gray chiffon," she said. "I could see the wall and chair behind it, and it started to come toward me. I was frightened, and I thought it might be you ... it just hung there in mid-air, waving slightly.... Then it backed away and faded out quickly." She asked if it was really me, and I said I thought it might be.

"Well, next time, say something so I'll be sure it's you," she answered. "Then I won't be so scared." I assured her I would. [It seems] I'm not a very bright-hued ghost, and I don't have [a] human shape—sometimes.[42]

Psychical researcher Raymond Bayless gives us another example:

On February 5, 1955, I was seated on a couch at my home, when I saw a peculiar shadow form which was trapezoidal in shape and approximately the height of a man. It leaned at an angle to the right and seemed to have no connection with the floor. As I watched it in astonishment, it rushed—the only word I can really use to describe its strange motion—through two glass doors which were in an opened position and into the living room, where it suddenly disappeared. I automatically checked the clock and saw it was 6.15 p.m.

I left my home and went about eleven miles to the studio of Mr. Attila von Szalay [a psychic whose paranormal powers Mr. Bayless was studying]. When he met me at the door, I said, "Guess what happened to me?" He replied that I had seen him, and in the course of the following conversation stated that he had deliberately attempted to project himself to my home so I could prove to myself that astral projection was a reality.[43]

Still other subjects do not see themselves as being contained in any sort of shape or form, human or otherwise. For example, they may describe themselves as "a disembodied consciousness," "a pinpoint of presence," or as "looking at [myself] from nothing." Here is one woman's experience:

> At first I thought it was very funny; it couldn't be possible. I'm up here yet I'm lying in bed down there. I wondered if I could wake my husband up and tell him *but I seemed to have no hands to shake him or touch him; there was nothing of me—all I could do was see.*[44]

Solid, transparent, human, oval, a small circle, a magnetic field, a piece of filmy chiffon, a trapezoidal shadow, a disembodied consciousness, a pinpoint of presence? How are such variations possible? Why does one person have form while another is formless? Robert Monroe's courageous explorations beyond his body have supplied data which can provide an answer to these questions. On a September afternoon in 1960, Monroe left his body.

> Again I noticed the strange rubbery elasticity of this other body. I could stand in the middle of the room and reach out to touch the wall some eight feet away. At first, my arm didn't come anywhere near the wall. Then I kept pushing my hand outward and suddenly, the ... wall was against my hand. Just by pushing out, my arm had stretched to twice its length.... When I relaxed the pushing out, the arm came back and seemed normal. This confirms the other evidence that you can make it just about whatever shape you think of, consciously or unconsciously.[45]

After many such experiences, Monroe concluded that this "second body" is completely responsive to thought and may take whatever shape or form is *transmitted by the mind* at any given moment. Since human beings are strongly habituated to having the appearances of their bodies, Monroe speculates that this is why so many projectors look exactly like their physical forms.

The evidence cited does not prove, but certainly suggests, that the human "self" is an energy form which may assume any shape from a small point in space to a precise replica of the physical body. Why our familiarity with the human form does not always produce it in the astral form is yet to be discovered. For reasons unknown, the mind does not always, perhaps, give the "order." For instance Monroe, after many hundreds of projections, noticed that at times his astral form had begun to lack limbs and assume a kind of ovoid, incompletely human shape.

As we have seen, the astral form may appear completely solid, transparent, or entirely invisible. Its visibility to its occupant varies similarly. One habitual projector, Oliver Fox, who states that he normally sees his OBE body, adds that "occasionally, I have not been able to see any astral body when I looked for it—no legs, no arms, no body!—an extraordinary sensation—just a *consciousness,* a man invisible even to himself."[46] Why should this be so?

One of the more spectacular types of spiritualist séance is the "materialization" séance. In order for "materialization" to occur, a medium must emit a white, jelly-like substance known as "ectoplasm." Chemical analyses have shown that it consists of albumin and amino-acids—in other words, it is protein. This protein can form a vapor, at which point some discarnates seem able to use it to make themselves visible to the embodied. According to Dr. Douglas M. Baker, all human bodies give this substance off in varying quantities.[47] Hence, the visibility of the astral form, both to other embodied persons and to its occupant, probably varies with the amount of physical substance brought with it from the physical body. If it carries none, the energy form of the "self" would be invisible both to others and to its own occupant. A larger quantity would make it visible to its occupant, but not to embodied persons; a still larger quantity would render it visible to both, and its shape would usually be determined by the thoughts of its occupant.

Astral clothes

Many skeptics are amused to learn that apparitions of the dead and the astral bodies of the living, when they are visible to the embodied, are fully clothed, including in their appearance such ghostly accessories as walking-sticks, jewelry, and so on. But like Monroe's arm, the substance of the astral body can be extruded and manipulated in accordance with the thoughts and desires of the projector. As he puts it "if you have been conditioned to acute awareness of nakedness, you will automatically think you are clothed—and so you are."[48] As Dr. Wiltse, when close to death, described the new body in which he found himself:

> I seemed to be translucent, of a bluish cast, and perfectly naked. With a painful sense of embarrassment, I fled toward the partially opened door to escape the eyes of the two ladies whom I was facing as well as others who ... were about me, but upon reaching the door *I found myself clothed.*[49]

Celia Green's survey of four hundred people who have had OBEs reveals that, when the astral body resembles the physical one "[it] *tends to be dressed normally, that is, in clothes that the subject is, or might be, wearing at the time.*"[50] That these clothes are in fact formed from the subtle substance of the astral body is proven by those cases in which projectors have actually witnessed their creation! Two habitual projectors, Sylvan Muldoon and Caroline Larsen, claim to have witnessed this process. According to them the astral form is surrounded by an emanation of light, which it generates, and which is usually called an "aura." Astral "clothes" are formed by the effect of either the conscious or unconscious mind on this "aura." Muldoon states that no one need be concerned about finding himself having an OBE in the nude:

> For his aura surrounds him, and no sooner does he begin to think about his clothing than he will discover that his thoughts have already formed or materialized clothing for him.
>
> On one occasion, I noticed the clothing forming itself out of the emanation surrounding my astral body ... and the clothing was exactly like that covering my physical body.
>
> One can awaken, from unconsciousness, in the astral [i.e., awaken to find oneself having an OBE], and find that he is already

> clothed! Thus, it is evident that … the subconscious mind … [may cause] the clothing to be brought into being … the *conscious* mind does not necessarily create the … attire.[51]

Similarly, during an OBE, Caroline Larsen entered the home of a neighbor who was very ill—in fact, dying. Several times, she observed his astral form rise from his physical body and then return to it, before leaving it for the last time. She reports that "each time he stepped out of his physical body his aura instantly covered him with a dress similar to a sack suit he always wore."[52]

Invisibility

The claim that the OBE body is invisible to embodied persons deserves some elaboration. Indeed, for someone having an OBE, it is one of the most astounding features of the experience. Dr. George Ritchie, the psychiatrist whose experience was described at the beginning of this chapter, was so invisible in his out-of-the-body state that an orderly carrying a tray of instruments in the hospital corridor walked right through him! Oliver Fox has stated that during his OBEs he was usually completely invisible to embodied persons. During one of his OBEs, he found himself on a street of red brick houses. He decided to enter one, curious as to whether the inhabitants would be aware of his presence. Passing up the stairs to the second floor, he entered a bedroom in which he found a young lady combing her hair in front of a mirror.

> I knew, from my previous experiences, that there was small likelihood of my being visible to her. It occurred to me that I would stand just behind her and look over her shoulder into the mirror. I wanted to see whether it would reflect my face. I stood so close to her that I was conscious of a pleasant fragrance emanating from her hair. In the mirror I could see her face—a good-looking one, I think her eyes were grey—but not the faintest indication of mine was visible.[53]

After three weeks of illness, Dr. George W. Kelley was pronounced dead by his doctor, although he later recovered. Finding himself out of his body, he tried in vain to get his wife's attention:

> I found communication impossible. I touched her but she seemed *unconscious of my presence.*[54]

These experiences are not unique to our society, as is clear from a passage which appears in the *Bardo Thödol* or *Tibetan Book of the Dead.* This Tibetan Buddhist work on the nature of death was first committed to writing in the eighth century A.D., although its teachings are much older. According to this book, after physical death has occurred the dead person will find himself out of his body and fully conscious in the "astral" or "bardo" body, from which he will witness the mourning of loved ones, while being unable to gain their attention:

> To all those who are weeping (thou shalt say) "Here I am, weep not." *But they not hearing thee*, thou wilt think, "I am dead!"[55]

Permeability

Another amazing, yet highly repetitive feature of these experiences is that the OBE body is usually completely permeable to matter—it passes right through it without the least impediment, without even any sensation! The effect of this on a person conditioned to making solid contact with physical objects can be extremely unsettling. Sylvan Muldoon had this experience for the first time during his first OBE at the age of twelve. Finding himself out of his body, frightened and astonished, he tried to leave his room in order to awaken the other occupants of the house:

> I attempted to open the door, but found myself passing through it. Another miracle to my already astonished mind! Going from one room to another I tried fervently to arouse the sleeping occu-

> pants of the house. I clutched at them, calling them, tried to shake them, but my hands passed through them as though they were but vapours.[56]

One of Celia Green's subjects, during his OBE, attempted to turn on the light in his bedroom:

> I pressed [the] switch down but my finger went right through the switch button. Tried this several times. I thought I would make a test. I put my flat hand not once but several times through the box ... where the wires are joined to [the] electric switch. It traveled right through the box.[57]

According to Green, this usually happens when a person having an OBE attempts to make tactile contact with his environment. Here is another example:

> Then something happened which puzzled me at the time and has continued to puzzle me ever since. I moved away from my body toward the door, thinking to open it and go out into the starlight; but to my surprise I found that the door was no obstruction whatsoever. I simply passed through it as the sun's rays pass through a pane of glass.[58]

In an OBE during sleep, one projector says:

> I found myself moving toward the wall and supposed that the wall would halt me, but [I] passed right through it into open air. Outside stood a tree and I passed through it [as well] without any resistance.[59]

Perhaps even more extraordinary is the sensation of passing without any resistance through the body of another human being, an experience which Sylvan Muldoon claims to have had repeatedly:

> One will dodge other persons at times. One may be walking along the street, and, on meeting someone in the flesh, will dodge unconsciously. On the other hand, one will at times pass right through earthly people—never think of colliding with them ... this is a thrill indeed when one does it for the first time![60]

And perhaps most extraordinary of all is the sensation, while traveling during an OBE, of passing through material structures! Robert Monroe says of his OBE travels:

> It's a little disconcerting when you rush headlong toward a building or tree and go right through it.... You never quite get over the physical-body conditioning that such things are solid.[61]

However, on rare occasions habitual projectors have stated that they found themselves unable to pass through matter, or that they did so, but with unaccustomed difficulty:

> When I came up against the wall, I seemed to be unable to penetrate it.... I pushed with my outstretched arms ... There was a moment of resistance, then I went through. But there was one difference. As I went through to the outside, I felt and identified every layer of material in the wall—the paint, the plaster, the lath, the sheathing, and finally the shingles on the outside.[62]

There are thus three different possibilities, each of them reported over and over again: most commonly, the OBE body passes through matter instantaneously, and without the slightest resistance; more rarely, matter is passed through with some resistance, or else cannot be passed through at all. The most plausible explanation for these variations lies with the amount of ectoplasmic material carried by the OBE body—which may render it invisible, transparent, or solid in appearance, and, correspondingly, permeable, semi-permeable, or impermeable to matter.

Traveling in the OBE state

Concerning modes of travel, again we find quite explicit and repetitive experiences. Habitual projectors state that one may imitate physical modes of travel by simply walking; one may "glide" just above the ground; one may also rise to a higher altitude and glide; or one may travel, seemingly in instantaneous fashion, to one's destination. But by far the most incredible feature of astral traveling is that *it may be done by thought.* Oliver Fox, attempting to rise to a high altitude, willed himself to ascend:

> The effect was truly surprising. Instantly the earth fell from my feet—that was how it seemed to me, because of the suddenness and speed of my ascent. I looked down on my home, now no bigger than a matchbox; the streets were now only thick lines separating the houses. I ... continued to ascend straight up. Soon the earth was hidden by white clouds. Up and up and up. Velocity ever increasing. The loneliness I felt was indescribable. I got really frightened.... I willed to descend. Instantly the process was reversed ... earth came into sight through the fleecy veil of clouds and rose up to meet my feet.[63]

Here are statements concerning "thought-travel" made by three habitual projectors:

> You "think" of the person at the end of your destination. In a few moments, you are there.
>
> The simple act of thinking will transport you wheresoever you wish.
>
> Imagine where you want to go and you will be there.

To those of us used to being bound to our bodies, this sounds delightfully entertaining, but it can be disconcerting, as the following experiences will show. Monsieur Semjonov awakened in the night to find himself standing in the middle of his room. Moving forward, he was terrified to note that he *passed through* the chairs in his room and saw his body still asleep in bed. What followed was scarcely more reassuring.

> Without cause, I think of Trocadero Place. Incredible as it sounds, I am [suddenly] there, right at the entrance to the Avenue Henri Martin! The appearance of the square, cold and dark under a rainy sky, impresses me painfully.... I think of you ... and instantly I am in your studio.[64]

In the OBE state, the tendency of thought to "accelerate" one toward the object of thought can be quite alarming:

> I ... got rather frightened, especially when I realized I only had to look at something and want to approach it, for me to start moving in that direction. I didn't have to put one foot in front of another. I just glided, in the upright position. It was the acceleration which frightened me.[65]
>
> I began to wonder what it would be like to go through the ward door. As I looked at the door handle, I found myself moving towards it, gathering speed so rapidly, I got frightened.[66]

Directing one's attention toward any person or place, however distant, can produce a virtually instantaneous journey. One man, during his first OBE, thought with curiosity of his neighbor's room and instantly found himself standing in it! A Miss Okenden on several occasions felt concern for a friend during an OBE, and no sooner had the thought formed than she found herself with that friend. A Mrs. Newby, finding herself out of her body, but still apparently in a reclining position, described what happened:

> I no sooner thought of getting up than I was in the centre of the room.[67]

The world of the dead

If astral travelers can travel, then where do they go? An analysis of more than one thousand cases of OBEs by Robert Crookall reveals that, in 85 percent, the "traveler" was right here with the rest of us in the physical world. In the other 15 percent, the traveler went to the world of the dead.[68]

For the projector to encounter and communicate with people whom he knows to be dead is a commonplace in OBEs, as are the two locales where they are met: right here on the physical plane, or in their own "astral" world. Robert Monroe, for example, met a dead woman in his own bedroom whom he was able to identify later from a photograph. Monroe had rented the house and been in residence about a week when, shortly after retiring one night, he felt himself floating out of his body:

> I noticed something at the doorway. It was a white form the general size and shape of a person. I could see that it was a woman of medium height, with dark straight hair and rather deep-set eyes, not young, not old.... She ... looked at me.... I could see the windows and drapes behind her and *through* her.... She smiled slightly ... and moved around the bed and out the door.

A few days later Monroe met his next-door neighbor, a psychiatrist named Samuel Kahn. From him Monroe learned that Mrs. W., now deceased, had been the former inhabitant. At Monroe's request, Dr. Kahn found a photograph of Mrs. W.—a group photograph in which she appeared with 50 or 60 other persons. There in the second row was a familiar face—the face of the "ghost." Was *that* Mrs. W., Monroe asked Kahn? The answer was yes.[69]

Many projectors claim to have met and communicated with dead friends and relatives in the world of the dead. Reading a few dozen accounts of visits to this world makes it clear that the same place is being described by different people. The following quotations came from eleven different projectors, each of whom tried to describe the world of the dead:

- a vast and lovely garden beneath an intensely blue sky
- a beautiful meadow
- an exquisite landscape with woods and hints of scattered waters
- a beautiful park-like area
- an exquisite garden scene
- a beautiful garden with trees
- a beautiful park-like area near a lake
- a marvelous world … filled with flowers and trees
- a beautiful landscape[70]
- beautiful trees and flowers[71]

Here is an account, by Dr. R.B. Hout, of his trip to this world during an OBE:

> After a brief sensation of drifting upward, I found myself in a new, but very natural environment—in a grove or park which seemed to extend as far as I could see.
>
> I saw a group of figures approaching.… They came closer and I was both surprised and elated when I recognized them. Old, almost forgotten friends from my home town were coming to greet me. The first was a gentleman who had died a year or two ago. With him was his son whom I had known well and his wife whom I had never met.… "Do you remember me?" I asked him. "I never dreamed of meeting you here."
>
> Turning, he made a little motion to two ladies coming up the path at my side. I turned and joyously met my grandmother, passed over about two years. With her was her friend … and neighbor [who] had made her transition a short while previously.
>
> I could only tell them again and again my extreme happiness to greet them.… Now the others, seemingly with one accord, fell

> back away from me a few steps.... My glance instinctively took me down the path toward which all of the others were looking. And there, coming radiantly toward me ... walked my ... mother. Toward her I sprang with outstretched arms ... and such a joyous reunion took place there! My being fairly blended with hers, and this moment seemed the supreme happiness of my existence.
>
> It was a triumph of spirit, as side by side we stood there together. She was in the glory of her ... spirit body, free and attuned to the plane of life upon which she was living.... Thus we were together for a time, reunited on one plane of life. Here were my friends and loved ones gone to the fourth dimension through death, and here also was myself, able to function actively there for a limited time and in a feeble manner.... I would like to emphasize the fact that these out-of-the-body experiences are real to me, objective and tangible, wherein I meet people living in a real world.... Until after my first visit I could not possibly have understood the actuality and objectivity of the plane of life upon which dwell my *dead* friends. Now I know they are living somewhere in this great universe of ours, in an *other place* existing beyond the limits of our ... earth plane.[72]

To many people, of course, the idea that the dead continue to exist in a beautiful landscape will seem nothing more than a fantasy by which the grim reality of death may be avoided. Were there only one source of evidence to support this claim, it would be easy to dismiss, but there are *three.* Fifteen percent of all OBE experiences involve visits by the living to this realm. Similar reports come from people who have temporarily died, and been resuscitated, and from the dead, who have transmitted their reports through mediums.

Perhaps at this point it would be well to remember the words of Heraclitus, written some 2,500 years ago, with which I began this chapter:

Because it is sometimes so unbelievable, the truth escapes becoming known.

The essential similarity of the living and the dead

Out-of-the-body experiences are crucial data for anyone who wishes to develop an adequate theory of life and death, for they link the two intimately. It is a common belief that the living and the dead are grossly different—hence our fear and horror in the face of death. But out-of-the-body experiences lead us to a startling conclusion—that the living and the dead are the same. Only the fact that the living temporarily possess a physical body prevents them from realizing that they are already as "dead" as they will ever be, because the essential selfhood dwells in the astral form and is only the temporary tenant of the physical.

Probably the best way to establish the similarity between the living and the dead would be to show that they can do the same things. And, in fact, they can, because a living person's OBE body is the same body inhabited by that person after death. An out-of-the-body experience by a living person must therefore be very similar to an after-death state, and permit a similar range of experiences. Both the living and the dead have *appeared as apparitions, been responsible for hauntings, communicated through mediums, appeared in death-bed visions, provided post-mortem accounts, spoken of a reincarnational past, and possessed the bodies of the living!* Although such cases are a relative rarity for the living, the existence of even one case of a living person doing, in an OBE, what the dead commonly do, establishes that it is in fact possible, and that the living and the dead are essentially the same.

Apparitions of the living

Usually apparitions of the living are the result of unconscious OBES, but, as shown earlier, living persons may also appear as visible apparitions while they are having fully conscious OBES. Research shows that apparitions of living persons are approximately twice as common as apparitions of dead ones.

Hauntings by the living

Although the following case is of a rare type, it illustrates the point that some "dreams" are actually projections while in a state of partial consciousness.

> Some time ago, my wife dreamed on several occasions of a house whose interior arrangement she was able to describe in all its details, although she had no idea where this house existed.... Later ... I leased from Lady B_____, for the autumn, a house in the mountains of Scotland.... My son, who was then in Scotland, took charge of the matter, without my wife or I ever seeing the house in question.
>
> When I went there alone later, to sign the contract and take possession of the property, Lady B_____ was still inhabiting the place. She told me that if I had no objection, she would give me a room which she herself had been occupying and which had, for some time past, been haunted by a woman who continued to appear there.
>
> Being quite skeptical about such matters, I replied that I should be delighted to make the acquaintance of the ghost. I went to sleep in the room, but did not see any ghost.
>
> Later, when my wife arrived, she was astonished when she recognized the house as the one of her dreams! She went all over it; all the details corresponded with those she had so often seen in sleep. But when she went back down into the drawing room again, she said: "But still, this cannot be the house I saw in my dreams, because there ought to be a succession of rooms that are missing here." She was told that the rooms actually existed, and that one could reach them through the drawing room. When they were shown to her, she remembered each one of them clearly.
>
> She said, however, that it seemed to her that one of the

bedrooms was not used for this purpose *when she visited it in sleep.* It was again explained to her that this room had not formerly been a bedroom, but had been changed into one.

Two or three days later my wife and I visited Lady B_____. Since they were unknown to each other, I introduced them. Lady B_____ cried out in amazement: "Why—you are the lady who has been haunting my bedroom!"[73]

Mediumistic communications by the living

In theory, a living person would be able to communicate through a medium if the astral body of that person took over the body of the medium. Mediums who have dealt with the dead have described the process of leaving their own bodies and observing them being entered and controlled by the astral bodies of the dead:

> I found myself standing in one corner of the room, looking on at the people gathered about the table.... I clearly saw my physical body sitting in its place there.... The spirit of a woman stepped back of my physical body, leaned over it, and seemed to melt into it.[74]

But has a living projector ever controlled the body of a medium and communicated through it? The answer is yes. Quite a number of cases are on record, involving several mediums and various living communicators.

For example Vincent Turvey, a habitual projector with an interest in mediumship, claims on many occasions to have controlled the bodies of mediums during his OBEs, and to have communicated through them in séances. These experiences are described at some length in his book *The Beginnings of Seership.*

Possession of the living by the living

This phenomenon is simply a variation of the above, with the difference that it is unintended by the projectors, and the persons possessed are usually asleep or severely ill. Robert Monroe has had several such experiences, which have alarmed him considerably.

> I thought I had made a normal return to the physical. I opened my eyes, and I was in a strange bed. A strange woman was beside the bed, and she smiled as she saw me awaken. An older woman stood behind her. They expressed happiness that I had finally come to, that I had been ill for a long time, but that now I would be all right. They helped me get out of bed, and I was dressed in some sort of robe (like a dressing gown) and I knew for sure I wasn't the person they thought I was. I tried to tell them this, but they only humored me and seemed to think I was still in some form of delirium. I asked what day it was, and they only smiled understandingly as if I wasn't yet fully oriented (I wasn't!).
>
> I was sure that I couldn't stay there any longer, and despite their strong objections, went out a door into the open air. I … tried to move upward … I started to rise slowly.… Suddenly … I was high in the air over a landscape of countryside dotted with houses. It looked familiar, and I thought I saw what was our house and buildings between road and river. I dove for the house and in the next moment I was merging with the physical. I sat up … and looked around gratefully. I was in the right place! [75]

A living person appears in a deathbed vision

In deathbed visions dead persons who are emotionally close to the dying appear at the bedside as if to welcome the dying into death. But it is in fact possible for the living to do the same thing in an out-of-the-body experience. Consider the following report:

> I found myself standing [in OBE form] … in a wretched garret in a city. It seemed barely dawn. At either side of me, supporting me, I saw … a form like myself.… They were holding me up a little. All three of us stood immediately in front of a low, miserable-looking bed, on which a woman of middle age lay dying.

> She turned her head and saw me—and I felt convinced I was the only form she saw.... I *knew* I had been called thus to convince this woman of a future life.[76]

Post-mortem accounts by the living

I have already discussed the fact that fifteen percent of all OBEs involve travel to the world of the dead. These journeys have produced many accounts of that world, accounts which are in basic agreement as to its nature. The only difference between living visitors to this world and dead dwellers in it lies in the fact that the living still have a physical form to which they return.

Reincarnational memories of the living and the dead

In Chapter 7 we will look at evidence that human beings carry deeply-buried memories of many former lives, memories which can be explored in detail by regression hypnosis. We will also see that, for a small number of people, these memories may become available without the use of any deliberate technique designed to retrieve them. Some dead communicators have reported vivid reincarnational memories, suggesting that the OBE state may make their retrieval easier. If this is the case for some of the dead, may it not also hold true for some living projectors? Two habitual projectors have had experiences which suggest that the answer is yes. Paul Twitchell has described how in some of his OBEs he had a vivid awareness of a succession of his past lives, "laid before me like a fan of cards on a table."[77] Robert Monroe has experienced similarly vivid past-life memories while projecting. He speaks of:

> the gradual flooding of the memory with events, places, people, and things that have no relationship in any way to one's current physical life activities or past experience.
>
> These memories ... are ... recalled while in the Second State [out of the body]. For example, I have a vivid memory of a place

> where I used to live—the roads leading up to it, the shape of the land, its location in relation to the road, and the surrounding landscape. It is not a good piece of land, but I seem to have worked hard for it and it was all I could afford. I had intentions of building a house on it someday.
>
> There is the memory also of three connected buildings on a city street—old buildings, some eight stories high. The top floors of these buildings . . . have been joined into one large living area, with large, high-ceilinged rooms. One has to step up or down slightly to go from one room to another due to the difference in floor levels. This was a place I visited, not too often, sometime, somewhere.[78]

Are the living and the dead the same?

It is certainly beginning to look that way. The study of hundreds of spontaneous OBE cases, and a much smaller number of experimental ones, clearly demonstrates that the ancient idea that human beings possess a soul has a firm basis in fact: human consciousness occupies a physical body, but does not require it for existence. If this knowledge seems astounding, perhaps astonishment now is easier to take than astonishment later. During a projection, Robert Monroe encountered a "dead" man who seemed to sense that Monroe was only temporarily, rather than permanently, projected. Addressing Monroe with an anger which reflected his bewilderment at the revelations that the death of his body had thrust upon him, he said:

> "Well, *now* are you ready to learn the secrets of the universe? . . . I hope you're ready," he went on, his voice rising in anger, "because nobody took the trouble to tell me when I was back there."[79]

CHAPTER FOUR

THOSE WHO ARE ABOUT TO DIE: DEATHBED VISIONS

They've come to take me into death.
– *dying patient*

I want to go back, let me go back.
– *dying patient, following a visionary experience*

PEOPLE WHO HAVE DIED suddenly and unexpectedly—by heart seizure, drowning, automobile accident—have often been brought back from death by the resuscitation techniques of modern medicine. Afterwards, they have described strange experiences during their temporary journeys into the realm of the dead: many report being "met" by dead friends and relatives, by "spiritual helpers," or by a "being of light."

Such experiences suggest how remote from us the world beyond death must be—if you can reach it only by dying. But in fact people have been able to enter this realm while still alive by dying slowly. Those who sink gradually into death from cancer, from disease, from degeneration of the body, have reported being met in advance! And, just as those resuscitated from sudden death have later described intense joy, serenity, and an after-death world of breathtaking beauty, those who die slowly report identical experiences just before death.

These experiences, which appear to be universal among human beings, are known as *deathbed visions.* They are found in the folklore of many societies, in literature and biographies from all ages, and have been regarded for centuries as a sign of imminent death. But just how likely is it that something like this will happen to you? Recent research suggests that perhaps as many as one-half to two-thirds of those who are in a state of reasonably lucid consciousness shortly before death can expect to have such experiences!

What are these experiences actually like?

Wilma Ashby was involved in an automobile accident which pinned the lower part of her body beneath tangled wreckage. After being hospitalized in critical condition, she continued to bleed severely, and, despite their best efforts, her doctors were unable to stop the hemorrhage. Relatives were summoned and told of her impending death. Her twin brother, Willard, to whom she had been very close, had died a premature death just four years earlier. At eight o'clock in the evening, fully conscious, she had just finished a prayer of thanks that her family, who had been with her in the car, had been spared any serious injury.

> Suddenly, something compelled me to open my eyes. I was astonished to see the gray wall in front of me changing. In the middle of a beautiful purple mist stood my twin brother.... He was smiling the same kind of infectious smile he used to smile when he teasingly called me his "sin-twister." His arms outstretched, he moved slowly forward. I reached out my arms to embrace him.
>
> My brother had reached the foot of my bed and our fingers were about to touch when my husband entered the room. My twin instantly vanished. I began to cry. "Willard was here but he left before I could touch him." My husband looked amazed. "When I opened the door," he said, "it was as if an electric shock passed through my body."[1]

Mrs. Ashby recovered; her doctor called it "a miracle."

Similar encounters have been reported by many others who, like

Mrs. Ashby, have come to the very brink of death but have not died. They are even more common just before an actual death. Note the striking similarity of the following case, recently reported from India by parapsychologist Karlis Osis. A Hindu boy in his teens was dying from leukemia. His mother had died years before when he was very young. Doctors and nurses who were present at his death told Osis:

> He often talked about [his mother].... He mentioned her ... very affectionately. The day he died he had no fever but he said, "My time has come," to his father. "My mother is calling. She is standing there with her arms open." At that moment his state of mind was clear. He was conscious of his surroundings and talked to his father until the last moment. Then, with one hand holding his father's and the other pointed toward where he saw his mother, he said, "Don't you see my mother? See! ..." Then he died—stretching forward to [her] ... almost falling out of bed. He was so happy to see her![2]

In 1925, the assistant head nurse of an Indian hospital in Saskatchewan, Canada, had the following experience with a patient in the hospital who was dying of tuberculosis.

> He was a Cree Indian lad, about 20 years of age, son of Chief Papewyn, of a neighboring Reserve.... At last the ... day arrived. It was evening and I was with him. He was lying quietly in his bed when suddenly he sat up, stretched forth his arms with a yearning gesture, while an ecstatic smile broke over his face. It was not simply a smile of pleasure, but something far beyond it ... no one who was looking on could fail to realize that it was a glorious vision that met his gaze. He then lay back in his bed, looked at me with a smile, and passed away. He had been calm and collected during the day, there was no delirium.[3]

It is extraordinary that an American woman, a Hindu adolescent, and a Cree Indian should have such uncannily similar experiences just before death. These are examples of "apparitional" deathbed visions: the person appears to be greeted shortly before death by someone from the "other side" with whom he has strong emotional ties, who has appeared in order to take him into the world beyond physical death. Strange though such experiences may seem, they have their own compelling logic. If human beings do survive bodily death, and continue to take an interest in the living (and there is plenty of evidence to support both contentions), then what more logical time for the dead to "appear" than when a loved one is dying?

But the dying undergo two other fascinating experiences as well—actual "visions" of the world after death, and medically inexplicable mood rises to a state of exhilaration and exaltation. Consider these examples.

A dying seventy-eight-year-old German-born mill foreman suffered very severe angina pain. One of the medical people attending him was so struck by his experiences that she remembered them vividly:

> When he had visions the pain would disappear and all you could see was a smile on his face. [He would say] "It was so beautiful, you just can't tell anyone. It was a breathtaking scene, more so than anything in real life." That was all he could say.[4]

A dying woman in her late seventies was described by her nurse as always nasty, a very mean person:

> One night she called me to see how lovely and beautiful heaven is. Then she looked at me and seemed surprised: "Oh, but you can't see it, you aren't here [in heaven], you are over there. She became very peaceful and happy ... and she permitted her meanness to die.... I don't think these are hallucinations, they are ... very real.[5]

These visionary glimpses of a post-mortem world can in fact involve such inexpressible beauty and be so deeply gratifying that the patient abandons the will to live and prefers to "die into" the vision rather than to continue living without it.

A typical reaction to such experiences is a sudden feeling of exaltation and exhilaration. But, strangely enough, doctors and nurses at deathbeds have also reported these mood rises in patients who were completely unable to explain them. For example, the last hours of a fifty-nine-year-old woman who had pneumonia and a serious heart condition were described as follows by a nurse:

> The expression on her face was beautiful; her *attitude* seemed to have changed entirely. This was more than [just] a change of the [depressed] mood I had seen her in many times before.... She was always moody but for the past year she was really depressed. It seemed as if there was something [here that was] just a little beyond us ... [it] was not natural.... There was something which made us feel that ... she [had] some contact with the beyond and it had a happy effect on her.[6]

A strange reaction, indeed. People who are dying usually suffer. Terminal patients often endure agonizing pain and indignity, rendered helpless by their failing bodies. And yet, inexplicably, some patients who are sunk in such intense misery will "light up" as death approaches, suddenly exhilarated, exalted!

We are thus confronted with three unusual kinds of deathbed experiences: visits by apparitions of the dead; visions of a paradise-like afterlife; and medically inexplicable mood rises to states of exhilaration, joy, and serenity, all occurring shortly before death. These experiences so compellingly suggest that there may be something "beyond" death, that half a dozen studies of them have been published during the past century.[7] Again and again, the same striking characteristics reappear in the hundreds of reported cases: the patient is lucid, and well oriented to his surroundings, not in a fog of delirium; the experience is often of exceptional intensity, having a profound effect on the patient and even, at times, on observing medical personnel; the experience is completely unexpected (patients are often astonished at what is happening to them) and it is frequently regarded as medically inexplicable by attending physicians and nurses.

The clarity of consciousness of the dying persons who have had these experiences baffles medical observers and suggests that the experiences cannot be explained away as ordinary hallucinations. Consider, for example, the following Victorian case of a middle-aged woman dying of heart disease. According to her doctor, who was at the deathbed:

> Her mental action was perfect. She conversed, a few minutes before dying, as pleasantly and intelligently as ever. There was no stupor, delirium ... or ... symptoms indicating cerebral disturbance.... After saying a few words, she turned her head upon her pillow as if to sleep, then unexpectedly turning it back, a glow, brilliant and beautiful ... came into her features; her eyes, opening, sparkled ... at the same moment, with a tone of emphatic surprise and delight, she pronounced the name of the [dead person] ... dearest to her; and then dropping her head upon her pillow ... [died].[8]

This clarity of mind is in some cases so pronounced that the dying person is able to carry on two conversations—one with an apparition unseen by anyone else; the other with the people surrounding the deathbed. In 1918, Dr. E.H. Pratt of Chicago described the death of his sister Hattie. While away at school, she became ill with diphtheria and was brought home to be cared for. Her bed was in the living room, where she was surrounded by relatives and friends during her last hour of life. Pratt describes her death:

> She knew she was [dying], and was telling our mother how to dispose of her little personal belongings among her ... friends ... when she suddenly raised her eyes as though gazing at the ceiling toward the farther side of the room, and after looking steadily

> and apparently listening for a short time, slightly bowed her head, and said, "Yes, Grandma, I am coming, only wait just a little while, please." Our father asked her, "Do you see your grandma?" Seemingly surprised at the question she promptly answered, "Yes, Papa, can't you see her? She is right there waiting for me."... She pointed toward the ceiling in the direction in which she had been gazing. Again addressing the vision she evidently had of her grandmother, she scowled a little impatiently and said, "Yes, Grandma, I'm coming, but wait a minute, please." She then turned once more to her mother, and finished telling her what of her personal treasures to give to different ... [friends]. At last giving her attention once more to her grandma, who was apparently urging her to come at once, she bade each of us good-bye. Her voice was very feeble and faint, but the look in her eyes as she glanced briefly at each one of us was as lifelike and intelligent as it could be. She then fixed her eyes steadily on her vision [and] so faintly that we could ... just catch her words, said, "Yes, Grandma, I'm coming now."

The girl then died. She and her grandmother, who had died a few years previously, had always been very close. Of this experience, Dr. Pratt later said:

> She was so clear-headed, so positive of the ... presence of her grandma, with whom she talked so naturally, so surprised that the rest of us could not see [her], the alternation of her attention and conversation between her grandma and father and mother were so [distinct] ... that it seems impossible to [explain] ... on any theory except that her grandma was alive and so completely like herself while on earth that Hattie's recognition of her was instantaneous.[9]

Deathbed visionary experiences can be so intense that they can profoundly affect the lives of others. A Florida physician who witnessed one later confessed that it had changed his whole outlook on life. Dr. Wilson of New York, a physician who was present at the death of the American tenor James Moore, later said that he would remember what happened for the rest of his life:

> It was about four o'clock and the dawn for which he had been watching was creeping in through the shutters, when, as I bent over the bed, I noticed that his face was quite calm and his eyes clear. The poor fellow looked up into my face, and taking my hand in both of his, he said, "You've been a good friend to me, Doctor. You've stood by me." Then something which I shall never forget to my dying day happened.... While he appeared perfectly rational and as sane as any man I have ever seen, the only way that I can express it is [to say] that he was transported into another world ... for he said in a stronger voice than he had used since I had attended him, "There is Mother! Why, Mother, have you come here to see me? No, no, I'm coming to see you. Just wait, Mother, I am almost over. I can jump it. Wait, Mother." On his face there was a look of inexpressible happiness, and the way in which he said the words ... firmly convinced [me] that he saw and talked with his mother ... [it was] the strangest happening of my life.[10]

The power of deathbed visions is eerie. We find this same, inexplicable intensity over and over again. Patients who are in pain, wretched and frightened, are suddenly transformed, glowing with exaltation, eager for death. Dying in a coma, a sixteen-year-old American girl became clearly conscious just before the end:

> "I can't get up," [she said] and ... opened her eyes. I raised her up a little bit and she said, "I see him, I see him. I am coming." She died immediately afterwards with a radiant face, exultant, elated.[11]

An experience which can lead a sixteen-year-old girl from a coma to a "radiant" death must be an incredibly powerful one and it has some further fascinating variations which we will now explore.

Childhood cases

Although skeptics will be tempted to explain the previous cases as "hallucinations" induced by religious beliefs about death, it is more difficult to dismiss similar experiences of young children, to whom adult ideas of death are unknown.

Consider, for example, the case of a young Italian girl, three-year-old Hippolyte Notari, who was present at the death of her baby brother. According to the parents and grandmother, about fifteen minutes before the death of the baby

> little Hippolyte stretched out her arms, saying, "Look, mother, Aunt Olga." The parents asked, "Where do you see Aunt Olga?" The child said, "There, there!" and tried insistently to get out of bed to go to her aunt. They let her get up, she ran to an empty chair and was much discountenanced because the vision had moved to another part of the room. The child turned round and said, pointing to a corner, "Aunt Olga is there." Then she became quiet and the baby died.[12]

Aunt Olga, a sister of the child's mother, had died a year before.

A recent example of this very striking type of case concerns an eleven-year-old girl dying of congenital heart disease. The child's mother was already dead.

> She was having another bad episode with her heart, and said that she saw her mother. She was very happy and smiling, told me to let her get up and go … [to her mother, who] was ready to take her on a trip.[13]

This vision, which lasted for half an hour, left the girl serene and peaceful for her death, four hours later.

Collective cases

Understandably, skeptics will dismiss deathbed visions as hallucinations. But what about those cases where the apparition of the dead visitor was seen by more than one person? Although such cases are rare, they are important precisely because they cannot be hallucinations. The following examples were observed over nearly a century—from 1864 to 1949.

In 1903, Hugh G., a little Yorkshire boy, lay dying after a long illness. His mother had recently died, and he was being cared for by his oldest sister and a close friend of his mother. In a written account which she later gave to the British Society for Psychical Research, and which both witnesses signed, the friend describes what happened.

> On Sunday evening, June 28th, 1903, about 9 o'clock, I and the sister were standing at the foot of the bed, watching [Hughey], who was unconscious, when suddenly I saw [his] mother distinctly. She was in her ordinary dress as when with us, nothing supernatural in her appearance. She was bending over her boy with a look of … love … and did not seem to notice us. After a minute or two she quietly and suddenly *was not there.* I was so struck that I turned to speak to the sister, but she seemed so engrossed that I did not think it wise to say anything.
>
> [Hughey] grew gradually worse, until on Tuesday evening, June 30th … he passed away. After rendering the last offices of love to the … little body, the sister and I again stood, as on the Sunday, when I said, "I had a strange experience on Sunday evening here." She quickly replied, "Yes, mother was here; I saw her too; she came and kissed Hughey."[14]

In the next case, a deathbed apparition was seen by four persons—the dying woman and three relatives who were caring for her. In November of 1864, Harriet Pearson, who was fatally ill, was being nursed by three relatives, a Mrs. Coppinger, Mrs. John

Pearson, and Emma Pearson, who prepared a written account of what took place on the day of her death.

> Harriet … slept in a large three-windowed bedroom over the drawing-room. The room behind was occupied by Mrs. Coppinger and myself.… On the night of December 22nd … Mrs. John Pearson was in [Harriet's] room, Mrs. Coppinger and myself in the back room; the house lighted up on the landings and staircases, our door wide open.
>
> About 1 or 2 a.m. on the morning of December 23rd, both Mrs. Coppinger and myself started up in bed; we were neither of us sleeping, as we were watching every sound from the next room.
>
> We saw someone pass the door, short, wrapped up in an old shawl, a wig with three curls each side and an old black cap. Mrs. Coppinger called out, "Emma, get up, it is … Aunt Ann" [Harriet's dead sister]. I said, "So it is." We jumped up and Mrs. John Pearson came rushing out of the room and said, "That was … Aunt Ann. Where is she gone to?"[15]

Harriet Pearson died at 6 p.m. that day, but before she did, she too said that she had seen her dead sister, who had "come for her."

The next case involves a well-known historical figure. Horace Traubel, a close friend and biographer of the poet Walt Whitman, lay dying in a remote vacation lodge in Ontario owned by a wealthy Canadian mining family, the Denisons. What happened at the deathbed was witnessed by Lt.-Col. Moore Cosgrave.

> [On September 6th, 1919, two days before Traubel's death] about 3 a.m. he grew perceptibly weaker, breathing almost without visible movement, eyes closed and seemingly comatose. He stirred restlessly towards the further side of the bed, his lips moved, endeavoring to speak, I moved his head back, thinking he needed more air, but … his eyes remained riveted on a point some three feet above the bed. My eyes were at last drawn irre-

> sistibly to the same point in the darkness, as there was but a small shaded night lamp behind a curtain on the further side of the room. Slowly the point at which we were both looking grew gradually brighter, a light haze appeared, spread until it assumed bodily form, and took the likeness of Walt Whitman, standing upright beside the bed, a rough tweed jacket on, an old felt hat upon his head and his right hand in his pocket … he was gazing down at Traubel, a kindly … smile upon his face. He nodded twice as though reassuringly, [his] features quite distinct for at least a full minute … toward the end of his appearance, while Horace and I were gazing at him, [Whitman] moved closer to Horace from the further side of the bed, [and] Horace … said, "There is Walt." At the same moment, Walt passed apparently through the bed towards me, and appeared to touch my hand, as though in farewell. I distinctly felt it, as though I had touched a low electric charge. He then smiled at Horace, and passed from sight.[16]

In 1949, Margaret Moser, a nurse from Jamaica, Long Island, saw—several times—the same apparition her dying patient did, and saw it so clearly that she was later able to identify the apparition's son by his strong resemblance to the face of his dead mother. In her account of these uncanny incidents, Mrs. Moser writes:

> In the winter of 1948-49 I nursed a very sick old lady, Mrs. Rosa B. She was a very clever, well-educated, and highly-cultured [woman] … who had lived for many years in New York City. She was residing at that time at the Savoy Plaza Hotel on Fifth Avenue, and up to the last she was mentally competent.
>
> Early one afternoon I had put my patient to bed for a nap and was sitting at my little table beside the window writing in her chart. I was facing her bed, the door at my back. Mrs. B. had been asleep, but suddenly I saw her sit up and wave happily, her face all smiles. I turned my head toward the door, thinking one of her daughters had come in; but much to my surprise it was an

> elderly lady I had never seen before. She had a striking resemblance to my patient—the same light blue eyes, but a longer nose and heavier chin. I could see her very clearly for it was bright daylight; the window shades were only slightly lowered. The visitor walked toward my patient, bent down, and, as far as I can remember, they kissed each other. But then, as I got up and walked toward the bed, she was gone.
>
> Mrs. B. looked very pleased. She took my hand and said, "It is my sister!" Then she slept peacefully again. I saw the same apparition twice later on, but never as clearly and always from another room. But every time she came the patient was obviously elated.[17]

Some weeks later Mrs. B. died, and at her funeral Margaret Moser was startled to see a man who so strongly resembled the apparition that she asked one of Mrs. B.'s daughters who he was. He was the son of Mrs. B.'s dead sister.

"Peak in Darien" cases

> Then felt I like some watcher of the skies
> When a new planet swims into his ken;
> Or like stout Cortez when with eagle eyes
> He stared at the Pacific—and all his men
> Looked at each other with a wild surmise—
> Silent, upon a peak in Darien.
>
> – *John Keats*, "On First Looking into Chapman's Homer"

These fascinating cases take their name from this poem by Keats, which expresses the awestruck amazement of someone who has just made an important discovery. And they are striking *because the apparition is of someone who is not known to be dead.* Skeptics regard deathbed visions as mere hallucinations caused by the dying person's desire to rejoin dead loved ones after his own death. The Darien cases are important because they can't be explained away as wishful thinking on the part of the dying, since the person appearing as an apparition is thought to be still alive!

The following Darien cases span nearly a century in time from 1889 to the present. The first involves two little American girls eight years of age—Jennie and Edith—who were close friends. In June of 1889, both caught diphtheria, and at noon on a Wednesday, Jennie died. Edith was so sick that her parents decided not to tell her that her friend had died. Shortly before Edith herself died, she asked her parents to give Jennie two photographs and to say goodbye to Jennie for her. According to witnesses, Edith

> had … bidden her friends goodbye. She appeared to see … friends she knew were dead.… But now suddenly, and with every appearance of surprise, she turned to her father and exclaimed, "Why, Papa, I am going to take Jennie with me! … Why Papa! You did not tell me that Jennie was here!" And immediately she reached out her arms as if in welcome, and said, "Oh, Jennie, I'm so glad you are here!"[18]

The second Darien case concerns two sisters. On January 12th, 1924, Doris B. experienced heart failure after giving birth to a child in Mothers' Hospital in Clapton, England. Her sister Vida had died more than two weeks earlier, on Christmas day. Because Doris had been dangerously ill at the time of Vida's death, the head nurse at the hospital, Miriam Castle, advised the family not to tell Doris of her sister's death. What happened to Doris shortly before her death was witnessed by her husband, by her mother, and by Miriam Castle. Just as Doris was sinking into death, she suddenly exclaimed, "I can see Father; he wants me."

> She spoke to her father, saying, "I am coming," turning at the same time to look at me, [her mother] saying, "Oh, he is so near." On looking at the same place again, she said with rather a

> puzzled expression, "He has Vida with him," turning again to me saying, "Vida is with him."[19]

No wonder Doris was puzzled to see her sister Vida with their dead father—she thought that Vida was still alive!

But surely such things don't happen today? They can and they do. While in the hospital having a baby, Maxine, a young woman who lives in Anaheim, California, had a *double* "Peak in Darien" experience. Resting after having the baby, she was astounded to see her father standing in an upper corner of her room, near the ceiling, holding a baby in his arms. This was incredible enough, but what he said to her was even more baffling: "Don't worry. I'll take care of the baby." Then he disappeared.

> Maxine immediately rang for a nurse and asked about her baby. She was told it was doing fine. Given one excuse after another every time she inquired, she grew more and more suspicious that her vision of her father must have meant something very important. Finally she insisted [that] her husband … tell her the truth, no matter how painful it might be to her. He told her that the baby had been stillborn, and that her father had died suddenly while she was in the hospital.[20]

Another dramatic modern case involved Natalie Kalmus, a pioneer developer of the technicolor process. Natalie's sister Eleanor was dying, and Natalie was beside her in her last moments of life.

> I sat on her bed and took her hand. It was on fire. Then Eleanor seemed to rise up in bed, almost to a sitting position.
>
> "Natalie," she said, "there are so many of them. There's Fred and Ruth—what's she doing here?"
>
> An electric shock went through me. She had said Ruth! Ruth was her cousin, who had died suddenly the week before. But I knew that Eleanor had not been told of the sudden death.… I felt on the verge of some wonderful, almost frightening knowledge....

> Her voice was surprisingly clear. "It's so confusing. There are so many of them!" Suddenly her arms stretched out happily. "I am going up," she murmured.[21]

And Eleanor died.

The above cases prove that knowledge of another's death can come in a deathbed vision. Witnesses are shocked by such encounters—and are even more amazed when the death is confirmed!

One hundred thousand deaths

Parapsychologist Dr. Karlis Osis knows more about deathbed visions than anyone else in the world. Since 1960, he has investigated over one hundred thousand human deaths, and revealed the results in two books, *Deathbed Observations by Physicians and Nurses* (1961), and *At the Hour of Death* (1977). As the title of the first suggests, his information was gathered entirely from doctors and nurses, an ideal source because of the number of deaths they witness, and the fact that their medical training requires them to observe and record patients' reactions.

What happens to people just before they die? According to the information his medical sources provided, only about ten percent of those who die are conscious shortly before death, and thus able to report deathbed events. Of this group, how many undergo the kinds of experiences discussed above? Unfortunately, Osis's research does not directly answer this question, but a careful examination of his statistics suggests that from one half to two-thirds of conscious dying patients have these experiences! Such frequencies are unique to the dying, for only 10-17 percent of people in normal health ever have hallucinations of any kind! What exactly happens to the dying? Three things: *apparitional visits from dead loved ones, glimpses of the "next world," and medically inexplicable moods of elation.*

But aren't they just hallucinations?

It is tempting to explain these experiences away as mere hallucinations. After all, it seems highly reasonable that people who are close to dying might see things that aren't really there: their bodies, and presumably their minds, are breaking down, disintegrating, dying. Dr. Osis, a hard-headed, tough-minded scientist, tried to explain away these strange occurrences as simple hallucinations. As we will see, he was unable to do so.

The first thing that Dr. Osis noticed was that these hallucinations were very unusual ones, with frequencies and qualities which are unique to people who are dying. Furthermore, most of the doctors and nurses who reported these experiences to Osis agreed that they were peculiar: two-thirds did not feel that these experiences could be explained either by the physical condition of the patient, or by medication he had been taking.[22]

Apparitional visitors

The overwhelming majority of the apparitions seen by the dying are either dead people to whom they were close in life, or religious figures such as Christ, angels, or the Virgin Mary. In three surveys Osis conducted of deathbed experiences (two in the United States and one in India), he found that 75 percent of the apparitions seen by the dying were of this nature.

Of the human apparitions seen in deathbed visions, the vast majority—91 percent—were dead relatives of the patient, and 90 percent of these were close relatives—parent, spouse, child, brother or sister. This is very much in contrast with the hallucinations of mental patients, or drug-induced visions, which are seldom of close relatives.[23] Why do these apparitions appear? Quite often, the apparitions told the dying why they were there: to take them into the world beyond death.

Apparitions of "religious figures"

For a person in normal health to hallucinate at all is uncommon—only 10-17 percent report such experiences.[24] But seeing a *religious apparition* is an even rarer event among the general public; of this small 10-17 percent group, only 2-4 percent have ever done so.[25] Once again, what happens to the dying is something very different: dying Americans are 3 to 10 times more likely to see religious apparitions than are those in normal health.

But just who are these "religious figures?" The dying don't seem to be in any doubt. Americans claimed to be seeing Jesus, angels, or the Virgin Mary, whereas Indians usually saw Yama (the Hindu god of death), or some other Hindu deity such as Krishna or Shiva. We could conclude that such experiences are merely delusions, or that the patient is right, and the supernatural figures of our religious mythology really do descend to take us into death. But neither conclusion would be warranted. Resuscitated patients frequently report that while temporarily dead, they were met by a "being of light." Many decided later that he was Christ, others that he was an "angel," and still others that he was simply a "being"—though of an obviously superior type. In short, who they thought he was depended on their religious background—or lack of it. Thus when a dying person sees the radiant figure of an unknown man or woman who evokes intense feelings of serenity and exaltation, he will probably assume that he has been visited by an angel, Jesus, or God, or if he is a Hindu, by Yama, Krishna, or Shiva. But *we* don't know *who* these beings actually are. If we decide they are probably real (and evidence I will present suggests they are), then all we need conclude is that they are what they claim to be—discarnate beings who help people die.

For example, a male patient in his fifties had had a hip operation, and was due to be discharged from the hospital. He had no fever and was not receiving any medication. When he developed chest pain, his doctor was called. Describing what happened, the doctor said:

> When I came he told me he was going to die.... Then [he] told

> [me] how immediately after the pain in the chest started ... he saw Christ coming down through the air slowly. Christ ... waved his hand that he should come to him [and] then ... disappeared.... The patient told me he would die within a few minutes. He seemed quite happy ... "I am going," he said, and [he died].[26]

Reactions to apparitions

How do people who are dying respond to their apparitional visitors? In a most astounding way. When the apparition appears to take them into death, most patients want to go. Some even bitterly reproach doctors and nurses who manage to resuscitate them. The truth is that these encounters with messengers from the "other world" are so compelling that all desire to continue living is abandoned. For example, consider the apparition experience of a businessman in his sixties, who was dying of a painful infection.

> It was an experience of meeting someone whom he deeply loved. He smiled, reached up, and held out his hands. The expression on his face was one of joy. I asked him what he saw. He said his wife was standing right there and waiting for him.... He became very quiet and peaceful.... He died.[27]

In fact, Osis found many cases where the "call" of the apparition was more powerful than the medical diagnosis, and the patient died when his doctors expected him to live. Consider the case of a ten-year-old girl in a Pennsylvania hospital who was recovering from pneumonia. Her fever was gone, and her doctor concluded that she was recovering satisfactorily.

> The mother saw that her child seemed to be sinking and called [us nurses]. She said that the child had just told her she had seen an angel who had taken her by the hand—and she was gone,

died immediately. That just astounded us because there was no sign of imminent death.[28]

The core of what we have discovered, then, is this: people who are clearly conscious just before death often see apparitions of dead close relatives or religious figures who want to take them into death. And when this happens, most of the dying want to go.

Visions of another world

Being visited by someone from the world of the dead is one thing. But some of the dying also claim to actually *see this world*, in a landscape vision. We've seen that there are dramatic differences between the apparitions seen by the living, and those seen by the dying. A similarly dramatic difference exists for landscape visions, which are rarely seen by people in normal health, but are very common among those who are dying.

The big question, of course, is whether these landscapes are real glimpses of a world beyond the grave, or mere hallucinations. And if they are real, then what do they tell us about this world? What, exactly, do the dying see in their landscape visions?

They see a landscape of compelling beauty, a beauty of such an extraordinary kind, so heightened in its unearthly intensity, that in the extremest cases, patients who have been revived from a state of clinical death lose all will to live and prefer to "die into" this kind of experience rather than continue living without it! After a vision of this type, a resuscitated man, reacting typically to this experience, pleaded with his doctor: "Let me go back!"[29]

The wife of a Pennsylvania doctor was depressed, dying of a liver disease, when she had a landscape vision. She found herself in beautiful surroundings, with green grass and flowers. Her depression disappeared and she died, serene and happy.[30] This is a typical vision of the "afterworld." Her reaction to it is also typical: a serene, happy death.

The dying agree that "heaven" is intensely beautiful, and they react to their visions of it with exaltation. But, strangely, what they *actually see* often differs. If the world of the dead really exists as a specific place, then why is it described in so many different ways?

A rather down-to-earth, unemotional woman, a buyer for a department store, was dying of cancer. Her doctors and nurses described her consciousness as very clear, and her judgment as in no way impaired. Suddenly

> she saw open gates and felt she was going to a place with flowers, lights, colors, and a lot of beauty. She was annoyed with me for disturbing her and accused me of not permitting her to get into this place. She was thrilled with [the vision] and angry at me.[31]

Another woman, suffering from cardiac failure, was

> an unusual patient, very alert and intellectual, keen sense of humor … a down to earth person. That morning … she told me that … she [had seen] beautiful, endless gardens [with] all kinds of flowers. She said that she had never seen anything like it, it was gorgeous. She did not want to return [from this place].[32]

These three "heavens" do seem rather similar. But the next two are different. A nurse reported the vision of a rather unemotional woman in her sixties who worked as a hospital purchasing agent.

> The patient said, "It looked like a great sunset, very large … and beautiful." The clouds suddenly appeared to be gates. She felt that somebody was calling her to them, that she had to go through [them].[33]

The patient had been afraid of death, but after this vision, became very serene. A pneumonia patient in her fifties

> found herself up in the sky. It looked like clouds. She was walking on clouds. She saw many castles there. They were in bright light, very beautiful. She was so impressed with their beauty.[34]

Visibly calmed by this experience, the woman died a tranquil death.

Indian visions were equally varied. In fact, a partial list of the ways in which "heaven" was visualized by dying Indians and Americans would include flowers, trees, gardens, streams, gates, buildings, castles, palaces, and temples. But these were not perceived as ordinary scenery. Illuminated in brilliant light, their beauty heightened, perfect, "beyond this world," these visions were so intensely gratifying that the dying didn't want to return from them to this life and this world.

How can such experiences be explained?

What we really want to know about deathbed experiences is this: are the apparitions, visionary landscapes, and exalted moods experienced again and again by the dying real, or are they merely hallucinations? Since they are usually seen only by the dying person, what else could they be but hallucinations? The answer is that they could be *psychic experiences.* Being very close to death may heighten the perception of the dying so that they become temporarily psychic. And in fact there are cases which support just this explanation, cases in which psychics who were present at deathbeds *have seen the visions which were visible to the dying, but invisible to the others present.* Joy Snell, a nurse who was psychic, wrote a book about her deathbed observations in which she reported such experiences as the following:

> It was about six months after I began work in the hospital that it was revealed to me that the dying often really do see those who

have come from the realms of spirit life to welcome them on their entrance into another state of existence.

The first time that I received this proof was at the death of Laura Stirman, a … girl of seventeen, who was a … friend of mine. She was a victim of [tuberculosis]. …

A short time before she [died] I became aware that two spirit forms were standing by the bedside, one on either side of it. I did not see them enter the room; they were standing by the bedside when they first became visible to me, but I could see them as distinctly as I could any of the human occupants of the room. I recognized their faces as those of two girls who had been the closest friends of the girl who was dying. They had [died] a year before....

She recognized them immediately. A smile … lit up her face. She stretched forth her hands and in joyous tones exclaimed, "Oh, you have come to take me away! ..."

As she stretched forth her hands the two [girls] extended … a hand, one grasping the dying girl's right hand, the other her left.… Their faces were illumined by a smile … radiantly beautiful.

... She did not speak again, but for nearly a minute her hands remained outstretched, grasped by the hands of [her friends], and she continued to gaze at them with … the smile on her face.

Her father, mother, and brother, who had been summoned that they might be present when the end came, began to weep ... for they knew that she was leaving them. *From my heart … went ... a prayer that they might see what I saw, but they could not.*[35]

In other words, in a typical deathbed experience the dying may be made temporarily psychic by a heightened consciousness created by impending death, and are able to see what, normally, only those who are psychic can. This theory also explains why the visions of heavenly landscapes seen by the dying can be different, and why some of those who die without deathbed visions experience a mysterious exhilaration just before death.[36]

The case for hallucination

Could these experiences be mere hallucinations? That certainly seems a reasonable conclusion. Dr. Osis did his utmost to prove that this was all that was happening. He tried to think of every possible cause of hallucinations among the dying, and carefully checked each one of them against his data. What did he find?

Anoxia

If you're suffering from "cerebral anoxia," your brain isn't getting enough oxygen to operate normally. Cerebral anoxia was often mentioned by doctors and nurses as one of the likeliest explanations for deathbed visions. To see whether this condition was the real cause, Osis separated all of the dying people who had had visions into two groups: those who, in the opinion of doctors and nurses, were suffering from cerebral anoxia, and those who weren't. It turned out that anoxia made no difference. The visions of dying patients with cerebral anoxia were indistinguishable from those of other patients.[37]

Cerebral anoxia could not, therefore, be the cause of these experiences.

Drugs

People who are dying sometimes receive large doses of drugs. As some drugs are known to cause hallucinations, could drugs be the explanation for these experiences? Osis looked into this possibility, with interesting results. Only a small minority of those who had deathbed visions had been given drugs which could cause hallucinations. Furthermore, this minority had visions no more frequently than did other dying patients.[38] Drugs could not be the cause of these experiences.

Fever

People with high fevers often become delirious and begin to hallucinate. Could this be the explanation? Osis found that the majority of patients who had deathbed visions had normal temperatures, and only a small minority had fevers high enough to cause delirium.[39] Fever cannot explain the experiences.

A "sick brain"?

Diseases which affect the brain, or injuries to the brain, can cause hallucinations. Could this be the explanation for deathbed experiences? The answer turned out to be no, because only a small minority of those who had deathbed visions—10-13 percent—had such diseases or injuries in the first place.[40] And this small group was, on the whole, *less likely* to have the kinds of deathbed experiences we've been talking about. Therefore such experiences are definitely not caused by sick brains.

The hallucinogenic index

Dr. Osis, a cautious man, decided to make a final decisive check before coming to any conclusions. From the group of dying patients who had had visions, he selected all who had any medical condition which might cause hallucinations, and compared these with the rest. (They included patients affected by drugs, or fever, alcoholism, senility, mental illness, kidney disease, brain disease or injury, or any condition, such as stroke, circulatory disease, hemorrhage, bodily injury, or surgery, which might in any way reduce the supply of oxygen and blood to the brain.)[41] These patients did not have more experiences of "afterlife" visions than the others.[42] In fact, Osis found some evidence that they had fewer: medical conditions that reduced clarity of mind tended instead to produce ordinary hallucinations that had nothing to do with death, such as reliving past memories.[43] Medical factors do not cause afterlife visions.

Psychological and cultural factors

Does this mean, then, that afterlife visions are real? Not at all. Maybe people see, on their deathbeds, what their minds want them to see, or what their religious or cultural backgrounds have taught them to expect. Dr. Osis investigated these possibilities.

Stress

People who are under severe stress sometimes hallucinate. As dying patients may be under great stress in coping with their impending deaths and enduring intense pain, might not stress, rather than psychic perception of another existence, be the real cause of their afterlife visions? Osis gathered information from doctors and nurses on the patients' mood the day before the vision. He felt that patients who were in positive or normal moods were probably not under much stress, whereas those who were anxious, angry, or depressed, probably were. The results are interesting. Patients suffering from stress saw the same number of afterlife visions as patients who were not.[44] Therefore stress cannot be the cause of such experiences.

Desire

Perhaps, then, the dying person's desires are responsible for the visions, and patients see what they want to see, just as someone dying of thirst in the desert might "see" water where it didn't really exist. To investigate this, Osis asked doctors and nurses the identities of those people the patients had wanted to see the day before the hallucination. In some cases, there had been a very strong desire to see a particular person. But only 3 percent of the apparition cases involved such a person. In other words, such desires did not create the vast majority of afterlife visions.

Fear

Another powerful cause of hallucinations might be fear of dying. Patients who expected to die might try to relieve their fear of death by creating otherworldly fantasies, whereas patients who expected to live would not. But the facts did not support this theory. Dying patients who expected to die and those who thought they would recover were equally likely to see landscape visions of the next world.[45] The same proved true of apparitions: both kinds of patients were equally likely to see apparitions who had come to take them into death.[46] And often, these apparitions contradicted the expectations of both patients and doctors: patients who expected to live, with doctors who also expected them to live, would die after seeing apparitions calling them to another existence. The meaning of these findings is clear: fear cannot have been the cause of these visions.

Religious beliefs

It seems reasonable to expect that religious beliefs could be the cause of afterlife visions, and Osis looked into this possibility carefully, by comparing the deathbed experiences of Protestants, Catholics, Jews, Hindus, Muslims, and those who were not members of any religious group. All were equally likely to have afterlife visions. Religion, in other words, has no effect on these experiences.[47] Interestingly, these religions hold very different views of the nature of life after death. Therefore, if religious ideas about "heaven" are the real cause of deathbed visions of the "next world," these visions should imitate such ideas. But this didn't happen. Only a small minority of landscape visions showed any influence from religious ideas. The great majority—5 out of 6—did not.[48]

Are those who are very religious more likely to have deathbed visions? According to Osis, they aren't.[49] How about belief in a life after death? Are believers more likely to have these experiences? Again, the answer is no.[50] The conclusion is inescapable. Religious beliefs do not cause these experiences.

Osis found himself running out of "explanations," but he still had a couple of possibilities up his sleeve.

Education

How about education? Perhaps these experiences are caused by various superstitious beliefs about death. If so, relatively uneducated people should have most of them. They didn't, though. The educated and the uneducated were equally likely to have afterlife visions.

Observer bias

Then isn't it possible that the doctors and nurses who reported these experiences might be biased by their own beliefs? If, for example, they believed in life after death, or were religious, wouldn't this cause them to misinterpret what was happening to the patient so that it supported their own beliefs? This was carefully checked, but in vain. Osis discovered that the beliefs of doctors and nurses did not influence the kinds of experiences they reported.[51]

Cultural background

Cultural background can have a powerful influence on human attitudes and behavior. Therefore, if deathbed visions are mere delusions created by the human mind, we would expect them to be heavily affected by cultural background. If, on the other hand, deathbed experiences are real, we would expect them to be relatively unaffected by this background. With this in mind, Osis gathered data on deathbed experiences from two radically different cultures—the United States and India. His findings will give skeptics an unpleasant shock. Although there were some relatively minor differences between the deathbed experiences of Americans and Indians, *the core phenomena were the same.* In both India and the United States:

- most of the apparitions seen by the dying were "otherworldly"—dead close relatives and religious figures;

- most of them were there "to take the dying away to another existence";

- most of the dying were eager to accept the invitation and "go"—by dying;

- most landscape visions were of "otherworldly" scenery of such compelling beauty that the dying did not wish to remain in this world;

- medically-inexplicable mood elevation occurred in some patients shortly before death.[52]

What can we conclude?

Our efforts to "explain" deathbed experiences by finding normal, ordinary causes for them have ended in complete failure. They cannot be explained by the medical condition of the dying person, nor by the state of his mind, nor by his religious or cultural background. How, then, can we explain them?

The only remaining possibility is that these are genuine *psychic experiences.* Being close to death can apparently create an altered state of consciousness, making the dying temporarily psychic and enabling them to see what, normally, only mediums, psychics, and clairvoyants can see. Psychics have always claimed that they can "see" the dead, who appear as vividly real to them as any person with a body. Some of them have "seen" the dead at deathbeds, waiting to guide the dying into the world in which they now live. In addition, some psychics claim to have seen the dead standing in the landscape of this next world. The dying describe their apparitional visitors and their visions of otherworldly landscapes in the same terms.

If we can accept these experiences as glimpses into the life beyond death—and Osis's research strongly suggests that we have no alternative—then we are ready to venture further into this astounding world.

CHAPTER FIVE

WHAT IT'S LIKE TO DIE: RESUSCITATION EXPERIENCES

Nobody's ever come back to tell us about it.
– *popular saying about death*

It opened up a whole new world for me that I never knew could possibly exist. It just opened me up to a whole new world.[1]
– *resuscitated patient, speaking of his death experience*

THE VIEW that no one has ever "come back" to tell us about death is an extremely popular one—but it is also untrue. The experiences which we will now examine come from the world beyond death. They happened to people who were technically dead—whose hearts had stopped beating, whose lungs had ceased to breathe, whose blood pressure had dropped so low that it was unreadable, whose pupils had dilated, whose body temperature had begun to sink. They are "experiences" in the sense that they are detailed accounts of what people say happened to them between the time their bodies died, and the time they were resuscitated. Such experiences are no longer rare: advances in medical techniques of resuscitation have in recent decades brought many thousands of people back from death. The testimony of those who return from death reveals that two quite different things happen when that awesome boundary is crossed. Some report that they lacked any trace of consciousness and so experienced nothing but a "blank"; the rest report extremely vivid experiences. There are people who, having died and been resuscitated more than once, have reported *both* types of experience. Why these variations occur we do not yet know.

The study of these experiences has already upset two groups of professionals with differing orthodoxies to defend. Most scientists assert as an article of faith that it is "impossible" for consciousness to continue after the death of the body, whereas many clergymen hold equally strongly that the nature of "life after death" can and should be discovered—only through traditional theological writings. There is, however, another source of information on the death experience—those who have died and been resuscitated. Many have described what "happened" to them, and these actual experiences of hundreds of ordinary human beings exist on their own quite independently of any theological or scientific authority.

By the standards of the normal, everyday, body-centered consciousness with which each of us has learned to view the world, the following narratives may seem utterly incredible. The standards of normal experience, however, are completely unsuited to judging them, for with clinical death we enter a realm beyond the body and beyond anything we have ever undergone in it. The word "beyond" has been used deliberately, because it implies something vaster, something greater, higher, and more dramatic, than anything we have yet encountered. The stories of those who have traveled beyond life and returned to the living to describe this most mysterious of all journeys actually resemble those of early geographical explorers. In the ancient world:

> When the Mediterranean Sea was the centre of civilization, explorers occasionally sailed through the Straits of Gibraltar and along the coast of northern Africa.... One venturesome captain, on returning from such a voyage, not only described landscapes, peoples, animals, ... but also made the statement *that eventually the sun had shone from the north!* ... this phenomenon was

> unknown to Mediterranean peoples. The captain was laughed to scorn. But today we cannot doubt that he had been where he claimed to have been—that he had, in fact, sailed south of the equator.[2]

Similarly, reports that conscious existence continues after clinical death are not accepted by contemporary medicine and science, and people describing such experiences are assumed to be suffering from hallucinations caused by the trauma of temporary death. But in opposition to this popular modern view of death is a very ancient human tradition which holds that the death of the body does not bring one's personal existence to an end.

> According to this ... tradition, some aspect of the human being survives even after the physical body ceases to function and is ultimately destroyed. This persistent aspect has been called by many names, among them psyche, soul, mind, spirit, self, being, and consciousness. By whatever name it is called, the notion that one passes into another realm of existence upon physical death is among the most venerable of human beliefs. There is a graveyard in Turkey which was used by Neanderthal men approximately 100,000 years ago. There, fossilized imprints have enabled archaeologists to discover that these ancient men buried their dead in biers of flowers, indicating that they ... saw death as an occasion of celebration—as a transition of the dead from this world to the next. Indeed, graves from very early sites all over the earth give evidence of the belief in human survival of bodily death.[3]

For most contemporary scientists, such beliefs are nothing more than pathetic delusions by which unsophisticated people shield themselves from the brutality of death. *The possibility that these ideas might, on the other hand, be based not upon delusions but rather upon actual experiences of human beings in the past* seems not to have occurred to contemporary thinkers. Let us, therefore, examine some experiences in which people who have actually died and returned to life tell us what happened to them. And as we will now see, whether death was by drowning or by freezing, by hemorrhage, by heart seizure, or by shooting, the post-mortem experiences which befell the dead were overwhelming in their power; so overwhelming, in fact, that it is not unusual for mature, emotionally stable adults to break down and weep while recounting death-experiences that may have happened thirty years before!

Death by drowning

Caresse Crosby drowned when she was seven years old, but was resuscitated:

> When my head plunged beneath the water's surface, I took one long frightened gulp and I never got another breath of air, my lungs expelled once and refilled with tide water. The blood rushed from my toes to my nose and suddenly my head seemed to expand and explode, but softly as though it were a cotton ball fluffing out and out and out. Into my ears the waters poured strange sea lullabies and little by little, there beneath the flood, a dazzling prismatic effulgence cleared my vision—not only did I see and hear harmony, but I understood everything. And slowly, as a bubble rises to the surface, I rose to the surface, rose up through the wooden platform, rose to where I could dominate the whole scene spread out beneath me. I watched my father at work on his boat, my brothers deathly frightened hanging on to my spindly heels and I, my hair like seaweed, pulled flat against the submerged bottom of the float. Thus, while I drowned I saw my father turn and act; I saw my frightened brothers run homewards; I saw the efforts to bring me back to life and I *tried not to come back.*
>
> It was the most perfect state of easeful joy that I ever experienced, then or since. There was no sadness or sickness from

which I wished to escape. I was only seven, a carefree child, yet that moment in all my life has never been equalled for pure happiness. Could I have glimpsed, while drowned (for I was drowned), the freedom of eternal life? One thing I know, that Nirvana does exist between here and the hereafter—a space of delight, for I have been there.[4]

Death by freezing

Dr. Russell Noyes, a professor of psychiatry at the University of Iowa College of Medicine and a student of death-experiences, obtained the following account from a woman, then twenty years old, whose car stalled in a snowbank one sub-zero night on a deserted country road. Realizing that she was in grave danger, she made strenuous efforts to rescue herself. When these failed, however, she returned to her car, where:

> I was overcome by excruciating pain as the cold penetrated the depths of my body. The pain shut off all thoughts but soon gave way to a warm glow, which softly enveloped me. The pain was replaced by indescribable comfort and warmth of my innermost being. Then I heard magnificent music, not of this world but from unseen stars, creating a harmony of such rapturous beauty as to lift me to a transcendence of my being. The music is still audible in my mind, even after forty-seven years, it was of such beauty and harmony. At the same time I saw a soft glow of light—how shall I locate it—on the horizon. For a moment I was one with the Universe. Time, space, and myself were one and the same. I experienced ecstasy as I saw the unity and beauty of the Universe.
>
> When I awoke in a hospital I struggled against those who were working to save me. I did not want to come back. However, my body soon became filled with painful "pins and needles" and I again found myself fighting for life. The process of freezing to

death was one of agonizing pain, but "death" itself was so beautiful that the word "pleasant" is almost inane.[5]

Death by hemorrhage

David Wheeler, another student of such experiences, interviewed a woman who, after the very difficult birth of a baby girl, hemorrhaged and died, but was successfully resuscitated. Describing her death-experience, she told Wheeler:

> For a second everything went totally black. Not really black like the color, but a voidlike black.... Something jerked me out of my body. I was carried, or pushed, through this long tunnel.... I saw a strange light.... A bright cloud enveloped me for an instant, then ... I found myself floating ... in the delivery room watching ... their attempts to bring me back to life. The body on the white table—deathly white—it was me!
>
> There was my body on the bed and here I was floating above it watching the whole thing like it was a movie. It was very real. I could actually float through the wall of the delivery room, and I drifted down the halls of the hospital. I don't know what I looked like for sure. I think I was a transparent cloud but regardless of my looks, no one seemed to notice that I was gliding through the air near them. I suppose that I was invisible to them although I could see and hear them very well. I came back to the delivery room. There seemed to be something pulling me back to my body. The entire experience of floating out of my body was very good. It may seem strange but I really did not want to join with that body on the table. But I was jerked very forcefully to it. I remember ... re-entering it. After that I can't remember a thing until I came to hours later in my bed in an intensive care unit.... That was twenty-five years ago. I remember the incident ... as clear as anything.... I know that I died and I would like to do it again. It was very pleasant.[6]

Death by cardiac arrest

Kenneth G. was stricken with a heart attack while on his way home from an afternoon at the racetrack. He collapsed on the street, and was unconscious, though still alive, upon his arrival at the hospital. When he regained consciousness in the Intensive Care Unit and appeared to be doing well, he was placed in one of the regular hospital rooms. Although he was fine when checked by a nurse at 10:30 p.m., he was found ten minutes later slumped out of bed, dead. In the words of one of his doctors:

> The patient's body was black in spots, indicating that the blood had ceased flowing.... [It] had already started to settle in the body's lower portions.... If I had not known Elizabeth [Kenneth G.'s daughter] personally, I do not think that we would have attempted to resuscitate the man. He was as dead as anyone that I have ever seen. I saw no real hope but decided to go ahead as though there was.[7]

To the amazement of the doctor, Kenneth G. was successfully resuscitated. But he was not happy to be "back," and told those around his bedside, "When I go again, please leave me alone." In an interview, he described vividly the overwhelmingly powerful experience that befell him during the minutes that he was dead.

> I found myself in the most enchanting place you could ever visit. The beauty was far beyond anything that I had ever seen before in my life. It was so luxuriant that there is absolutely no way to express to you the intense enjoyment I felt with the place.... I know that I was transported there by dying.... I discovered myself drifting down to a huge valley. It sloped downward from low, gently rolling hills. There were miles upon miles of ... flat rolling plains.
>
> [I] was ... floating down ... very slowly like a man with a parachute. I drifted out of the sky and landed softly in a field of

grass which came up to my waist. It was a delightful sensation. Then I saw that this meadow went on forever. I saw dense forests in the far distance.... The only word I seem to be able to use to talk about that place is beautiful.... As I stood there in the middle of this lush, green field, I could see animals, flowers, and trees. It was the flowers that I especially liked. I'd never before seen anything like the profusion of growing beautiful plants and flowers in this place.

For a while I stood in that waist-high grass, listening to the gentle rustle of grass being blown by a light breeze. That, for a while, was the only sound. Then I heard a voice calling to me. It was at first so faint that I just felt that someone was trying to talk to me. It got a little louder. I did not see the person calling to me, but I recognized the owner of the voice. It was my father, who had died ten years ago. "What is he doing here?" I thought to myself. "Here I am in a strange meadow. I don't know where I am, and my dead father is calling to me." I accepted things as they were—what else could I do? The voice kept faintly telling me, "Kenneth, don't be afraid. Do not worry, I have come to help you with your journey. Don't be afraid of this. I've helped others."

Then, some joyous laughter rolled across the meadow and caught my attention. I looked across the grass and up the slight curvature of the hill in the distance. There, in a broad expanse which was separated from the trees, I saw children playing in an amusement park. They looked very familiar.... The park was like one that I remembered as a child ... Steeplechase Park in Coney Island.... But all my old playmates were there, just like they were sixty years ago.... None of them noticed me; they continued to play in the amusement park as we had done half a century ago.... I was a little boy again, reliving [my] youth ... God, it was beautiful!

Death seemed to have blended the hereafter with the fondest memories I carried through life. I know I went to heaven with

> my most cherished childhood memories.... How wrong it was for them to bring me back from such a wonderful ... place.[8]

Death by shotgun

After a shotgun was discharged into his abdomen at point-blank range, Arthur Sanders was pronounced dead on his arrival at the hospital. But doctors managed to restore his heartbeat and he underwent a five-hour operation, during which he died, and was again resuscitated. Speaking of his death-experience, Sanders states that it gave him a glimpse of what he calls "the other world" beyond death, a world in which, he says:

> I never felt so happy in my entire life. During the time that ... I died ... I had an experience that has completely transformed my life. I suddenly felt myself floating up away from my body. I seemed to be out in an open landscape of beautiful scenery which was glittering with an incredible, brilliant golden light. There was a clean, blue sky above me and I seemed to be ... led on by a kind of shining mist that hovered near. I felt such a sense of joy and exhilaration as I had never known ... this sense of utter happiness has not left me.... One thing I'm certain of and would like to share with everybody—I'll never, never be afraid of death again. It was quite incredible.... What happened ... has changed my whole way of thinking.... The 23rd Psalm is my favorite now. You know how it says, "Yea, though I walk through the valley of the shadow of death, I will fear no evil"? Well, that's taken on tremendous meaning.... I now know it is true. There is no evil to fear because we're going to a far, far better place.[9]

These five narratives make it clear that some extremely powerful things happen to people who die. We will now look more deeply into these death-experiences by examining a large number of cases. And what we will find is that although the same features are reported again and again, they will often appear in an unpredictable combination, or in an unusual sequence. The reason for this variability is still unknown.

The stages of death

Down a tunnel

It is common for death to begin with the experience of a very rapid passage through a long, dark enclosure, variously described as a tunnel, tube, shaft, hole, funnel, cave, well, trough, valley, or cylinder. A sixty-five-year-old man who suffered a cardiac arrest later said:

> The first thing that I was aware of was moving very rapidly down this endless tunnel. There was a bright light at the end of it. I sort of felt like I was in a low sports car doing about 120 miles an hour. Then I came to a light.[10]

One woman who was resuscitated said it was as though she were rushing along through a pitch-black tunnel. Dr. B. Kirkwood, who had been given up as dead, but was revived, said of his encounter with death:

> I was hurried off at great speed. Have you ever looked through a very long tunnel and seen the tiny speck of light at the far end? ... Well, I found myself ... hurrying along just such a tunnel or passage.[11]

Another informant states:

> I had a very bad allergic reaction to a local anaesthetic, and I just quit breathing—I had a respiratory arrest. The first thing that

> happened—it was real quick—was that I went through this dark, black vacuum at super speed. You could compare it to a tunnel, I guess. I felt like I was riding on a roller coaster train at an amusement park, going through this tunnel at a tremendous speed.[12]

Another says:

> Suddenly I was in a very dark, very deep valley. It was as though there was a pathway, almost a road, through the valley, and I was going down the path.... Later, after I was well, the thought came to me, "Well, now I know what the Bible means by 'the valley of the shadow of death,' because I've been there."[13]

I was out of my body!

When the dying person emerges from the tunnel down which he has been speeding, he undergoes what is undoubtedly one of the most astounding phenomena which can befall a human being: meeting his own body face-to-face—in an out-of-the-body experience. Alternatively, there may be no tunnel effect at all, and death may *begin* with an OBE. And it is fascinating to note that the out-of-the-body experiences of the temporarily dead are, at first, exactly the same as those experienced by living persons during sleep, voluntarily, or as the result of a trauma to the body which does not cause clinical death. Dr. Raymond Moody, a physician who has interviewed more than one hundred people who have undergone clinical death, was given this description by a woman patient:

> About a year ago, I was admitted to the hospital with heart trouble, and the next morning, lying in the hospital bed, I began to have a very severe pain in my chest. I pushed the button beside the bed to call for the nurses, and they came in and started working on me—I was quite uncomfortable lying on my back so I turned over, and as I did I quit breathing and my heart stopped beating. Just then, I heard the nurses shout, "Code pink! Code

pink!" As they were saying this, I could feel myself moving out of my body and sliding down between the mattress and the rail on the side of the bed—actually it seemed as if I went *through* the rail—on down to the floor. Then, I started rising upward, slowly. On my way up, I saw more nurses come running into the room—there must have been a dozen of them. My doctor happened to be making his rounds in the hospital so they called him and I saw him come in, too. I thought, "I wonder what he's doing here." I drifted on up past the light fixture—I saw it from the side and very distinctly—and then I stopped, floating right below the ceiling, looking down. I felt almost as though I were a piece of paper that someone had blown up to the ceiling.

I watched them reviving me from up there! My body was lying down there stretched out on the bed, in plain view, and they were all standing around it. I heard one nurse say, "Oh, my God! She's gone!", while another one leaned down to give me mouth-to-mouth resuscitation. I was looking at the *back* of her head while she did this. I'll never forget the way her hair looked; it was cut kind of short. Just then, I saw them roll this machine in there, and they put the shocks on my chest. When they did, I saw my whole body just jump right up off the bed, and I heard every bone in my body crack and pop. It was the most awful thing! As I saw them below beating on my chest and rubbing my arms and legs, I thought, "Why are they going to so much trouble? I'm just fine now."[14]

One of the most fascinating aspects of this experience can be the unfamiliar appearance of one's own body. An informant says:

Boy, I sure didn't realize that I looked like that! You know, I'm only used to seeing myself in pictures or from the front in a mirror, and both of those look flat. But all of a sudden there I—or my body—was and I could see it. I could definitely see it, full view, from about five feet away. It took me a few moments to recognize myself.[15]

This unexpected feature took a rather comical turn in one account. A physician who was clinically dead found himself beside the bed looking at his own corpse, which had taken on the ashy-grey hue characteristic of dead bodies. Understandably confused and upset, the deceased doctor tried to decide what he should do. Eventually he chose to beat a hasty retreat, as he was not at all happy contemplating his own body. His grandfather had told him ghost stories as a child, and therefore, as he put it, "[I] didn't like being around this thing that looked like a dead body—even if it was me!"[16]

The well-known Dr. Elisabeth Kübler-Ross, a psychiatrist who has worked extensively with dying patients and their families, gathered hundreds of accounts of death-experiences after her interest was aroused by an incident which occurred during a seminar on death and dying which she was conducting at the University of Chicago Hospital.

> The seminars were set up so that doctors, nurses, anyone who was involved with helping the dying, could listen behind a screen while terminally ill patients talked to me about how they felt about their approaching death. They understood that they were teaching us and that we regarded their conversation as their final gift to us. One of the patients was a housewife in her late forties who had suffered for years from Hodgkin's disease, and who had been near death many times. About ten minutes before the end of our interview, she began to describe an experience she had never told anyone else.
>
> About a year earlier ... this woman had been taken critically ill to a hospital and put in intensive care. One afternoon a nurse saw that she was dying and rushed out of the room to summon help. Meanwhile, this woman felt herself float out of her body. In fact, she said she could look down and see how pale her face looked. Yet at the same time she felt absolutely wonderful. She had a great sense of peace and relief.
>
> The remarkable thing about this experience was that she was able to observe the doctors at work on her body. She heard what

> they said, which members of the team wanted to give up trying to revive her and which did not. Her recall of details was so acute that she was even able to repeat one of the jokes an attendant had cracked to relieve the tension. She wanted to tell them to relax, that it was okay. But her body showed no vital signs—no respiration, no blood pressure, no brain-wave activity. Finally she was declared dead … later, she returned to her body and recovered.

At the end of the interview, Dr. Kübler-Ross joined her audience of doctors, nurses, medical students and clergymen.

> "They all leaped on me because I refused to label the woman's story as hallucination. They all wanted me to give this woman's experience a convenient psychiatric label so they could forget it."[17]

Because our society does not generally "believe" in such experiences, the individual who has one is forced to try to understand what it means alone and unaided. Many do not at first connect the astounding condition in which they find themselves with physical death, and even when they do, their bewilderment may continue:

> I thought I was dead, and I wasn't sorry that I was dead, but I just couldn't figure out where I was supposed to go. My thought and my consciousness were just like they are in life, but I just couldn't figure all this out. I kept thinking, "Where am I going to go? What am I going to do?" and, "My God, I'm dead! I can't believe it!" ... And so I decided I was just going to wait until all the excitement died down and they carried my body away, and try to see if I could figure out where to go from there.[18]

The "dead" thus find themselves separated from their physical bodies, yet fully conscious and able to see and hear. But what, without bodies, do they find themselves "in"? Interviews with dozens of resuscitated persons simply confirm what other researchers of the out-of-the-body experiences of the living have already learned: that there are three possibilities. Some of the "dead" report that they did not seem to be contained in any form, but were simply "points" of consciousness occupying a particular position in space. Most, however, did find themselves in a "form." Some of these discovered that they were human in shape, and looked like the physical bodies which they had left behind. Others, to their amazement, found that they entirely lacked their familiar human appearance, and were roundish, globular, or amorphous "clouds."

The experiences which now befall the dead are of a very dramatic character, and are *identical* to those reported by living projectors: they find that they are invisible and inaudible to embodied persons, able to penetrate matter, and able to travel by thought.

> The doctors and nurses were pounding on my body to try to get I.V.'s started and to get me back, and I kept trying to tell them, "Leave me alone. All I want is to be left alone. Quit pounding on me." But they didn't hear me. So I tried to move their hands to keep them from beating on my body, but nothing would happen. I couldn't get anywhere.... I couldn't move their hands. It looked like I was touching their hands and I tried to move them yet when I would give it the stroke, their hands were still there. I don't know whether my hand was going through [them], around [them], ... or what. I didn't feel any pressure against their hands when I was trying to move them.[19]

Another informant reports:

> People were walking up from all directions to get to the wreck. I could see them, and I was in the middle of a very narrow walkway. Anyway, as they came by they wouldn't seem to notice me. They would just keep walking with their eyes straight ahead. As they came real close, I would try to turn around, to get out of their way, but they would just walk *through* me.[20]

The vision and hearing experienced while out-of-the-body are described as being either as good as or better than that in the physical body. Many people report that their surroundings look and sound completely normal. In other cases, people whose bodily senses were defective are now able to function perfectly. Dr. Kübler-Ross recalls a case involving a chemist who had been blinded a year earlier in a laboratory accident. During a death experience, however, he floated out of his body and was able to see perfectly everything that happened in the vicinity of his body.[21] Identical reports have been made by people who had OBEs without undergoing death: although suffering from deafness or poor eyesight in their bodies, they have found themselves seeing and hearing perfectly while "out." And both Kübler-Ross and Moody have found cases in which people who died and were revived after losing limbs in accidents reported that they were out of their bodies in forms which were completely intact and included the missing limb. Reports of paranormally superior vision and hearing are common for both regular and death-induced OBEs. These remarkably consistent similarities make it clear that, in their first stages, the OBEs of the dying are identical to those of the living. The following cases are typical:

> One man says that while he was "dead" his vision seemed incredibly more powerful and, in his words, "I just can't understand how I could see so far." A woman who recalled this experience notes, "It seemed as if this … sense had no limitations, as if I could look anywhere and everywhere."[22]

Among living projectors, reports of being able to see in the dark, to see in all directions at once, and to see through solid objects such as walls, are commonplace.

In addition, both the living and the dying frequently describe themselves as having expanded mental powers during OBEs. Moody's resuscitated informants repeatedly stated that they could think more rapidly and clearly while out of their bodies. Surveys of out-of-the-body experiences and writings by habitual projectors contain identical claims. These intriguing findings rather strongly suggest that whatever else we may be, we are not our bodies.

Audiences to whom I have presented such material often recoil at this point with a kind of fascinated horror. A typical reaction is: "But how horrible! To see that you're dead, but to be unable to communicate with anyone, that would be awful! If I have to survive death as an invisible ghost floating around on the ceiling, then I'd rather not survive it!" But as we shall see, the events that have been described are followed by others even more astounding.

Greetings from beyond

Upon being born into physical existence, human beings are met and cared for by others. As this book will make clear, death is actually a kind of "birth" into another form of existence. And in death, too, we do not find ourselves alone. Four different researchers, engaged in quite separate studies of death-experiences, have made this same discovery: Dr. Raymond Moody, Dr. Charles Garfield, Dr. Elisabeth Kübler-Ross, and David Wheeler. A resuscitated patient told Wheeler:

> It was a tremendous feeling to die.... I was in a lot of pain.... I died.... I saw myself on the operating table. The doctors were frantically trying to bring me back, but I did not want to come back. I drifted farther and farther away ... and I saw the spirits of some of my dead friends. They seemed to be coming toward me. I was about to join them when I was slammed back into this world.[23]

One of Raymond Moody's informants said:

> I had this experience when I was giving birth to a child. The delivery was very difficult, and I lost a lot of blood. The doctor

> gave me up, and told my relatives that I was dying. However, I was quite alert through the whole thing, and even as I heard him saying this I felt myself coming to. As I did, I realized that all these people were there, almost in multitudes it seems, hovering around the ceiling of the room. They were all people I had known in my past life, but who had passed on before. I recognized my grandmother and a girl I had known when I was in school, and many other relatives and friends. It seems that I mainly saw their faces and felt their presence. They all seemed pleased. It was a very happy occasion, and I felt that they had come to protect or to guide me. It was almost as if I were coming home, and they were there to greet or to welcome me. All this time, I had the feeling of everything light and beautiful. It was a beautiful and glorious moment.[24]

These experiences, however, show some variability. Many of the resuscitated, but not all, report them, and they may happen at different times during the process of dying. Usually the dying are met by people to whom they were close in life, but who are now dead. In other cases, the dying encounter beings who are unknown to them, but who identify themselves as "spiritual helpers." In still other cases, the "greeters" are not visible to the dying and do not identify themselves. A sixty-five-year-old heart-attack victim said, "I felt the presence of another being, but I never saw anyone."[25] Another said:

> While I was dead ... there were people around me ... I could feel their presence ... though I could never see anyone. Every now and then, I would talk with one of them.... And whenever I wondered what was going on, I would always get a thought back from one of them, that everything was all right, that I was dying but would be fine.... I always got an answer back for every question that I asked.[26]

However incredible such encounters may seem to those who have never undergone them, the dying themselves, upon returning to their bodies, are in no doubt about their meaning: *they are being welcomed into death.*

Ascending into light

For many of us death is a horror; we imagine ourselves sinking inexorably into darkness, the darkness of the grave. But if we will accept the experiences of those who have passed through that dreadful gate, we will find that we have chosen the wrong metaphor: death is far more likely to be experienced, not as a descent into darkness, but as an ascent into light. After dying, Charles Ritchie found that his hospital room began to fill with light. Leslie Sharpe, whose heart stopped beating and who left his body, found himself floating in a bright, pale yellow light. John Van Luyk, a fifty-two-year-old aeronautical design technologist who suffered a cardiac arrest in the hospital and was dead for three minutes, told me: "I was floating, floating upward, with all of my senses intact, in a brilliant, beautiful beam of light; it was all light!"

The two events which the dying now describe will seem utterly incredible to many readers, for not only are they completely beyond anything we experience in normal bodily consciousness, they are also remarkably similar to some traditional religious ideas about death. Two interpretations of this are possible. The first is that the experiences are hallucinations and the religious ideas are fantasies. The other is that the experiences are not only real, but were the original basis, far back in time, for the religious ideas. What happens next is that the light becomes *personified.* It is transformed into a "being," a "being of light," who shows the dying *a "movie" of their lives.*

Both Dr. Kübler-Ross and Dr. Moody have gathered many accounts of encounters with this being[27] from their resuscitated subjects, and it is this feature of the death-experience which typically has a more profound effect on the dying than any other. This light, usually dim at first, quickly becomes unearthly in its brilliance, and despite the fact that, in normal bodily life, "light" is not personified, Dr. Moody says:

> not one person has expressed any doubt whatsoever that it was a being. Not only that, it is a personal being. It has a very definite personality.[28]

The encounter between the dying person and the being of light involves emotions which are so intense and powerful that they are beyond bodily experience: the total love, emotional warmth, compassion and complete acceptance that emanate from the being of light to the dying person are so profound they are indescribable, beyond words, and he finds himself irresistibly drawn to the being.

The being now speaks to the dying person, apparently often by "thought" rather than by audible voice, asking him to assess his life. And in this request there is no trace of condemnation, threat or accusation, for the being continues to radiate a completely loving acceptance. One person, who collapsed after suffering a ruptured appendix and then left his body, describes his encounter with this being:

> I floated … down the hall and out the door onto the screened-in porch … and then I floated right straight on through the screen, just as though it weren't there, and up into this pure crystal clear … white light. It was beautiful and so bright, so radiant, but it didn't hurt my eyes. It's not any kind of light you can describe on earth. I didn't actually see a person in this light, and yet it has a special identity, it definitely does.… I felt as though I were surrounded by an overwhelming love and compassion.[29]

In another experience, the "light" is more intensely personified:

> I knew I was dying and that there was nothing I could do about it, because no one could hear me.… I was out of my body, there's no doubt about it, because I could see my own body there on the

operating room table. My soul was out! All this made me feel very bad at first, but then, this really bright light came. It did seem that it was a little dim at first, but then it was this huge beam. It was just a tremendous amount of light.... And it gave off heat to me; I felt a warm sensation. It was a bright yellowish white—more white. It was tremendously bright; I just can't describe it. It seemed that it covered everything, yet it didn't prevent me from seeing everything around me—the operating room, the doctors and nurses, everything.

At first, when the light came, I wasn't sure what was happening, but then it asked ... me if I was ready to die. It was like talking to a person, but a person wasn't there. The light's what was talking to me, but in a *voice*.... From the moment the light spoke to me, I felt really ... secure and loved. The love which came from it is just unimaginable, indescribable.[30]

My life passed before my eyes

The idea that, after death, people are "judged" for their earthly actions and rewarded or punished accordingly might seem to us today to be a rather naive religious fantasy. However, the reports of many resuscitated persons indicate quite clearly that this idea is a somewhat distorted reflection of some actual human experiences.

Is there really, then, a "Day of Judgment" after death? The answer seems, incredibly enough, to be "yes," except that it doesn't last a "day." Instead, it takes just seconds, and only somewhat resembles the traditional religious idea. Such experiences, however fantastic they may sound, have been discovered under conditions which force us to take them seriously: six different researchers—Dr. Raymond Moody, Dr. Russell Noyes, Dr. Robert Crookall, Prof. Albert Helm, Dr. R.C.A. Hunter and Father Herbert Thurston[31]—all working completely independently, have gathered numerous, highly similar accounts of this experience from many different people who have had an encounter with death.

The "being of light," after asking the dying person to assess his life, helps him to do this in the most practical way possible: by showing him a "movie" of it—an astonishingly vivid visual depiction of his own past. For example:

> When the light appeared, the first thing he said to me was, "What do you have to show me that you've done with your life?" ... And that's when these flashbacks started. I thought, "Gee, what is going on?" because, all of a sudden, I was back in my early childhood ... when I was a little girl, playing down by the creek in our neighborhood, and there were other scenes from about that time—experiences I had had with my sister, and things about neighborhood people, and actual places I had been. And then I was in kindergarten, and I remembered the time when I had this one toy I really liked, and I broke it and I cried for a long time. ...
>
> The things that flashed back came in the order of my life, and they were so vivid. The scenes were just like you walked outside and saw them, completely three-dimensional, and in color. And they moved. For instance, when I saw myself breaking the toy, I could see all the movements. It wasn't like watching it all from my perspective at the time. It was like the little girl I saw was somebody else, in a movie, one little girl among all the other children out there playing on the playground. Yet, it was me. I saw myself doing these things, as a child, and they were the exact same things I had done, because I remember them.
>
> The light ... disappeared as soon as ... the flashbacks started, and yet ... he was there with me the whole time, ... because ... he made comments here and there. He was trying to show me something ... he was picking out these certain flashbacks of my life and putting them in front of me ... he kept stressing the importance of love. The places where he showed it best involved my sister.... He showed me some instances where I had been selfish to my sister, but then just as many times where I had really shown love to her.... He pointed out to me that I should try to do things for other people, to try my best. There wasn't any accu-

sation in any of this, though. When he came across times when I had been selfish, his attitude was only that I had been learning from them, too.

He seemed very interested in things concerning knowledge, too. He kept on pointing out things that had to do with learning, and he did say that I was going to continue learning.[32]

A lightning-swift visual presentation of one's own life, although startlingly unlike anything that happens in normal bodily consciousness, seems simple enough if we can accept it as real. But in fact, the research of these six men shows that this "review" can involve many variations. One of the most startling is the fact that clinical death is not required to induce it; it can be triggered by two other things as well: simply being close to physical death, or feeling utterly convinced that death is imminent. For example, a man who was very sick, but not clinically dead at the time of his "review" experience, describes it:

I had had a slight fever and had not felt well for about two weeks, but this night I rapidly became very ill.... I found myself in a completely black void, and my whole life kind of flashed in front of me. It started back when I was six or seven years old.... I went from grammar school to high school to college, then to dental school, and then right on into practicing dentistry. ...

This flashback was in the form of mental pictures ... but they were much more vivid than normal ones. I saw only the high points ... it was so rapid it was like looking through a volume of my entire life and being able to do it within seconds. It just flashed before me like a motion picture that goes tremendously fast, yet I was fully able to see it, and ... comprehend it ... the emotions didn't come back with the pictures.... I didn't see anything else during this experience. There was just blackness, except for the images I saw. Yet, I definitely felt the presence of a very powerful, completely loving being there with me all through this experience.[33]

In the following cases, death was incorrectly believed to be imminent and unavoidable.[34] John Gerard, a priest, was skating with a friend when the latter fell through the ice. In attempting to rescue him, Gerard was also pulled under the ice. He said:

> There flashed [before] me, along with the realization that death was, apparently, immediately inevitable, a perfect picture of my past life in every detail.... Everything seemed to be included, however trivial.[35]

Albert Helm, a distinguished Swiss professor of geology, undertook a study of the "life review" phenomenon after undergoing it himself. An experienced mountaineer, he was climbing in the Alps when a gust of wind blew off his hat. Impulsively lunging for it, he slipped from a steep precipice and began to fall helplessly to what he realized was probably his death:

> I saw my whole past life take place in many images, as though on a stage at some distance from me. I saw myself as the chief character in the performance. [It was] ... a rapid, profuse succession of images that were sharp and distinct ... [and] almost instantaneous.... As though I looked out of the window of a high house, I saw myself as a seven-year-old boy going to school. I then saw myself in the 4th grade classroom with my beloved teacher Weisz. I acted out my life as though I were an actor on a stage upon which I looked down from the highest gallery in the theatre.... I saw myself industriously working in the sketching studio of the Canton school, matriculating examinations, making a mountain journey, and sketching my first panorama from Zurichberg.[36]

In his article "Memory at Death," Herbert Thurston says of such experiences:

> In almost every case, the range, the minute detail and the incred-

ible rapidity of the vision came as a complete surprise. Nothing in their previous knowledge of their mental processes had prepared them to believe that such a lightning flash of illumination was possible.[37]

A number of other variations in the "life review" may take place:

- The review may occur at different points in the sequence of events involved in the death experience (or it may not occur at all), and it can take place with or without the presence of the "being."

- The life-events which it depicts may appear in chronological order, or they may all be experienced simultaneously.

- The individual may feel strongly that every single thing he has ever done, from the most trivial to the most important, was depicted, or he may see only the principal events of his life.

- The emotions which accompanied what is seen may be relived, or the experience may be emotionless and almost impersonal.

- Although all agree that the visualizations involved are unbelievably vivid, the images may seem flat as if being projected, or they may be completely three-dimensional and apparently externalized in space—as if the person were watching a play with living actors.

- The experience may be interpreted as an educational effort to help the person understand the meaning of his life, or he may be completely baffled as to its purpose.

- Finally, if the "being" is present during the review, he may

> or may not "teach" the dying person a "lesson" concerning his life—as he did, for example, in the case of the woman who was told that acquiring knowledge and learning to love others were the purposes of life.[38]

According to Moody, there is remarkable agreement among his subjects, after their death-experiences, that these last two goals are the main purposes of embodied existence. The type of love which the being encourages is, however, of a somewhat unusual sort: it is the kind of profound, compassionate, and unconditional acceptance which he himself gives to the dying.

"Dying is the most beautiful experience you can have"

One of the most dramatically unexpected revelations to come from this research is the frequency with which death is described as a *positive* or even *ecstatic* experience. So often is this the case, that many of the resuscitated are angry and distressed to find themselves back in their bodies. They may even request that they be permitted to die, and may feel an intense nostalgia for the realm in which they found themselves after clinical death. John Van Luyk, who had a cardiac arrest and died for three minutes, said of his experience of death:

> I can hardly find words for it—the most beautiful experience of my life. I had the most peaceful, contented feeling—but I wish there were different words available to describe it. If you called it peaceful to the 10th power—that would be getting close to it. When they jolted me out of that, I was really mad. The experience changed my whole outlook on death. I think very differently of it now—I'm not afraid of it at all. As a matter of fact, I sometimes tell my kids that dying is the most beautiful experience you can have but they look at me as if I'm some kind of nut. So far as death is concerned, I can recommend it to anybody.[39]

A drowning victim described death as

> the most perfect state of easeful joy that I ever experienced, then or since.... That moment in all my life has never been equalled for pure happiness.[40]

Another clinically dead survivor reports:

> I never felt so happy in my entire life ... such a sense of joy and exhilaration as I had never known.[41]

And one young woman who resisted efforts to revive her said:

> I have no fear of ... death. Having once experienced the beauty and rapture of it, the fear of death has been removed for all time.[42]

Others who have been resuscitated simply say that they had a pervasive sense of calmness, peacefulness, and well-being, which they did not wish to relinquish by returning to their bodies. In fact, Dr. Kübler-Ross, who has interviewed hundreds of resuscitated patients, says that such positive feelings are so often associated with death that she has been afraid that publicizing them will encourage suicides. And these positive experiences can occur without clinical death: *being convinced that you are about to die, or simply being in an out-of-the-body state*, are also highly likely to cause them.

Dr. Russell Noyes has made a study of fifty-nine people who had a close encounter with death, incorrectly believing that they were about to die. He reports that, initially, they made every possible effort to save themselves, but when they recognized that these efforts were in vain, they accepted their imminent deaths. Much to Noyes's surprise, this acceptance of death was instantly followed by profound feelings of peacefulness and joy.[43] One gentleman described the peace and calm which overcame him during his near-death episode as "the most blissful feeling he had ever experienced."[44]

Out-of-the-body experiences regularly produce similar states, as we can readily see from the published literature on them.[45] Celia Green's survey of four hundred people who had had OBEs revealed that feelings of elation and exaltation often accompany them.

> One subject, for example, refers to having experienced "a tremendous feeling of exhilaration." The following are typical expressions of delight experienced by ... [OBE] subjects:
>
> Excitement and wonder at what was happening, delight in my sense of freedom and power....
>
> Both occasions were so happy, ecstatic almost, that I have never stopped wishing that I could repeat them. There was a quality of extreme joy....
>
> The whole experience was absolutely wonderful, and I wish I could experience a similar one again....
>
> I had no further interest in my physical body, or indeed my physical life. I only wanted to pursue and prolong this happy state of being where everything was more bright, vivid and real than anything I had previously known.[46]

Many of the people Moody interviewed had had highly positive death experiences. Some had been so ecstatic that the person lost all interest in returning to his body and to physical life, and felt intense longing for the after-death state:

> After I came back, I cried off and on for about a week because I had to live in this world after seeing that one. I didn't want to come back.[47]

Not surprisingly, these encounters with death lead to a dramatically new view of it as a positive or even supremely gratifying experience—a transition to a higher state of existence. This conception of death as a desirable transformation was expressed by people who likened dying to awakening, to graduating, and to escaping from jail.

> I don't feel bad at funerals anymore. I kind of rejoice at them, because I know what the dead person has been through.
>
> After you've ... had the experience that I had, you know in your heart that there's no such thing as death. You just graduate from one thing to another—like from grammar school to high school to college.
>
> Life is like imprisonment. In this state, we just can't understand what prisons these bodies are. Death is such a release—like an escape from prison. That's the best thing I can think of to compare it to.[48]

Exhilarating though this positive view of death may be, it has some chillingly obvious negative implications. If the discovery that death is a marvelous experience becomes widely publicized, what is to prevent those millions of people who yearn for a more joyous existence from seeking it immediately by committing suicide? The answer may be found in the after-death experiences of those who tried to kill themselves. The most extensive research done on suicide experiences shows that they are:

> uniformly characterized as ... unpleasant. As one woman said, "If you leave here a tormented soul, you will be a tormented soul over there, too." In short, they report that the conflicts they had attempted suicide to escape were still present after they died, but with added complications. In their disembodied state they were unable to do anything about their problems, and they also had to view the unfortunate consequences which had resulted from their acts. A man who was despondent about the death of his wife shot himself, "died" as a result, and was resuscitated. He states: "I didn't go where [my wife] was. I went to an awful place.... I immediately saw what a mistake I had made.... I thought, I wish I hadn't done it."
>
> Others who experienced this unpleasant "limbo" state have remarked that they had the feeling they would be there for a long time. This was their penalty for "breaking the rules" by trying to

> release themselves prematurely from what was, in effect, an "assignment"—to fulfill a certain purpose in life.[49]

None of the resuscitated people with whom Moody spoke actively sought death as a result of their resuscitation experiences. They all seemed to realize instinctively that while they remained physically embodied and alive, they were supposed to continue living life and trying to learn from it. For this reason, none of them would consider suicide as a way of returning to the world they entered during their temporary deaths.

But it can't be true!

Just how strong a case can be made that these experiences are real? The basic position taken by skeptics is that the events described in death-experiences are hallucinations caused by the effects of the trauma of death on the brain. But the fact is that hallucinations are extremely variable for different people, whereas death-experiences are not—they are highly similar, often virtually identical. The major difficulty with the hallucination theory, however, is that many of the most dramatic early events in the death-experience cannot be hallucinations. Hallucinations are not objectively real—they are things that *aren't there*, except in the mind. But when patients who undergo clinical death have out-of-the-body experiences, what they see while dead is typically *what actually happened in the vicinity of their bodies, and is verified as accurate by the living people who were present.* These perceptions cannot, by definition, be hallucinations.

Thus patients with no medical training or knowledge have baffled their doctors by describing accurately, and in great detail, from the vantage point of an OBE, the resuscitation procedures used on them while their doctors knew them to be dead. *We are therefore dealing not with hallucinations, but with real perceptions.* Since the out-of-the-body part of the death experience can be established as real, and not illusory, the events which follow may well be equally real.

But even accepting that the OBE part of the death-experience is real, surely, says the skeptic, what the dying person undergoes after that will simply be a hallucination caused by his religious beliefs: he sees what his religion tells him he will see. This argument is not, however, supported by the facts. In the first place, what happened to the resuscitated while they were dead was not at all what their religious backgrounds would have led them to expect, and many stressed this point. For example, one woman said:

> The strange thing was that I had always been taught in my religious upbringing that the minute you died you would be right at these beautiful gates, pearly gates. But there I was hovering around my own physical body, and that was it! I was just baffled.[50]

Furthermore, if beliefs about death did influence the experiences of the dying person, we would expect the religious and the non-religious to have very different kinds of experiences. But they don't—the experiences of the two groups are identical.

Let us take a more extreme skeptical position: that OBE perceptions of the vicinity of the body are real, but the rest of the death-experience is only a hallucination caused by drugs given to the dying, oxygen starvation of the brain, malfunctioning of the nervous system caused by the trauma of death, or a psychosis or some other mental disorder of the dying person. Yet not even these arguments can deal with the facts. Drug-induced hallucinations, when studied, turn out to be quite different from the events of the death-experience. Further, many death-experiences occurred among people who had had no drugs prior to these events, so drugs could not have caused them. And if we group the experiences of those who were drugged and compare them with the experiences of those who were not, we find that they do not differ in any discernible way.

Perhaps, then, these experiences are the hallucinations of an oxygen-starved brain, or of a nervous system damaged by the trauma of death? But it turns out that they cannot be, for all of the death-experiences reported by resuscitated people—the tunnel, the OBE, the life-review, the being of light—have also been reported as occurring in other cases *before* any physical injury took place, or by people who mistakenly thought that they were about to die, but who were, in the end, not physically injured in any way.

Could they not, then, be fantasies or hallucinations created by the dying person to lessen the terror of death—a kind of temporary psychosis? The difficulty with this explanation is that the experiences of the dying simply do not show the tremendous variety of imagery that is characteristic of hallucinations. Instead, the great similarity of the events reported, and their sequence, is striking.

The skeptics, however, have one last, decisive card up their sleeves. These experiences, they will say, however interesting, cannot really tell us anything about what happens to human beings after death, because the people who had them *did not die*. Granted, they were close to death, but so long as it was possible to *revive them*, to restore them to full physical life, then they were not truly dead, for true death is a state from which a person cannot be revived. Therefore the stories of the resuscitated can give us no information about real death. That is an experience we can never learn anything about, because anyone who can come back to life and tell us what happened to him wasn't really dead. From this point of view, then, the only possible source of accurate information on after-death states would be the accounts of people who are actually in their graves. If, say the skeptics, it were possible to obtain accounts from the dead of what it was like to die, and if the accounts of the dead were found to be in agreement with the accounts given by the resuscitated, then and only then would we be able to say that the experiences of those revived from death are genuine.

Intriguingly enough, a large body of communications claiming to come from the dead does exist, transmitted to the living by psychics. These communications contain numerous descriptions of the death-experiences of the communicators. Coming through many different psychics, they claim to be first-person accounts of the deaths of hundreds of human beings. When these communications are examined, something quite astounding is revealed: despite the diversity of both the communicators and the psychics, *these accounts agree in every detail with the experiences described by the resuscitated.* In fact, no fewer than thirteen identical features can be found in the death-experiences of the dead and the resuscitated. The dead describe: going down a tunnel; having an out-of-the-body experience; experiencing confusion as to what was happening to them; being unable to gain the attention of the living; being met by friends or relatives who were already dead; experiencing a "light"; encountering a spiritual "being" or "guide"; undergoing a vivid "review" of their past lives; finding that their consciousness had expanded beyond what it was in bodily life; discovering that death was a highly positive experience; finding themselves in scenery of paradise-like beauty; being unwilling to leave the post-mortem state and return to their bodies; and being surprised that death was not what they had expected.[51]

Had only a few death experiences been gathered by one eccentric and presumably deluded researcher, they would be relatively easy to dismiss, or at least ignore. But instead we are confronted with the fact that some or all of the phenomena described in this chapter have been discovered independently by no fewer than eight researchers—Doctors Kübler-Ross, Moody, Noyes, Garfield, Helm, Hunter and Crookall, and Father Thurston—and gathered from hundreds of people of highly diverse religious, educational, and social backgrounds. Their stories are uncannily repetitive.

Thus, the most strenuous efforts of the skeptics have proven to be in vain. It is obvious from the evidence presented that we are dealing not with hallucinations but with real experiences.

> Now all this was three years ago, but it is still just as vivid as it was then. It was the most fantastic thing that has ever happened to me.... I'm not trying to make a big explosion in your life, and I'm not trying to brag. It's just that after this, I don't have any doubts anymore. *I know there is life after death.*[52]

The foregoing material has led us inexorably toward this stupendous conclusion. And as the rest of the book will show, there is much further evidence that it corresponds to the truth.

CHAPTER SIX

I WANT A BODY: POSSESSION EXPERIENCES

> The refusal of modern "enlightenment" to treat "possession" as a hypothesis to be spoken of as even possible, in spite of the massive human tradition based on concrete experience in its favor, has always seemed to me a curious example of the power of fashion in things scientific. That the … theory will have its innings again is to my mind absolutely certain.
>
> – *William James*

MY TEACHING ASSISTANT looked worried. Entering my office at the University of Toronto, she gazed at me somewhat uncertainly, walked toward the window, and turned around.

"A friend of mine has had a horrible experience. She's very, very upset about it, but she doesn't dare talk to anybody. It has to do with something 'psychic.' Now you know something about that kind of thing, and you're interested in it. If you could talk to her, you might be able to calm her down. Would you be willing to come to dinner on Friday and meet her?"

"Sure, I'd like to. But what happened?"

"I'd rather she told you. She's psychic, and has had quite a few experiences. She seems to have been able to handle them okay. But this time, things got a little out of hand."

That Friday I took a commuter train out to a suburban stop. My teaching assistant's husband picked me up and we drove to an elegant, modern home. We entered a sunken living room, and there I met Ann, a vivacious, attractive blonde, with hair sweeping down to her shoulders. No beads, no incense, no hippy robes. Someone less like the popular image of a "psychic" would have been hard to imagine. Ann held a graduate degree in economics and an executive position at a major corporation. She was so wholesome she looked like a cheerleader. Bright and outgoing, she chatted easily, but beneath that exterior, she seemed nervous. Her eyes kept sliding away from mine. Finally I asked her what had happened. In a trembling voice, she told me. As she began, her eyes filled with tears. Before she had finished she was sobbing.

> I was seated at the table after dinner, talking to some friends. I was idly watching a candle flame on the table, and I must have put myself into some kind of trance state. Suddenly I became aware of a discarnate masculine "presence" descending toward me. He was saying "I want a body! I want a body!" I remember that I felt feelings of sexual arousal. Then everything went blank. When I came to the room was in a state of complete disorder and my friends were holding me down.

Her friends had been terrified by the incident. They told her that her face had suddenly changed to that of a man, and the voice in which she spoke was male. They would not repeat to her the terrible things that the "voice" had said. They said she had gone berserk, had knocked over the dining room chairs, had flung glasses and dishes to the floor. She found her face covered with deep, bleeding scratches. They had been self-inflicted.

I was thunderstruck. Ann had ventured into a realm of experience of which I knew practically nothing. I asked her what had happened afterwards. Had he tried again? Angrily, her voice trembling with emotion, she said that he had, half a dozen times. He had "appeared" with the same grisly message—that he wanted a body—hers.

"What do you do?"

"I get angry and I tell him to get lost."

"What does he do?"

"He just presses harder. But I resist him. I get really angry. I keep telling him to get lost! After a while, he gives up and leaves. He can't get into my body unless I relax and let him. In the weeks after that first experience, he tried six times. Finally, he gave up. He's gone away."

And that is how I first became interested in possession.

This possession experience was of a particular type—brief, violent, and hateful. But as we will see, there are many, many other kinds.

It wasn't easy for me to take the hypothesis of possession seriously. How can anyone in the late twentieth century truly believe that "spirits" can influence the bodies and the lives of the living? It wasn't an idea in which I *wanted* to believe. It was frightening, irrational, crazy. And when I looked into it, I found out what others before me had also discovered—that it was true.

What is it like to be possessed?

Ann was unconscious during her possession. She doesn't remember what happened—it's all a blank. Such blackouts are not uncommon when possession occurs. The invading intelligence puts you "out," and then takes over your body. In Ann's case, the visit of this unwelcome guest was brief. But many others who are possessed remain conscious while being partially or fully controlled by the "other," whose tenancy may be brief or prolonged. How does it feel to be possessed—and aware of it?

In 1965, author and editor Alan Vaughan was possessed. It made a profound impression on him. It was an experience he will never be able to forget:

> For a long time afterward I could not bear even to talk about it;

> reliving that experience in my mind would rekindle a sense of terror; my voice would tremble; and anxieties would flutter in my stomach. Somewhere in the back of my mind was the apprehension that if I so much as thought of *her*, she might return to possess me once again.[1]

It all began in late 1965 when Vaughan was working as a science editor for a New York publisher. He and a colleague named Delores often used to discuss psychic phenomena, in which he did not believe. His skepticism, he now admits, was based on ignorance—an ignorance which got him into some very serious trouble. One day the subject of ouija boards came up, and Delores described the strange "messages" she and a friend had received while playing with the board. Vaughan was not impressed. It was a kind of self-delusion, he told her. The "message" simply came from the subconscious minds of the people involved. Nevertheless, he was curious. He bought a board and tried it out with two friends. Nothing happened the first time. They tried again on a Sunday evening in November, and this time the board worked. The pointer flew from letter to letter, spelling out answers to their questions. Dorothy Kilgallen, the newspaper columnist, had recently died, apparently of a heart attack, and they asked the board whether that was true. The answer was interesting. "No," said the board; "poison." This turned out to be correct—alcohol and barbiturates, not a heart attack, had caused her death. Vaughan was fascinated. How could the subconscious mind provide information which was unknown to it?

He was hooked, and the board became his constant companion. One evening, he and three friends contacted a "spirit" who called himself "Z." Although Z revealed little about himself, he did admit to being male, and had a peculiar, old-fashioned vocabulary. Vaughan was amazed to realize that he had a very convincing sense of Z's presence.

> The next morning ... my enthusiasm for the ouija prompted me to try it alone. I wasn't alone for long. A spirit appeared on the

> board who called herself "Nada." ... She said ... that she had died in 1919.... Other details about her life were sparse. When I asked her where her husband was buried, she replied, "churchyard." And she kept repeating the phrase, "You are living, I am a spirit." She seemed to be jealous of my living body.
>
> Marveling at the strong force she exerted on the planchette [pointer], I telephoned ... a friend's house to ask him to come over and observe this amazing phenomenon. There was no answer. *And then I did the stupidest thing in my life. I asked Nada to come into my body and guide me to where the friend was.*
>
> No sooner were the words out of my mouth than I felt a strange sensation in my brain. A force of some sort now was uttering words I could hear in my mind. "You are living, I am a spirit," she repeated.
>
> Guided by Nada, I left the house in search of the friend. My body became a puppet for her whimsy. I would be walking along when suddenly she would turn my direction, whirling me around. The sensation in my brain I can only liken to the odd feeling one gets when holding magnets together of opposite polarity. Like a mechanical man I tromped erratically through the neighborhood, ... searching for the friend. It finally dawned on me that Nada didn't know any more than I did where he was.[2]

Occasionally, he heard her voice in his head. That evening, he took the board to a friend's apartment, and "Z" came through. Rapidly, the board spelled out a message—a chilling one:

AWFUL CONSEQUENCES—POSSESSION

With horror he realized that he had let Nada "in"—that he was possessed. She was in his head all of the next day. That evening, "Z" came through again:

> Each of us has a spirit while living. Do not meddle with the spirits of the dead. It can lead to awful consequences.

That message was a terrifying one—but it saved him. He suddenly realized that *he* had a spirit, too.

> Instantly I felt a strange, powerful sensation … rising up within my body. I was like a container being filled with … energy, working its way up until it filled my mind and even extended beyond the confines of my skin. Instantly … Nada … [was] pushed out.[3]

Fortunately, she was unable to return. Vaughan was master of his own body and mind once again. But as we will see later, things do not always end so happily.

Robert Swain Gifford was an American artist. Frederic L. Thompson was a goldsmith. They were not well acquainted—in fact, they met only twice. Despite that fact, they developed a very intense relationship and became full "partners"—*after Gifford's death*. Dr. James Hyslop, a professor of philosophy at Columbia University, investigated this case. It was the first research he ever did on possession, and it convinced him, beyond any possibility of doubt, that it could happen.

During the summer and fall of 1905, Thompson, who was not an artist, was seized by an irresistibly strong impulse to draw and paint pictures. This proved to be highly disruptive to his career as a goldsmith, and almost jeopardized his ability to earn a living at his trade. His will, in fact, no longer seemed to be quite his own. He soon found he could not work as a goldsmith any longer, because when he did he felt nauseated. Nor was his desire to paint anything like a normal impulse: it was accompanied by numerous, hauntingly vivid visions of trees and landscapes which he felt *compelled* to paint. These hallucinations were so frequent, and so overwhelmingly powerful, that he sought Hyslop out for help. He feared for his sanity.

When he did these paintings—which, despite his total lack of artistic training, were from the start of a thoroughly professional standard—he often "felt" that he *was* Mr. Gifford. In January of

1906 Thompson saw a notice of an exhibition of paintings by Robert Swain Gifford at a gallery, and went to see them. It was only then that he learned Gifford was dead. He had died six months before the mysterious "impulse" began. And as he stood looking at Gifford's paintings, he told Hyslop, he heard a "voice" say,

> You see what I have done. Can you not take up and finish my work?[4]

After that, the impulse and the visions grew relentlessly stronger, until he feared that he was going mad. Hyslop was, in fact, inclined to agree with him. Presumably Thompson *was* going mad. But at this point Dr. Hyslop had an intriguing idea. Much of the material published by the British Society for Psychical Research seemed to suggest that the dead could, at times, contact and even influence the living. And if Thompson's hallucinations really did emanate from the dead Gifford, then there was a very simple way to test that theory: take Thompson to a medium. If Gifford was involved, the medium would probably "pick him up."

And so they went to a medium whom Hyslop knew. They told her nothing whatever of their purpose, beyond the fact that Thompson, whose identity was not revealed, wanted a "reading." Nothing further was said. They all sat down and the reading began. Almost immediately the medium stated that a "man" was standing behind Mr. Thompson. He was, she said, "fond of painting." She described this man's appearance so precisely that Thompson was easily able to identify him as Gifford. The medium then described, in detail, a group of oak trees, a powerful vision of which had haunted Thompson for the last eighteen months. When she had finished this description the man spoke to her. He told her that this scene, which he had "impressed" on Thompson, was to be found on an island off the New England coast, and that he wanted Thompson to go there and paint it. He described the location of the island, and Thompson later went to it, found the group of trees, and painted them. On this island, which he later learned was one of Gifford's favorite places, he found several of the scenes which had appeared to him as hallucinations. Visiting the environs of Gifford's home, he found several more. He was shaken by this, but even more shaken by what he found when he visited Gifford's old studio, which Mrs. Gifford showed him. There, on easels, were three preparatory sketches for oil paintings which Gifford had done before his death. *They were identical to three "visions" which Thompson had had, and had felt compelled to draw.*

Dr. Hyslop took Thompson to several other sittings with mediums, always concealing their purpose in coming. Each time, Gifford was described as present. And always, it was said of him that he had been and still was influencing Thompson to paint. On one of these occasions Gifford spoke to Thompson through the medium, with rather remarkable results. After referring to the efforts which he had made to influence Thompson to paint, Gifford said:

> Ask him if he remembers an incident when, standing on a bridge and looking down, he saw pictures in the water like reflections and a great desire came over him to paint? I was there and followed him for some time.[5]

In fact, Thompson remembered the incident vividly. He had seen visions of landscapes in the water, and had been overwhelmed by an ecstatic desire to paint. This powerful experience led him to search the island on which it had occurred. And when he did, he discovered, and painted, many of the visions which had haunted him. Needless to say, he did so—as, strangely, he did all of his paintings—in the style of Robert Swain Gifford.

These three "possessions"—of an executive, an editor, and a goldsmith—certainly seem to indicate that the bodies of the living can sometimes be taken over by the minds of the dead. But even if, as these incidents suggest, such things *sometimes* happen, surely they can't happen very often?

In fact, there is a good deal of evidence that experiences like this are not particularly rare. This conviction began, in my case, with personal experiences. As soon as it became "known" among my friends, acquaintances, and students that I was interested in "psychic" aspects of death, people began to approach me—always very quietly and privately, always with personal anguish, to confide their possession experiences to me. These experiences were highly disruptive of their personal lives. When they were not openly terrified at what had happened to them, they were very badly frightened. Although all were desperate for help, not one had seriously considered consulting a psychiatrist, since, they explained, the "influence" affecting them was external. It did not come from their minds—its source was discarnate, but they had no hope of convincing any psychiatrist of this. They knew they would be told that they were having hallucinations, or a psychotic or schizophrenic episode, and that they should have medication and perhaps hospitalization. It was not merely that they had no confidence in such judgments; they *knew* them to be untrue. And one of them said something to me that I will never forget. He said, "The most terrifying thing for me was that you were going to tell me it was all in my head." I was his last hope for a non-psychiatric understanding of what he knew was happening to him—that he was being taken over.

Some of the experiences recounted to me involved such anguish that I found myself haunted by them. I had to learn more. I began to read. I was astounded by what I discovered—that we have had exorcists in our midst all along. Of the seven whose published works I examined, five had either M.D.s or PH.D.s and the other two were also literate, intelligent, and well-educated. I had always associated the word "exorcism" with the demonological fantasies of medieval Christian theology, fanciful tales of the casting out of assorted devils, demons, and evil spirits. This I simply could not take seriously. But not one of these men ever referred to devils or demons. They simply claimed that "possession" was caused, for a variety of reasons and in a variety of ways, *by the spirits of the human dead.*

These men found themselves approached by people who were seeking help, people who confided that, no matter how "crazy" it might sound, they were being bothered by spirits, spirits whose voices they heard in their heads, who sometimes took over their bodies, who interfered with their lives, who gave them "blackouts" during which they might do things they did not wish to do. Some of these men, because of their rather unusual intellectual backgrounds, found such claims credible; others, because of their scientific training and rationalist orientation, were skeptical. All, however, were willing to give the patient the benefit of the doubt, and proceeded with treatment *as if what the patient were saying might well be true.* The results were interesting, to say the least. When these modern exorcists used psychics, as five of them did, deceased human beings, whose existence and death could be verified, often "spoke" through the psychic. Their motives and state of mind were highly varied. Many were badly confused about what had been happening to *them.* But regardless of their state of mind, most could be reached by the exorcist, reasoned with, and persuaded to leave the victim alone. These conversations, many of which have been recorded, are very similar to those which have been held with haunting ghosts. *But the "possessing" dead, unlike the haunting dead, do not haunt a place—they haunt a person!* The results of these conversations were very similar, as well, to those which had occurred with haunting ghosts. The phenomena ceased, and the victim was free.

Do we have any idea how common such experiences are? Not really. But we can get some indication by looking at the experiences of these seven modern exorcists. Two of them dealt only with a few cases which came their way in the course of their work as scholars or therapists. Others dealt with dozens, and sometimes hundreds, of cases. One, retired Anglican cleric John Pearce-Higgins, dealt with *several hundred* cases during the 1970s. None of these men believe that the theory of possession can account for all mental illness—but they do believe, on the basis of their personal experiences, that it can account for some.

Many people regard spiritualists as foolish and credulous people—and indeed, some of them are. But as a result of their religious beliefs, they have had a lot of experience in dealing with the "possessing" dead. And because these experiences seem very similar to those of non-spiritualist, scientifically-oriented "exorcists," we should be prepared to take them seriously.

According to spiritualists, possession is caused by the "earthbound" dead. People who die and are "earthbound" do not undergo the experiences described by the resuscitated. They are not "met" by a guide and taken to the post-mortem world. They are "stuck," in various states of mind, "right here." How often does this happen? Spiritualists, who form "rescue circles" to contact and release such entities, affirm that it happens quite often. The experiences of non-spiritualist exorcists suggest the same. And so do some very vivid personal experiences, a few of which I will describe.

Joy Snell, a psychic who was able to leave her body and enter the realm of the dead at will, describes the bewildered earthbound dead as she has personally perceived them:

> They all ... appeared to be irresistibly impelled to seek something which they could not find.... They hurried hither and thither ... glancing ... about them ... as though some faint hope that they were near the object of their search had come to them, for they would then cease their ... weeping and sighing.... Though occasionally two or three of them would come together as they chanced for a brief space to pursue the same direction, ... they never engaged in conversation that I observed. Each individual seemed so absorbed in his own woes that he took no notice of anybody else.[6]

In fact, other evidence we will examine suggests that such entities fail to communicate with each other not from unwillingness *but because their state of consciousness is such that they literally cannot see each other.* If Joy Snell's account stood alone, we could dismiss it as the fantasy of a lunatic. *But it doesn't.*

In his interviews with resuscitated patients, Dr. Raymond Moody came across several similar experiences. A number of resuscitated patients told him that they had seen other human beings who seemed to be confused and "trapped" in a distressing after-death state. Their accounts agreed on a number of points. It seemed to them that these spirits were still "bound" to the physical world—to some person, object, or habit. This "bondage" appeared to cause a "dimming" or "dulling" of consciousness. A woman who was clinically dead for fifteen minutes told Dr. Moody that these entities were surrounded by a "dull" atmosphere, in contrast to the "brilliant light" which she perceived elsewhere. She said:

> Their [heads were] bent downward; they had sad, depressed looks; they seemed to shuffle, as someone would on a chain gang … they looked washed out, dull, gray. And they seemed to be forever shuffling and moving around, not knowing where they were going, not knowing who to follow, or what to look for … they didn't even raise their heads to see what was happening … just this absolute, crushed, hopeless demeanor…. They seemed to be forever moving, rather than just sitting, but in no special direction. They would start straight, then veer to the left and take a few steps and veer back to the right. Searching, but for what they were searching I don't know.
>
> **Dr. Moody:** Would you say they were in between the physical world and what you were in?
>
> After I left the physical hospital [died] … I rose upward and … it was *before* … I entered the spiritual world where there is so much … brilliant light that surrounded everything [that I saw them]. But in this particular place [where they were] there was the dullest, drab gray…. They seemed to be … looking back; they didn't know whether to go on or to return to [their] bodies…. They [seemed) to hover; they kept looking downward and never upward. They didn't want to go on to see what was awaiting them. *There seems to have been a great huge array of them around.*[7]

Other resuscitated informants told Dr. Moody that they had had this same experience, but had, in addition, seen some of these beings trying, evidently without success, to communicate with living people. One man, while "dead" for an extended period, had observed many such cases. For example:

> he saw an ordinary man walking, unaware, down the street while one of these dulled spirits hovered above him. He said he had the feeling that this spirit had been, while alive, the man's mother, and, still unable to give up her earthly role, was trying to tell her son what to do.[8]

Moody asked a resuscitated woman who had had similar experiences whether she had seen any of these "dull" spirits trying to communicate with the living. She replied:

> You could see them trying to make contact, but no one would realize that they were around; people would just ignore them.... They were trying to communicate, yet there was no way they could break through. People seemed to be completely unaware of them.[9]

All of this strongly suggests that to be "earthbound" after death, at least for a period of time, is not at all unusual. And it is from the ranks of these dead, it seems, that those who "possess" the living come.

Our earlier picture of death, derived from research on resuscitation experiences, portrayed it as an enthralling, ecstatic "trip" to a far more fascinating plane of existence than that available in the physical world. The implication was that everyone who died could look forward to this enchanting sequence of events, and that, consequently, a fear of death—for either the dying or the bereaved—was absurd. But the data on hauntings put a bit of a damper on such optimism. As that data made clear, some of the dead, at least, got "hung up" after death, and might stay that way for long periods of time—even centuries—unless helped by knowledgeable, living people who were willing to communicate with them and explain their condition. But at least they need not be feared; although they were "ghosts," they could be talked to, understood, helped. Now even this view must be altered. *As we will see, the "possessing" dead are indeed to be feared.*

Twentieth-century exorcism

The idea that there are sane and responsible people in this century who have actually removed the spirits of the dead from the bodies and minds of the living may seem incredible. To make it less so, I will describe in detail several modern exorcisms taken from the published writings of the seven exorcists I referred to earlier. Just who are these mysterious men? Four are Americans: Dr. Carl Wickland, a physician; Dr. Walter Franklin Prince, a psychologist; Dr. James H. Hyslop, a professor of philosophy at Columbia University; and California psychologist Dr. Wilson Van Dusen, now a professor at Kennedy University and former chief psychologist at Mendocino State Hospital. (Although Dr. Van Dusen performed only one exorcism, which was successful, he is included because his research on hallucinating mental patients led him to the conclusion that many of his patients' hallucinations were caused by discarnate personalities who had invaded their victims' consciousness.) One is a Brazilian psychiatrist, Dr. Inacio Ferreira. The other two are British: John Pearce-Higgins, an Anglican cleric, and Paul Beard, president of the College of Psychic Studies in London.[10]

Dr. Carl Wickland, a physician who practiced in Chicago and Los Angeles, published an account of his exorcism experiences in 1924 entitled *Thirty Years Among the Dead.*[11] It must be admitted from the start that much of Wickland's book is credulous and naive. Wickland was a dogmatic spiritualist who communicated with the dead through his wife Anna, a trance medium. Much of his work with his wife was devoted to communicating with "possessing" entities and displacing them from the bodies and minds of their victims. In other words, he was an exorcist. But when we read the detailed, stenographically-recorded conversations which he conducted with the "dead," we cannot help but be struck, in many instances, by their obvious falsity. The spirits, often speaking with an almost identical idiom and phraseology, faithfully produce the kind of dialogue that Wickland obviously wanted to hear. They are duly converted to the view that they should leave their victims alone, and gratefully depart for better things. The dramatizing capacities of trance mediums are well-known: appropriate personalities are often produced, it seems, subconsciously rather than as the result of deliberate fraud. And Wickland, in some ways a naively dogmatic spiritualist, seems to have been unaware that, on numerous occasions, this obviously happened in his wife's trance communications.

Such a criticism, which I am convinced is true, would seem to be so damaging that it would clearly prevent any confidence being placed in anything that Wickland published. But things turn out to be a little more complicated than that. For *many of Wickland's cases appear to be quite genuine.* The dialogue is convincingly individualized, and the activities and state of mind of the "spirit" involved closely parallel the findings of the other exorcists whose work I have examined.

Wickland first became interested in possession after observing the frequency with which people who regularly used ouija boards or engaged in "automatic writing"[12] underwent drastic and harmful character changes, sometimes to the point of requiring hospitalization for mental illness. Curious as to why this happened so often, Wickland consulted discarnate intelligences through the mediumship of his wife. He was told that possession of the living by the "earthbound" dead was the cause, and that he could alleviate the condition of the victims by following their instructions. He was told to construct a "Wimhurst" machine, a device which generates static electricity by means of glass discs. The charges of electricity from this machine were to be applied to the body—particularly to the spine and head—of the victim, while Mrs. Wickland was in a trance. All of this Wickland faithfully did for some thirty years, with rather striking results.

Frequently a "voice," which would turn out to belong to an identifiable deceased person, would begin to speak through the mouth and body of the entranced Mrs. Wickland, complaining initially of the intense discomfort caused it by the static electricity. Characteristically, the "voice" would be unaware that it was "dead," and would sometimes complain bitterly of continually being "bothered" by the victim, who was "always around." Wickland usually had a good deal of difficulty in convincing the deceased that they were in fact dead, as they seemed to themselves to be clearly existing, solid, and visible. The discomfort of life in the possessing state, however, is often such that the spirit can easily be persuaded to vacate, once convinced of its true condition. In reading the stenographic records of these conversations, we find the doctor undergoing a very curious experience—talking directly to a possessing ghost.

A ghost called Carrie Huntington

The victim in this case, a Mrs. Burton, was relieved of her unwelcome visitor through charges of static electricity, whereupon the "ghost" unwittingly gravitated to, and spoke through, the body of Anna Wickland. If death can be said to have a "lighter" side, then it certainly appears here, in this rather comical conversation. Because such ghosts often required physical restraint, Wickland usually took the precaution of holding his entranced wife's hands during the "interview," a situation which often caused some amusing misunderstandings. The ghost, Carrie, is completely unaware that she is occupying someone else's body:

Doctor: Tell us who you are.
Spirit: I do not wish you to hold my hands.
Doctor: You must sit still.
Spirit: Why do you treat me like this?
Doctor: Who are you?
Spirit: Why do you want to know?
Doctor: You have come here as a stranger, and we would like to know who you are.

Spirit: What are you so interested for?

Doctor: We should like to know with whom we are associating. If a stranger came to your home, would you not like to know his name?

Spirit: I do not want to be here and I do not know any of you … when I … sat down on the chair you grabbed my hands.… It has been a terrible time for me for quite a while. I have been tormented to death. I have been driven here, there and everywhere. I am getting so provoked about it that I feel like giving everything a good shaking.

Doctor: What have they done to you?

Spirit: It seems so terrible … I do not know what it is … it seems as if my senses were being knocked out of me. Something comes on me like thunder and lightning (Static treatment of the patient.) It makes such a noise … it is awful! I cannot stand it … and I will not…! I have had so much hardship.

Doctor: How long have you been dead?

Spirit: Why do you speak that way? I am not dead.

Doctor: Can't you realize what has been the matter with you? Understand your condition … that you have no physical body. You died....

Spirit: Could you talk to a ghost?

Doctor: Such things certainly do happen.

Spirit: I am not a ghost, because ghosts cannot talk. When you are dead, you lie there.

Doctor: When the body dies, it lies there. But the spirit does not.… When you leave here you will understand that you have been talking through another person's body. That person is my wife.

Spirit: What nonsense! I thought you looked wiser than to talk such nonsense....

Doctor: Do you want to go to the spirit world?

Spirit: What foolish questions you put to me.

Doctor: You have lost your body.

Spirit: I have not lost my body....

Doctor: Listen to what is told you ... you are ignorant of your condition. You lost your body, evidently without knowing it.
Spirit: How do you know?
Doctor: You are now controlling my wife's body.
Spirit: I never saw you before, so how in the wide world can you think I should be called your wife? No, never!
Doctor: I do not want you to be.
Spirit: I don't want you either!
Doctor: Now, Carrie, be sensible.
Spirit: I am sensible, and don't you tell me differently.
Doctor: Now Carrie!
Spirit: I am Mrs. Carrie Huntington!
Mrs. Burton: You listen to what the doctor has to say to you.
Spirit: I will not listen to anyone. ...
Doctor: Do you know you are talking through my wife's body?
Spirit: Such nonsense. I think that's the craziest thing I ever heard in my life.[13]

In many respects this is typical of the exorcism "dialogues" conducted by Wickland. It is obvious that the possession was unintentional rather than deliberate: Carrie had been pulled into the personal "aura" of Mrs. Burton, and was more or less imprisoned there, a fact which she bitterly resented and did not understand. She was unable to comprehend that she was dead, and speaking through Anna Wickland's body. Ironically, Carrie thought that it was *her* body that was being interfered with by Mrs. Burton. For her part, Mrs. Burton was continually tormented by Carrie's presence and efforts to influence her.

In a number of Wickland's cases, the spirits' intermittent efforts to control the body of the victim, in the confused belief that it was theirs, resulted in the victim being considered mentally unstable. One of his patients, a Mrs. L.W., became subject to "fits" in which she tore off her clothes, pulled out her hair, bit her hands and arms, and beat her face with a slipper. She was, understandably, declared insane and placed in a mental institution where she remained for a year without showing any sign of improvement. She proved a troublesome patient, escaping three times, and the institution's administrators were willing to let the Wicklands take charge of her. Dr. Wickland's exorcism succeeded where conventional treatment had failed, and Mrs. L.W. recovered her sanity. Interviews with the confused possessing spirit, a man named John Sullivan, revealed that he strongly objected to finding himself wearing a woman's clothing and hairstyle, a situation which provoked him to direct and violent action: he would tear the hair out and the clothing off. He had stabbed himself to death in a jealous rage over a woman whom he felt had been unfaithful to him. This emotional trauma had left him with a vengeful hatred of women, and, finding it intolerable that a woman (the victim) should "cling" to him constantly, he would attack her fiercely (or rather, cause her body to attack itself).

The spirit at first struggled furiously, and had to be restrained.

Spirit: What in the world are you holding me for? I'll make it pretty hot for you before I get through.
Doctor: You came to us as a stranger and at once started fighting. What else could I do but hold you in restraint? … Tell us who you are, friend. You seem to be a pretty strong girl.
Spirit: If you take me for a girl you had better look again! …
Doctor: How did you happen to come here?
Spirit: I don't know. …
Doctor: Where do you think you are now?
Spirit: Where? I don't care where I am.
Doctor: Where have you been living?
Spirit: … different places … from one place to another, until I am … disgusted with everything. I feel like running away so nobody can find me.… I got one woman down and I bit and kicked, and still she clung to me. (The patient, Mrs. L.W.) She has no business to hang around me like she does. Some day I shall kill her.… I took a chunk out of her wrist one day, but she clung to me just the same … I couldn't get rid of her.… she has

no business to hang on to me like she does.... She has no business to dress me up in woman's clothes and put woman's hair on my head.

Doctor: How long have you been dead?

Spirit: Dead! I'll show you that I'm not dead. Talk about me being dead! (Laughing harshly.)

Doctor: You are an ... earthbound spirit, hovering around the earth ... bothering a woman. You are now using my wife's body.

Spirit: I'm not using anybody's body but my own. Why did that woman hang on to me?

Doctor: You were doing the "hanging on." Since you have been taken away from her, the woman is getting along nicely. You have tormented this woman for three or four years. Try to understand. You have probably been dead many years. What city did you live in?

Spirit: St. Louis.

Doctor: Do you know you are in California?

Spirit: I know where I am. I am in St. Louis.

Doctor: What year do you think it is?

Spirit: 1910.

Doctor: It is the 13th of January, 1918.... You are a spirit now. Look around and tell us what you see,—be honest now.

Spirit: I see my mother, but I'm afraid of her.

Doctor: We are not afraid of you.

Spirit: Well, my mother's a ghost.

Doctor: Does she appear ghostly?

Spirit: No, but I am afraid. Why, here's my father, too![14]

Possessing ghosts, like haunting ghosts, are typically completely unaware of the passage of time since their deaths, as is clear in the above case. The "consciousness-raising" aspect of exorcism is also clear: from being unable to see anything but the physical world, this entity, John Sullivan, was finally able to see discarnates with whom he had emotional ties. In deathbed visions, the dying are met before death. In resuscitations, they are met after death. And in the cases of haunting and possessing ghosts, the exorcism can "clarify" the situation for the deceased, raising their "awareness" so that they, too, are "met"—at long last.

Being convinced of the validity of his procedures, Wickland often did not bother to verify the identities of the possessing spirits with whom he communicated; he *knew* that they were dead human beings, and if the world didn't believe him, so be it. But in a number of cases, actual identifications were obtained, as in the following instance, where again the possessing spirit is entirely unaware that he is dead:

> Several years ago, a friend of ours complained of the peculiar and erratic actions of a business associate, Mr. P., who had suddenly become extremely irritable and despotic to those in his employ, highly unreasonable, impossible to please, and subject to violent attacks of swearing.
>
> As obsession [possession] seemed indicated we concentrated for the gentleman in question, and after several weeks an irate spirit spoke through Mrs. Wickland and frankly admitted having tormented this man, wanting revenge for attentions which he claimed the latter had been paying to his wife. (The situation had existed during his life but he did not discover this until after his death.)
>
> The spirit gave [as his] name [that] of a man prominent in local business circles; he had [died] some time before but was not aware of the fact. He said that he had been sick for a long time, but could now go where he pleased without any trouble, for he had become well.
>
> He could not understand why his wife would no longer speak to him, or why his child, who had always been so affectionate, was now so cold toward him [as he was now invisible to them, they were completely unaware of his presence].
>
> He declared that some of his friends were false to him, and had for some time been paying attention to his wife, sending her gifts and flowers, [in connection with his funeral, and to ease her

> bereavement] but that he would have revenge on them as soon as he was through with his present victim.
>
> [He] said that he could not think very clearly, but supposed that was because he had recently taken an anaesthetic, which he thought also accounted for the peculiar lightness of his body, and a feeling of having no weight.
>
> He was puzzled by the fact that whenever he thought about any persons he immediately found himself with them and involved in their affairs ["thought travel," similar to that which occurs in out-of-the-body experiences]. Recently he had been around Mr. P., but could not get away from him [having been "drawn into" his aura, which can, it appears, act like a kind of "magnet"]. This had exasperated him exceedingly, he had "done a lot of swearing," kept the man awake, made him go to work "early," and had annoyed him in every way possible.
>
> After many explanations [he] finally realized that he had "died," although this was at first difficult for him to comprehend, for he "had always thought death ended all, and that was all there was to it."
>
> Being assured that activity and progression awaited him in the spirit world, and that matters would there be explained to him to his entire satisfaction, he left.
>
> The following day there was such a remarkable improvement in the conduct of Mr. P. [who, understandably, did not realize what had been happening], and his behavior was so wholly normal that the entire office force noticed the change, although Mr. P. himself never knew of the experimental effort which had been made in his behalf.[15]

Although an identification was made in the above case, it was veiled to protect the anonymity of the parties involved. In the following case of an "earthbound"—though not possessing—entity, it was entirely explicit. The case occurred in Chicago on November 15, 1906, early in Wickland's career as an exorcist:

> During one of our psychic circles, Mrs. Wickland, entranced by a strange entity, fell prostrate to the floor, and remained in a comatose condition for some time. The spirit was at last brought [to consciousness], and acted as though in great pain, repeatedly saying: "Why didn't I take more carbolic acid? I want to die; I'm so tired of living." In a weak voice the spirit complained of the dense darkness all about, and was unable to see an electric light shining directly into her face. She whispered faintly: "My poor son!" and when pressed for information said that her name was Mary Rose, and that she lived at 202 South Green Street, a street entirely unknown to us at that time.
>
> At first she could not remember any date, but when asked: "Is it November 15th, 1906?" she replied: "No, that is next week." Life had been a bitter disappointment to her; she had suffered constantly from chronic abdominal ailments, and finally, resolving to end her miserable existence, she had taken poison. She could not at first realize that she had succeeded in destroying her physical body, for, like most suicides, she was in total ignorance of the indestructibility of life.

Eventually, they convinced her that although she was dead, she still existed. This knowledge dispelled the "darkness" in which she had been immersed, and she dimly saw the figure of her dead grandmother, who had come to meet her.

The Wicklands made inquiries at the address she had given them, and discovered that a woman of that name had lived there, that her son lived there still, and that she had been taken to the Cook County Hospital where she had died the previous week. Upon investigation at the hospital they found further verification of these facts and were given a copy of the record of the case:

> Cook County Hospital, Chicago Illinois.
> Mary Rose.
> Admitted November 7th, 1906.

Died November 8th, 1906.
Carbolic Acid poisoning.
No. 341106.[16]

Cases such as these offer further support for the claim that the number of "earthbound" and "possessing" dead is probably substantial; the case of "Mr. P." also suggests that many victims of possession may be wholly unaware of the influence to which they are subject. In fact, in some instances clairvoyants have seen and described possessing entities who were actually recognized by their victims, victims who had been entirely unaware of both their presence and their influence. The following account by a child psychic is a perfect example:

> A rum-looking party called Miss Salt—what a funny name—is staying here. She has short hair like what papa calls a rat's back, and talks in a manny voice and has an old gentleman inside her (i.e., inside her aura). I thought this rather funny, so while we were sitting in the drawing room before tea with Cousin Agnes, I said "Why have you got an old gentleman sticking to you?" Then she jumped, and said, "God bless my soul! What *does* the boy mean?" And Cousin Agnes went all red as if I'd said something rude, and sort of laughed. And so I thought I'd better tell Miss Salt that the old gentleman had funny clothes a bit like in those pictures of Mr. Pickwick, but he wasn't near so jolly looking and had a nasty red mark on his cheek. "Good Gracious!" she cried, "Why that was Mr. _____ and she said a name I can't remember.
>
> While I was watching William, the nice gardener, who says everything is rum, Miss Salt came by, and said she was just going to take a little walk to the sea, and would I like to come with her. So I had to say yes, so as not to be rude. When we got to the seashore we sat down on the ... sand, and she said, "Tell me, how did you know about the old gentleman?" So I said I could see his face in her lights. Then she asked me, what did I mean by her lights, which surprised me very much, because the old lady is not

> blind, and doesn't wear spectacles. So I said, "Why, the colours round people, of course."[17]

It is clear that the boy was not yet aware that most people cannot see auras.

Dr. Walter Franklin Prince and the case of Mrs. Latimer

As an exorcist, Prince operated on an infinitely more modest scale than Wickland, conducting, so far as I have been able to determine, only four exorcisms. Although two were apparently unsuccessful, the two in which he succeeded provide striking evidence of *deliberate, malevolent possession.* Here is one of them:

In May of 1922, Prince, a psychologist, was consulted by a Mrs. Latimer, who pleaded with him to help her. She said she felt certain that she was possessed by the spirit of a dead man.

> A male cousin, Marvin, who had died two years previously, had known her well. A day or two after his death she began to hear a voice that sounded like his and insisted it was his. The voice spoke to her hatefully, explaining that it wanted to make her suffer and that it had reasons for this. At first the voice sounded completely "outside," as if an invisible person were in the room, but soon it became an "inner" voice, though no less realistic or distressing. It continued to plague her for two years and made her life nearly unbearable. She was often told, "You made me suffer and I will make you suffer." She could not understand the reason for this and asked for an explanation, which finally came. The voice sought to revenge a certain occasion when, without her knowledge, Marvin had seen her writing a letter. The letter contained a remark about him that had hurt his feelings profoundly ... just before his death. She recalled ... the letter....
>
> The voice scolded her for not having sent flowers to his funeral. She had sent roses for the coffin and thought that they had been arranged upon it, but on checking she discovered that

> they had not been placed visibly. Her nights were almost never peaceful. Scarcely a day passed without these persecutions. Prince diagnosed her condition as a serious case of paranoia or persecution mania. He had been able to help patients with various forms of psychic troubles through psychotherapy, but "in no instance where there was what is known as the delusion of persecution accompanied by auditory hallucinations was instruction, persuasion, analysis, or suggestion of any avail whatever." He determined to attempt a completely different treatment. He explained that he was not convinced that there was such a thing as a possessing spirit, but, on the other hand, facts suggested that it might really exist.

He therefore agreed to try an experiment, based upon her belief that she really was possessed. With Mrs. Latimer present, Prince spoke, in a friendly but serious manner, directly to the claimed "spirit." He asked that the entity release his cousin from the torment she was suffering and forgive her, after which it would be free to move on to a higher realm.

> Review the whole matter with the desire to do this woman justice. Try to look at it from her viewpoint. Consider her sufferings.... And see how efforts to help her, to be good to her, affect you. You may begin to experience glimpses of a happiness you have not known since you left this earth. If so, you will surely go on, and the time will come when your life will become so transformed that you will be very thankful for the suggestions I make today.[18]

And what were the results of this attempt at "consciousness-raising"? Complete and instantaneous—from that moment forward the phenomena ceased, never to return.

The ouija board and the case of Gustav Adolf Biedermann

Some spiritualists conduct what are known as "home circles," where they meet on a regular basis in order to communicate with the dead. Mediumship, automatic writing, and ouija boards are employed and a good deal of this communication involves "rescue work," in which "earthbound" dead are contacted, instructed, and freed. Some of these cases involve possession either merely attempted or successful—by the earthbound. In this particular case, the entity attempting possession was identified in detail and the apparent reason for his "earthbound" state was revealed in a fascinating conversation conducted through a home-made ouija board made of a piece of board round which the letters of the alphabet had been burned with a poker. Those present lightly placed their fingers on an upturned glass which "moved" from letter to letter, spelling out a message. Two members of the circle, Miss E. and Mrs. D., realized that they were being "bothered" by an unidentified discarnate who seemed to take particular pleasure in "taking over" their ouija board whenever they attempted to use it. Because this was a nuisance, and more significantly because such phenomena are frequently a prelude to "possession" attempts, they asked for help from the rest of the circle, and a sitting was arranged. The board was operated by Mrs. W.G. and Mrs. G.J. The "victims," Miss E. and Mrs. D., were present, as was R.W. A regular communicator through the board, an entity calling himself "Peter," came through first. His comments refer to the "interfering" entity. He advises them to "talk to him."

Question: Is it a man, then?
Answer: Yes. Humor him. Get to know him. We can then deal with him from here.... I am leaving now. No worry. No harm [meaning the troublesome entity is not regarded as dangerous].
Question: [Addressing the unknown entity] You know you are on the spirit plane?
Answer: Yes. I am.
Question: What is your ... name, do you remember?
Answer: Yes. I will not say.
Question: We want to help you.
Answer: I do not want your help. I was happy with the ladies

["the victims," Miss E. and Mrs. D.] and I am not going to be bloody well pally with you. Mind your own business. I did not come to talk to you.

Question: You must take your business elsewhere and not worry these dear people.... Can you see anyone standing near you? ["Peter" had stated initially that Stanley, R.W.'s deceased brother, would remain with them to help deal with the communicator.]

Answer: Yes. Man.

Question: Well, that is my brother and he is a good chap. He will help you.... There are people who will help you.

Answer: Only Hitler can help. He is the master mind.

Question: What is your ... name?

Answer: What has that to do with you? Shut up blast you. I am going.... You make me sad....

Question: I'd rather make you pleased.

Answer: Keep quiet.

Question: I want you to stop worrying our friends here.

Answer: Sorry.

Question: That's better. That's the reply of an intelligent man, which I am sure you are.

Answer: I go now.

Question: Go with the thought of friendship with us. What is your nationality?

Answer: German ... I am German and my name is Gustav.... I am Gustav Adolf Biedemburg....

Question: What made you come to us? Why not a German circle?

Answer: I lived in London.... You welcome me.... My house was Charnwood Lodge. ...

Question: Ask ... Peter to help you.

Answer: I am going now with a kind friend who will listen and talk.

Three days later, they held another sitting. ["Peter" begins.]

Question: Now about Gustav. Wait ... ["Gustav" takes control of the glass]:

Answer: I offer my humble apologies and add to them my grateful thanks.

Question: We are glad to have been of help. Come when you like, you will find friends here, and Mrs. D. and Miss E. will welcome you too.

Answer: I want to help. I am not lonely now. I will tell you my correct name. Adolf Biedebmann [a misspelling: "Biedermann" was the correct name]. I always was known and called Gustav.

Question: Shall we call you Gustav?

Answer: Please. I was a rationalist.

Question: What exactly is that?

Answer: A type of religion to follow only the reasoning of one's own mind. It puts a barrier around.

Question: That is why you have been so lonely and found no companions?

Answer: Yes. Partly.

Question: Is there anything more we can do to help you?

Answer: Peter will help me. Your Stan showed me how to reach him. I am so grateful. I was turned seventy when I passed away.

Question: We had an idea you were much younger than that.... I think it was because of your reference to Hitler. [The sittings were held in January of 1943.]

Answer: I did that to hurt. I am sorry. I am forgiven and we are friends, yes?

Question: Of course.

Answer: Thank you. Goodnight.

["Peter" writes:] Not so ferocious. He is very good at heart. A new friend for Peter.

This communicator made his last appearance on February 4th, 1943.

Answer: I hope you will welcome me as friend. Gustav.

Question: Yes, of course, Gus. How are you?

> **Answer:** I am happy and that means more than I can express ...
> **Question:** What are you doing?
> **Answer:** I am working on myself. I ... remember my earth life.... I am happy.... I am forgiven for my lapse?
> **Question:** Yes, of course. ...
> **Answer:** Thank you all. Goodnight.[19]

The members of this "circle" made no effort to verify the identity of this communicator. They took him at his word, and were happy to have helped him. But in 1964, British S.P.R. researcher Alan Gauld decided to see whether or not such a person had ever really existed. He had. Biedermann had been a psychologist, and virtually everything he said about himself was verified as correct. A man who had known him described his personality as "blunt, arrogant, obstinate, and aggressive," which certainly comes through clearly in his communications.

In fact, this entire, rather moving dialogue is a classic example of the "consciousness-raising" process so frequently encountered in exorcisms, and one of Biedermann's statements provides support for a theory widely held by spiritualists; namely, that your personal attitude toward death can have a great effect on what actually happens to you after death. Biedermann states that he was a "rationalist" during his life, and thus a person who would regard as utter nonsense the idea that conscious existence continues after death. This belief apparently created an after-death "barrier" which prevented him from leaving the physical world. Many similar communications have been received. Dr. Karl Novotny's post-mortem account of his own death, given through a medium, provides another example. He had gone for a walk feeling very tired, and was rather startled when, suddenly, he felt completely "energized" and in the best of health:

> I turned back to my companions and found myself looking down at my own body on the ground. My friends were in despair, calling for a doctor and trying to get a car to take me home. But I was well and felt no pains! I couldn't understand

> what had happened. I bent down and felt the heart of the body lying on the ground. Yes, it had ceased to beat—I was dead. But I was still alive! I spoke to my friends, but they neither saw nor answered me. I was most annoyed and left them. When my body had been put into the coffin, I realised that I must be dead. But *I wouldn't acknowledge the fact; for, like my teacher, Alfred Adler, I did not believe in an afterlife.*[20]

He adds that once he was able to accept the fact that, although physically dead, he continued to exist, his consciousness was "raised" and he was able to see his dead mother who had come to "meet" him.

Dangers of the ouija

In looking at published accounts of possession cases, I have been struck again and again by how often such cases result from experimentation with ouija boards and automatic writing. The act of deliberately "opening" yourself to communication with the dead, in innocence and without due regard for the danger involved, seems to attract many of the sort of dead you would never want to meet. For dying apparently does not change your basic character. If you are a vicious, cruel person, consumed with hatred during life, so you will be in death. Spiritualists and others with much experience of communication with the dead have long maintained that those most likely to be earthbound are those who are filled with negative emotions and hatred, which prevent the "consciousness" of the dead from perceiving anything but the physical realm after death. In addition, having to operate on the earth plane without a physical body can be intensely frustrating. Physical desires, it seems, still exist; *what is lacking is a physical body in which they may be gratified.* And from this arises an intense need to "possess" the body of someone open to them.

I received my first personal lesson on this aspect of possession through a young man I met named David, and his psychic friend,

Sally. After a lecture I gave at a Canadian university in which I briefly mentioned possession, he approached me and described, with considerable anguish, how a dead young woman had for a number of years been able at times to take over his body. The result would be a homosexual "binge," for bizarre though it sounds, *she* was heterosexual and apparently frustratedly so.

She was able to use his body to induce him to have sex with males, which she found gratifying and he, later, devastating. His psychic friend, Sally, was very worried about him, but didn't know how to help. She told me that she could often "see" the figure of this woman "inside" or "on" his body, and sometimes separated from it. I suggested that the next time Sally "saw" this woman, she should explain to her that she would be a great deal happier if she would raise her consciousness and get away from the physical level, where she wasn't properly equipped to operate; if she would just go to the next level, she would find all sorts of gratifying possibilities available to her. Two days later, I got a call from Sally. She had seen, and talked with, David's possessing spirit. I will never forget what she said. "I just couldn't convince her that there is any more to life after death than what she is experiencing right here. I told her there was, I told her [as I had suggested] to call upon someone she loved, who was dead, for help, but she just wouldn't believe me. She wants a life, and she said she can only have it through David's body."

But why, I asked, only through his body? If she wanted to possess someone in order to gratify her sexual desires, why not a woman rather than a man, since her desires were heterosexual? Sally had apparently asked her this. The reply was that she and David were "attuned" in some mysterious way which she did not make clear, and it was therefore relatively easy for her to take over his body, but would be difficult or impossible with other people—so she "made do" with him.

Ouija-induced possession cases are, in my experience, highly similar to one another. At best, the entity is mischievous; at worst, diabolically malevolent. The motives of the possessing spirits often appear to be basically sadistic. They make elaborate efforts to get the sitter at the ouija board "hooked," and once this has happened, they may offer a great deal of highly destructive advice: the sitter should, for example, sell his house at once and go to Australia, where he will meet a great spiritual teacher who will guide him to the higher realms of knowledge. If the sitter is foolish enough to take such advice, as some are, it will turn out to be completely false. Or he may be advised that he will murder his wife in three weeks, or that his child will meet with a fatal accident, and so on. Invariably, such statements will turn out to be completely untrue. But if he has put his trust entirely in the entity—and elaborate efforts may be made to get him to do so—such messages can be devastating.

How does the receiving of such messages amount to possession? The victim often experiences irresistible urges to use the board or write automatically, at all hours of the day and night. Sometimes this is in response to a kind of inner "pressure," but often it is in response to a persistent voice, which may be heard externally in space, or, more often, inside the victim's head. Some such cases are dangerous enough to involve a direct threat to the life of the victim: the entity may urge the victim to "kill yourself so that you can join me." Some, tragically, have actually done so. One example of lethally dangerous possession involved the medium Geraldine Cummins. Raymond Bayless describes what happened:

> A young woman was introduced into a circle which made use of the ouija board. Miss Cummins sat with the newcomer, and within a few moments [her] "guide,"[21] Astor, wrote that extremely malignant spirits were occasionally in possession of the sitter and would prove to be a danger to Miss Cummins if she continued the sitting with her. The young lady and her husband did not see the strange message and, luckily, Miss Cummins refused to continue.
>
> It was subsequently revealed that the woman frequently was prey to insane attacks of rage during which she manifested an abnormal, evil desire to see blood and would attempt to stab anyone who was close to her.[22]

In the spring of 1972, Robert Ashby, then Research Officer at the College of Psychic Studies in London and now a director of the Spiritual Frontiers Fellowship, received a desperate telephone call from a lady in tears.

> Her story was that she had a friend who had been toying with a ouija board for some years and had, in her opinion, contacted various deceased relatives, friends, and eventually an "ascendant master" who revealed "higher truths." As a Christmas present, the friend gave this lady's seventeen-year-old daughter, Linda, a ouija board and urged her to try her luck. Linda and a high-school friend, Wendy, began sitting with the board the week after Christmas and within a few days, the pointer began to move and spell out some coherent messages amid the usual gibberish. To their question, "What is the name of the communicating entity?" the board spelled out "Joe." Intrigued by this, the girls began a daily practice of going to Linda's room as soon as they arrived home from school and spending two or three hours "communicating" with "Joe."
>
> As is typical in such instances, Joe proved to know correctly details of a family nature about the two girls, much to their amazement; from this, Joe became witty and the girls thought him really clever; from his innocuous witticisms, Joe moved on to slightly off-color suggestions which tickled Linda and Wendy further. His next stage was frankly sexual propositions that soon had the girls disturbed; but when they asked that he stop this, the messages became threatening, the warnings including something Joe termed "psychic rape" if they did not comply with his wishes. At this point, Wendy was so frightened that she stopped sitting at the board. Linda, however, was so "hooked" that she felt it more dangerous to stop than to continue, for Joe ordered her fiercely to keep on with the ritual. Eventually, ... Joe told Linda that she must drop out of school and stay home all day to communicate with him, for they were, he assured her, "soul-mates" from former lives. The punishment if she did not do his

> bidding was serious physical disfigurement or even death at his hands.[23]

At this point Linda had the courage to throw out the ouija board, but was unwilling to go to school or to seek any kind of therapeutic help, because Joe had warned her against doing either. The mother asked if Ashby could help. He was willing to try, but never got the chance. Linda refused to see him. Joe had whispered to her that he would kill her if she did. The sequence of events depicted in this case is quite typical.

Paul Beard, President of the College of Psychic Studies in London, England, has studied many such cases. They led him to certain chilling conclusions. First of all—as is clearly suggested by the experiences already described in this chapter—there are two basic varieties of possession: intentional and accidental. Most of Wickland's cases were accidental; the possessing entity had unintentionally become entangled with the aura of a living person and was trapped there, not knowing how to help himself. Most of the "ouija" and "automatic writing" cases, on the other hand, are deliberate, and the motives of the possessor, when not mischievous, are malevolent. According to Beard, the astral body generates a protective energy-emanation known to occultists as the "aura." Habitual use of a ouija board or automatic writing can bring about prolonged contact with a malevolent dead person, which can enable the dead entity to produce a "split" in the victim's aura. Once this has happened, the entity can make contact with the victim at any time by "talking," in a "voice" or through "thoughts," within the victim's head. The complete domination of the victim will then be sought, with practically continuous evil suggestions, which may even involve visual hallucinations. (An acquaintance of mine, for example, was for a time the victim of such an entity. He would show her vivid hallucinatory "movies" of herself torturing and murdering her baby. I asked her what the entity's purpose in doing this was. Her reply was that "he wants me to do what he shows me in the film.") The motives are apparently sadistic, and the victims of such assaults may be driven to suicide or mental breakdown. Such entities will typically show a truly diabolical ingenuity in maintaining contact and manipulating the victim. Beard writes:

> The first line of defense is … not … to [engage in automatic writing or use a ouija board] more than one hour a week. If the influence suggests [that the victim] write more [frequently], this should be considered … the strongest possible warning signal....
>
> In order to persuade the victim to continue writing, the influence will … [give him] facts … about … relatives, which are true, or alternatively … about things in ordinary life which the host is invited to check.… Warnings are likely to be given about the health of relatives in distant places. Frequently the host is told to go on journeys, which later prove to be useless.… It may suggest actions which violate health precautions, such as going without food, or undertaking night-long vigils; this is an attempt to bring about … physical and nervous exhaustion.
>
> The obsessor will not stop until it has obtained a complete and very unhealthy domination over the victim's whole being, even when it falsely represents that its intervention is benevolent and helpful. ...
>
> What the victim should do, in practical terms, is very simple: it is to deny any and all access to the influence, to "starve it out." … All attempts … to induce more writing must absolutely be forbidden, even though the most … urgent reasons be suggested.[24]

"Starving" the possessor out is best done, according to Beard, by focusing attention on the many diversions of everyday life: movies, television, visiting with friends, and so on. As a last resort, the possessor may plead that he himself needs help, but such entreaties should be ignored absolutely, as this is a calculated maneuver to maintain the relationship. Beard ends his advice with the following statement: "When in particular trouble the victim may mentally visualize being completely encircled in a cocoon of light."[25] I was particularly struck by this statement, because it reminded me of an extraordinary incident experienced by the psychiatrist Stanislav Grof.[26]

While engaged in research and therapy at the Maryland Psychiatric Research Center in Catonsville, Grof met a young patient with a number of psychiatric problems. She had failed to respond to more conventional therapies, and her doctors, as a last resort, had sent her for LSD treatment. During her first psychedelic session with Grof and other members of the staff, a truly startling event occurred. She underwent the classic symptoms of "possession." According to Grof, her facial features suddenly changed to those of an evil-looking male and her voice became deeply masculine. This "entity" spoke to the astounded therapists in an angry and threatening voice, stating that the young woman was "his," and clearly implying that her personal and psychiatric difficulties were attributable to his malevolent influence. In a terrifying display of paranormal facility, he revealed damaging and embarrassing incidents from the personal lives of the therapeutic staff present, including a number of things which they had never revealed to one another. He pointed out to them, quite accurately, that the status of LSD research was already in grave jeopardy, and threatened to destroy their entire research operation by revealing these incidents to the media in the most damaging way possible, unless they gave the patient up to him and ceased therapy. This harangue went on for some time. Attempting to reason with the "entity" proved fruitless. Finally, in desperation, Grof said that he remembered the occult tradition that such evil entities don't like "light," so he closed his eyes and meditated, visualizing himself, the patient, and the entire group surrounded by "white light." Instantly, the phenomena ceased; the face and voice vanished. Subsequently, the girl began to respond to therapy.

Among those who believe in life after death, but who have had little personal experience in "contacting" the dead, there exists a widespread assumption that since death turns the dead into "spirits," it also makes them "spiritual"—benevolent, wise, all-knowing. The cases I have cited in this chapter show that this assumption, as a generalization about the dead, could scarcely be less correct. The "borderland" between the worlds of the living and the dead appears to be a kind of psychic "jungle" or "territory," thronged with vicious, psychopathic personalities. If they can find and "attune" themselves to a victim, their destructive natures can operate with even less restraint than they did while embodied.

Possession can happen

I have used the recent personal experiences of many different people to demonstrate that possession is *not* a mere fantasy from the superstitious past. It can and does occur today, just as it always has. And it is my opinion that the legacy of such experiences, accumulating over the centuries, can go a long way toward explaining the extremely widespread human fear of the dead. As the experiences in this chapter show, we have every reason for fearing *some* of the dead.

Can we make any useful generalizations about the basic dynamics of possession? An examination of a large number of published cases suggests that we can.

Who causes possession?

Possession is caused, not by demons, not by devils, not by "evil spirits," but by the human dead.

In what "condition" are the possessing dead?

Here we have to distinguish between deliberate and inadvertent possession. Inadvertent or accidental possession usually seems to involve actual ignorance of one's own death, and can be accompanied by varied states of consciousness. Such possessing entities can be in an unconscious stupor, which may intermittently be inflicted on the victim. Or, they may be conscious, with either no, or minimal, sensory input. Some such complain of existing in "dense darkness" or in a "mist." Still others have a full, normal sensory awareness of the physical world with which they are completely familiar. Those who exist in mist or darkness frequently state that they have been drawn to a "light." This "light" seems most commonly to be the "aura" of a psychically sensitive person, but it can also be the aura of someone not known to be psychic. As the light seems to offer a refuge from darkness and permits visual perception, it may be "entered," an act which can apparently trap the confused entity within the aura. The possessing entity is now in a position to influence the embodied person, who may or may not be aware of this influence. As the "trapped" entity must now "go about" with the embodied person, intense anger and frustration may be directed at this person, who is seen as "imprisoning" the dead individual. The entrapment may proceed from the aura to actual blending with the body of the living person. The possessing entity may then regard the body as its own. In other cases, the "presence" is aware that there is another unwelcome tenant—the original owner—which it may try to drive out. All of this can be intensely distressing to the embodied person.

Deliberate possession, on the other hand, seems usually to be perpetrated by dead human beings who *know* that they are dead. This knowledge, however, does not prevent them from being "stuck" at the level of the physical world. All that they can perceive is what we perceive from the vantage point of our own bodies, although some can also see other entities in the same condition as themselves. Existence in this state proves highly frustrating, as it is normally impossible for them to manipulate the physical world in any way. As this state of impotence frequently seems to be accompanied by normal physical desires for sex, food, and so on, it leads, logically enough, to determined efforts to obtain control of a body in order to fulfill their needs. In the most malevolent cases, there is a sadistic desire to torture, dominate, and drive to insanity or suicide the originally embodied personality, using, if necessary, a diabolical capacity for deception.

But why do some of the dead end up like this?

Here we are on much less certain ground, although interested investigators have offered some generalizations. It is claimed that any intense personality trait or desire can "hold" you in one of the states described above:

- obsessive hatred for persons or specific situations;
- love for any person, object, way of life;
- earthly desires: for food, sex, liquor, drugs, power, money, clothing, life-styles, revenge, the physical or mental torturing of others, and so on;
- any negative general personality trait such as greed, lust, selfishness, religious fanaticism, exaggerated self-absorption, and so on;
- ignorance of the fact of life after death, or fixed but incorrect ideas about its nature.

It is also claimed that the victims of possession may in a sense bring it on themselves by having personal characteristics similar to those "holding" the dead; this "attracts" compatible deceased persons and makes it easier for possession to occur.

A good many cases can be cited in support of each of these generalizations. But we cannot say they are the only causes, because such qualities would, in various combinations, apply to virtually all dead and all living persons. And because other evidence proves that all of the dead are not possessors, and all of the living not possessed, we must simply confess our ignorance of the real causes of possession. Possibly it is a question of the degree, intensity, or nature of the commitment to these characteristics for both the living and the dead victims of possession which causes it to occur.

What do I do if it happens to me?

If you have reason to believe that you are being subjected, in a damaging way, to the influence of someone dead, there are several courses of action open to you. Some priests and clergymen are willing to perform exorcisms, and these procedures can be effective. Some spiritualist and psychic groups attempt to aid the victim as well as rescue the dead perpetrator, sometimes successfully. I know of instances in which prayer groups have been able to bring the phenomena to an end. I have found the College of Psychic Studies, with offices at 16 Queensberry Place in London, England, to be a knowledgeable source of advice and help. And finally, it must be said that not everyone who thinks he is possessed actually is. Possession can be a real state, externally caused by someone dead, or it can be a purely subjective delusion, a form of mental illness which has nothing to do with the dead and is generated solely by the mind of the victim. Psychiatrists can be effective in dealing with both kinds of cases. They can give medication such as tranquilizers to calm the patient and eliminate some of the most disturbing symptoms, such as the "voices." They can insist that automatic writing and the use of the ouija board be eliminated. And, whether the possession is genuine or not, they can also convert the patient to the view that it is "all in his mind." *In so doing, they can unwittingly help to break the hold of the dead.*

And what do you do if you find yourself in one of these distressing states *after death?* If you do, try to realize that you are now what the world calls "dead." Try to quiet your confusion and fear and call upon human beings whom you loved in life and who are now dead. Ask them for help, and put as much of an emotional "charge" on the request as you can. Do this repeatedly. It is a telepathic call—the post-mortem equivalent of picking up the phone. It enables those "called" to "locate" you. They will soon appear before you. And you will be led to the next phase of your personal existence.

CHAPTER SEVEN

BIRTH IS NOT A BEGINNING: REINCARNATION

> One day someone came … with a cinema camera. When he pointed it at Robert, turning the handle with a clicking noise, Robert screamed, "Don't! Don't! They killed me like that last time!"… he became so hysterical that I had to send for the doctor.[1]
>
> – *a little boy remembers his death by machine gun in World War I*

> Being born twice is no more remarkable than being born once.
>
> – *Voltaire*

WE KNOW a good deal about what it is like to be dead. Yet there are some questions still to be asked. As the saying goes, "You're a long time dead." But are you? Do you stay dead "forever?" Surprisingly, this question can be answered with a fair degree of precision. *You can expect to stay dead about fifty-two years.*

Most people in the West regard the idea of reincarnation as a fantastic superstition, and find it difficult to imagine how such an outlandish doctrine could have developed. The basis for this "doctrine" is, however, known. It is the same basis from which all of the ideas in this book have been derived: *actual human experiences.* And there is only one kind of human experience which could be the basis for the idea of reincarnation—memories of past lives.

The woman in the psychologist's office had been born in 1938. Deeply hypnotized, Anna was going back in time, year by year. Nothing—until 1917. Suddenly she found herself in a living room, looking out a window. Her voice was sad. She lived in a small town, and her life there bored her. But where was she? She didn't know. Pick up a newspaper and see, she was told. The town was Westfield, New Jersey.

> She described her feelings of attachment to the house she lived in and told me how she ... had made the curtains that hung at the windows. I took her to encounters with neighbors and friends and into shops on the main street of town, and she was able to give me many details.... she ... felt restless and dissatisfied ... wanting excitement, she found herself involved in a plot to sell World War I government supplies on the black market.... her husband was in the army ... overseas, but she expressed no strong attachment to him....
>
> I pressed for the kind of evidence ... I could check, and I was rewarded by an outpouring of details.... The name of the druggist on the corner, the description and name of the police chief ... the name of the town constable who had discovered the black-market plot.... Anna talked about her home, which she said was on Mud Lane, and gave other street names and places. She described the great fire of 1896, and told how the fire bell rang in her schoolroom though the fire was blocks away.
>
> I explored her involvement with the black market. Her voice shook with emotion as she described her fear of being exposed and her shame at the thought that she would be accused of profiteering while her husband fought overseas.... She talked about the hatred of Germans and the total involvement of her community in grandiose ideas of the glory of warfare. It seemed as though the ... feelings and attitudes of small-town America in 1917 came alive in my office. When I brought her to [her death in that life] I was shocked to find that she had killed herself.
>
> "I put the gun to my head and then all I see are magnificent

colors. I don't hear any explosion. Oh! I haven't escaped—I'm still aware of everything."[2]

The psychologist discovered that there was indeed a town in New Jersey called Westfield. Intrigued, she decided to visit it. Upon her arrival, she found that the historical records for the town were unusually good, and the local newspaper had been microfilmed as far back as 1885. With a sense of mounting excitement, she found confirmation for virtually everything Anna had said. The local newspaper revealed why the fire bell rang in the schoolroom—the school bell was the only one in town. Anna had said that Westfield's chief of police was a handsome man named O'Neil. An old newspaper photograph confirmed it—there he stood, handsome indeed, with a luxuriant moustache. Even the name of the druggist proved to be correct—and so it went, with even the smallest details checking out. But Anna had stated that she lived on Mud Lane, and it was not listed in the street directory. A little investigation showed why—in 1924 it had been paved; muddy no longer, it had been re-christened Crestwood Drive.

And finally there was but one detail left to check, the last for any life—a grave. In the local cemetery the psychologist found the family plot and the headstones of the family members whom Anna had named, but there was no headstone for her. Suicides, however, are sometimes interred in unmarked graves, and the cemetery records showed one in the family plot. Its occupant was unnamed. But the date on which this grave had received its body was recorded. *It was 1917.*

On January 19, 1951, Munna Prasad, the six-year-old son of Jageshwar Prasad, a barber in the Chhipatti district of the Indian city of Kanauj, was lured away by two neighbors, Jawahar and Chaturi, and brutally murdered. His throat was cut with a razor, and the body was decapitated before head and body were separately buried. A witness had seen Munna going off with the men shortly before his disappearance, and when the severed head of the boy was found, they were arrested.

One unofficially confessed, admitting that the motive for the crime was a desire to dispose of Prasad's heir so that one of the murderers, a relative, could inherit the barber's property. After being formally charged with the crime, however, he retracted his confession, and as there were no witnesses to the actual murder, the case could not be prosecuted and the two accused were freed.

> A few years later word reached … Jageshwar Prasad that a boy born in another district of Kanauj in July, 1951 (six months after the death of Munna), had described himself as the son of Jageshwar, a barber of Chhipatti District, and had given details of "his" murder, naming the murderers, the place of the crime, and other circumstances of the life and death of Munna. The boy, named Ravi Shankar, son of … Babu Ram Gupta … fully identified himself with Munna. His family and neighbors testified to his repeated demands for Munna's toys which he said were in … the house of his previous life … and to his wish to be taken to that home. He said he needed the toys. He complained that the house in which he lived was not "his house" … when rebuked, he ran out of his house, saying he would go to his former home. He often spoke spontaneously about Munna's murder to members of his family … neighbors and others. Ravi Shankar's mother and older sister … testified that he [began to make] such statements when he was between two and three years old.[3]

Ravi Shankar showed a highly detailed knowledge of Munna's life, his possessions, his relatives, and his murder. He stated correctly that on the day of his murder he had eaten some guavas before going out to play, was enticed away by the two men, and was murdered close to Chintamini Temple in an orchard near the river by having his throat cut with a razor. He was then buried in the sand. He knew Munna's name and address and showed an intimate familiarity with his toys and their location in Munna's home. He recognized Munna's watch and inquired after his ring. His recognition of Munna's father was very emotional, and he spontaneously identified Munna's maternal grandmother amongst a group of other women.

Ravi Shankar recognized Munna's murderers, for whom he showed extreme fear. He also became terrified when he was taken to the vicinity of Chintamini Temple, where Munna had been murdered. And Ravi Shankar was born with a very strange birthmark on his neck—a linear one closely resembling the scar of a long knife wound. When this birthmark was examined in 1964 by an American physician he described it as having "the stippled quality of a scar" and as looking "much like an old scar of a healed knife wound."[4] Interestingly, when Ravi Shankar talked about his murder in a previous life, *he would state that the birthmark on his neck had had its origin in the wounds of that murder.*

Memories of past lives may thus, as in Ravi Shankar's case, be perfectly clear and conscious ones. They may also be buried in the subconscious. If so—as in Anna's case—they can be retrieved, dramatically, by hypnosis.

Research on reincarnation should not be undertaken lightly. The claim that we have all lived before is a profoundly disturbing one, and cannot responsibly be made without painstaking investigation. Such investigation has, in fact, been conducted over the past dozen years, with scrupulous objectivity. And from all of this research has come a single finding: reincarnation is not merely a theory; it is a fact.

The leading student of *conscious* memories of past lives is Dr. Ian Stevenson, a highly respected professor of psychiatry at the University of Virginia. He has collected 1,700 cases of persons who have definite memories of a life prior to their present one. These memories, typically very vivid, are absolutely convincing to those who carry them. And, although some do not recall enough detail for a definite identification of their former selves, a good many others do!

In a typical instance, a child, as soon as he is old enough to talk (usually between the ages of two and three) begins to make persistent claims that he used to be someone else. Most parents make active efforts to discourage these revelations. But the child is adamant. He insists that what he says is true, even if he is punished repeatedly for doing so, and pleads to be taken to his former home, which he gives every sign of missing intensely. He will provide a great deal of detail about his former self, including his name and address. Where such claims have been checked, they usually turn out to be correct. Such a person did live and die where and how the child says he did. If the child is taken to his claimed former neighborhood, he will usually be able to take investigators to his former home, observing correctly any changes that have been made since his "death." The house, then white, is now green; a tree beside it has been cut down; a business across the street is no longer in existence. If ten friends and relatives of the dead man are lined up in front of him, along with ten people whom the dead man had never met, the child will be able to identify those he once knew. This identification often involves some very strong emotions. A three-year-old child may call his former wife correctly by a pet name, rush to embrace her, speak to her as a husband would to a wife, and state that he wishes to remain with her rather than with his parents. On encountering his children, who are of course a good deal older than he, he will address them and behave towards them in a way entirely appropriate to a parent. And in the most extraordinary cases, the child will bear on his body a birthmark closely resembling in shape and location a wound suffered by the dead man, either before or during his death.

Dr. Stevenson's meticulous investigation of thirty of the most convincing cases has established, beyond any doubt, that they are genuine. The person involved really did live, die, and become re-embodied. But such vivid conscious memories of past lives, although certainly not rare, are not the rule. The majority of us clearly do not have them. And this poses an obvious problem. Why do only some of us recall past lives? If reincarnation is, as I have claimed, a fact, then why should it have happened to a mere thirty, or even to a mere 1,700, of all of the world's millions? The answer is that it hasn't. Evidence gathered from some 1,500 hypnotized persons shows, beyond any doubt, that *it has happened to us all.*

Conscious memories of a past life

These memories can vary greatly in clarity and detail. Most commonly they appear as vivid fragments which do not contain enough detail to identify a specific historical personality. The memories may involve powerful emotions—often anguish—and are not sympathetically received by parents.

> As a child I often had such memories and sometimes tried to talk about them with Mother, who hushed me up and threatened me with a beating if I dared go on which such raving.... I remember it once came to me with incredible clarity that I was adult and had four children, a new-born I carried in my arms and three clinging to my skirts, screaming and sobbing. I found myself in church and round about me were people in strange, mostly gray clothes. All the women had very long full skirts, down to the ground, I had a very full one, too, a white blouse with side sleeves and a bodice which was done up in the front, and on my head a white hat with a wide brim turned up in front. I've seen a style somewhat similar in pictures from Holland. It was a little church on a hill and all these people had gone there in flight because of a battle, and we were being shot at ... from cannons, and ... the people screamed.... My children screamed and clung to me, then there was a terrible crash and everything was over.... I remember how I trembled and held my head and thought of running to Mommy and asking her, but then I remembered the whipping I'd get. I didn't dare go home for a long while, then was declared ill and put to bed. There I lay remembering everything so clearly and wondering and not being able to understand. Of course ... I never dared utter a word to anyone ... but I knew that I had lived before and kept it to myself. I didn't want to hear that I was talking crazy nonsense and didn't want to get a beating ... I suppressed it all.[5]

The above is a fairly typical example of this kind of memory. Here is another:

I was born in 1915, and what first dominated my mind was the feeling of homelessness. I experienced this consciously, the images didn't come until later.... I wept within myself, and it took several years before I taught myself to laugh and be happy. It was during that first lonely helplessness that the loss of my son first surfaced. He was a bit of myself torn away—I can't explain any better than that how it felt.

In my third year I began ... to smooth my pillow and lie down and caress the pillow as if it were my boy's cheek. In my memory pictures he was four years old, never older.... I used to hold myself very carefully upright, with my neck straight, and I felt I was grown up. So strong was my anchoring in the past that I felt exactly how the clothes covered my ankles and that my sandals were soft. I had a hard time learning to sit on chairs....

The pictures from the past ... came and went.... Only my love for that little boy remained there all the time, first as a pain in my soul, later as a kind of knowledge about that one particular little person. The pictures have been the same since early childhood ... [but] one ... remained burned into my mind....

The place we live in, in that memory picture, must be a very big house. The windows are high, like ordinary doors, with deep niches but no glass panes. I can't actually see that they have no glass, but I know it, definitely. The floor is made of thick polished tiles.... They look like marble ... red-brown and gray-green. If I were to stretch out my hand as I lie on my divan, I could touch a tile which has an unusually big red-brown design. It feels as if my divan is placed almost in the center of my room. To the left, diagonally behind my head on the same side as the two windows, a couple of steps lead to a roof garden with a dazzling white balustrade. There's no door, but half of the wall is missing, and there, in front of the opening, my son is playing. Sometimes he comes over and playfully traces his fingers over my face. That's the memory which gives such pain.... [He] is dressed in white, not Western style; he has bare feet. My clothes are thin, I'm resting on my left hip, and on my left foot I see the soft, lion-

> colored sandal. I lie there looking down at my brown wrist with the thin soft fabric around it. Though I can't really see it, I know I have white pearls in my black hair. Even in this present life, I "know" that my hair is black though it never has been black.... As a child I was always so disappointed when I saw my mirror image—I didn't recognize myself at all.... In my childhood I never heard about reincarnation....
>
> I began to suspect that it might have been India where I lived in [this] former life. A friend suggested that I read about that country because she found so much which could be connected with India in my images and personal characteristics. Then, with the joy of recognition, I found the lotus flower I had started to draw even before I went to school. But also OM, the holy sign, the symbol of God, was something I recognized and ... had mulled over in vain since the age of five, when I saw a beautifully stylized number 5 on my father's cigar box and was absolutely convinced that it had to be something other than a number, which my father told me it was.... I've never forgotten how I used to trace the number 5 on the wood of the box while deep inside I struggled to remember.[6]

In the majority of cases, such memories, although intense, don't provide enough detail on the identity of the former personality to permit them to be linked to a specific individual who lived in the past. A minority, however—as in the case of Ravi Shankar—do. And because these cases show so clearly that reincarnation does occur, I am going to give three examples.

Robert

Joan Grant, the English psychic whose memories of her former lives are so detailed that she has written remarkable books about them, was invited several years ago to visit a Belgian friend. The woman's grandson, a little boy of six named Robert, was staying with her, in preference to living with his parents. One morning soon after Joan's arrival, she awakened to find the boy studying her intently. With the abruptness of excitement, he told her he wanted to show her something, and asked her to come with him right away.

> He took me to a box-room where there was a large unopened packing-case. He foraged in a cupboard and handed me a hammer and cold chisel. "Open it, please. I cannot do it myself with one hand, and I have promised not to use the other one until the bone is quite mended. I broke it falling off my pony...."
>
> "Are you sure your grandmother wouldn't mind? It's addressed to her, and ... "
>
> "Please open it. Now!" He was quivering with impatience. "It's me in the packing-case."
>
> I thought he meant that it contained something which belonged to him.... I began to prise the nails from the wood. At last I got the lid off, and found that ... it held a large oil-painting. I propped it up against the wall and flicked sawdust from the glass. It was the portrait of a young man in khaki. Who was it? Obviously someone the boy knew very well, for he was gazing at it with intense excitement and a deeper emotion very close to tears. Then he turned and looked at me solemnly. "You will not laugh at me, will you?" I wanted to hug him, but I knew the matter was too serious. "I never laugh at true things." He nodded. "Then you will tell my grandmother that this is not just a picture of my Uncle Albert, it is a picture of me."
>
> I went at once to tell her. I think she had asked me there only for confirmation of what she already knew. Eagerly, as though it was a profound relief at last to accept evidence which her religion made it difficult to believe, she told me many things which substantiated Robert's story. Her elder son, Albert, had always meant far more to her than her younger son, John. She had separated from her husband, who was English, when both children were quite small. Albert had spent most of his time with her in Belgium, and had been killed in 1915, a captain in the Belgian

Army, at the age of twenty-three. John, just too young for the war, had been sent to school in England and had married an English wife. He saw his mother very seldom until she went to stay with them for a few days when Robert was two years old. To the other grandchildren she was still only an elderly woman whom they hardly knew. To Robert she was the only person who really mattered. If he was with her he was cheerful and healthy. With his parents he sulked or was violently disobedient until they were thankful to send him back to Belgium.

"Robert was always a brave little boy," she said.... "When he first saw a swimming-bath, and he was then only three, he ran along the diving-board and dived in. Albert too was a very fine diver. One day someone came here with a cinema camera. When he pointed it at Robert, turning the handle with a clicking noise, Robert screamed, "Don't! Don't! They killed me like that last time!" I tried to calm him, but he became so hysterical that I had to send for the doctor, who gave him a sedative. Albert went out alone into no-man's-land at night to stop a German post enfilading his men with a machine gun. There were eight bullets in his body when they found it, but he did not die very quickly. He had managed to crawl nearly back to our own wire before morning...." There were tears in her eyes, but she continued composedly. "There have been so many other things, pet names which Albert used to call me, likes and dislikes which used to be a private joke between us, trivial in themselves, perhaps, but altogether so certain. Now I shall hang up their portrait. I have kept it hidden all these years because even a snapshot of Albert made Robert behave so—so strangely. But now it is not strange to us any more that in 1915 Albert only left me for a little while."[7]

Altogether a very strange story. And were it the only such story that we have, it would have to be classified as an oddity, and dismissed. But it isn't.

The case of Corliss Chotkin, Jr.

In the spring of 1946, in Angoon, Alaska, Victor Vincent, a full-blooded Tlingit Indian, died. During the last years of his life, he had a very close relationship with his niece, Mrs. Corliss Chotkin. About a year before his death he told her that he would return to her as her next son. And so that she would know him, he said, this son would have two scars on his body which he himself now had. Both of these scars were the result of surgical operations. One was at the base of his nose on the right side. The other was on his back and was quite distinctive, as it included round holes left by stitches. Eighteen months after Victor's death, his niece gave birth to a son. The boy was named Corliss Chotkin, after his father. He was born with two birthmarks on his body—exactly the same in appearance and location as the two scars borne by Victor Vincent.

Dr. Stevenson examined these birthmarks in 1962. They looked exactly like old scars. The one on Corliss's nose was darker than the surrounding skin, and was definitely indented. Of the birthmark on his back, the Doctor said:

> It was heavily pigmented and raised ... [extending] about one inch in length and a quarter inch in width. Along its margins one could ... easily discern several small round marks outside the main scar. Four of these ... lined up like the stitch wounds of surgical operations.[8]

These birthmarks were interesting, to say the least. But they were followed by a series of even more extraordinary occurrences. When Corliss was thirteen months old and just beginning to talk, his family began trying to teach him his name. And one day when his mother was attempting to do this, a most startling event occurred. The little boy suddenly opened his mouth and said, in a Tlingit accent whose excellence was totally unexpected in a child of that age: "Don't you know me? I'm Kahkody." *"Kahkody" was the tribal name of the dead Victor Vincent.* And that was only the beginning.

When Corliss was two and being wheeled along a street in front of the docks, he suddenly saw someone and became greatly excited, jumping up and down and saying "There's my Susie." Susie was Victor Vincent's stepdaughter, and Corliss, in his present life, had never met her! What followed was just as strange. The two-year-old child hugged Susie affectionately, spoke (correctly) her Tlingit name, and kept repeating, excitedly, "My Susie, my Susie!"

A few weeks later Corliss was again out with his mother when he suddenly said, "There is William, my son." William Vincent was in fact the son of Victor Vincent and Mrs. Chotkin was unaware that he was in the immediate vicinity until Corliss spoke. At the age of three, his mother took him with her to a large meeting. Corliss remarked, "That's the old lady," and "There's Rose." Rose was Victor Vincent's widow, and Victor had always called her "the old lady." Corliss had picked her out of the crowd before his mother had noticed that she was present.

> On another occasion, Corliss recognized a friend of Victor Vincent, Mrs. Alice Roberts, who happened to be … walking past the Chotkins' house where Corliss was playing in the street. As she went by he called her correctly by her name, a pet name.[9]

In a similarly spontaneous way he recognized, at various times, other friends of Victor Vincent. He would accost them, call them by name, and display a familiarity toward them which was not only highly unusual, in that Corliss had never seen them before, but quite inappropriate for a child. In addition, he showed an inexplicable familiarity with other aspects of Victor Vincent's life. For example, on one occasion:

> Mrs. Chotkin and Corliss were at the home formerly occupied by Mrs. Chotkin and her family during the life of Victor Vincent. The boy pointed out a room in the building and said: "When the old lady and I used to visit you, we slept in that bedroom there." This remark seemed all the more extraordinary

> since the building, which had formerly been a residence, had by that time been given over to other purposes and no rooms in it could be easily recognized as bedrooms. But the room he indicated had in fact been occupied by Victor Vincent and his wife when they had visited the Chotkins.[10]

All of these events occurred before the child was six. But by about the age of nine, Corliss began to make fewer statements about his previous life as Victor Vincent, and these memories apparently began to fade. By the time Dr. Stevenson met him in 1962, when he was fifteen, he said he no longer remembered anything of his previous life. (Dr. Stevenson's research shows that these memories usually begin to fade at about the age of six, although they may be retained into adult life.)

When one examines a large number of cases such as this one, they quickly become rather repetitive. Yet they will seem so extraordinary to people unfamiliar with the evidence for reincarnation that I am going to give one more example.

The case of Parmod

Parmod Sharma was born in Bisauli, in India, on October 11, 1944. By age two and a half, he had learned to talk, and immediately began to make some very strange statements about himself. He told his mother that it was unnecessary for her to cook his meals because he had a wife in Morabadad who could do that for him. He declared himself to be one of the "Mohan Brothers," and said that he owned a large biscuit shop in Morabadad which also sold soda water. He added that he was wealthy, complained of his present poverty, and demanded to be taken to Morabadad. He had, he said, died in his previous life when he had eaten too much curd and become ill, dying "in a bathtub." These were his initial claims. More emerged when he was between the ages of three and four. He had four sons, and a daughter, and he owned a shop, a cinema, and a hotel in Saharanpur, where his mother lived. He said that his name was Parmanand. For about four years, from ages three to seven, Parmod strongly identified with his claimed previous life as "Parmanand." He showed a very strong and unusual interest in biscuits and soda water, and spoke in detail about his business activities. He strongly disliked curd, and advised his father against eating it, saying that it was dangerous. He also showed a strong aversion to being submerged in water, connecting this with his "dying in a bathtub."

Although Parmod's parents made no effort to verify these statements, word of them reached the members of a family called Mehra, who lived in Morabadad, and who found these claims of great interest. The brothers of this family owned a soda and biscuit shop (called Mohan Brothers) in Moradabad and another shop in Saharanpur. They had had a brother, Parmanand Mehra, who had died on May 9, 1943, as a result of a gastro-intestinal illness which he suffered after eating too much curd. He had been an affluent businessman and had owned, in partnership with three brothers and a cousin, the soda and biscuit shop and other businesses in Morabadad and Saharanpur, including two hotels, two shops, a cinema, and a biscuit and soda water manufacturing business which he had started and managed himself.

In 1949, when Parmod was five years old, the Mehra family got in touch with Parmod's parents and invited them to come to Morabadad with Parmod. They agreed to do so, with interesting results.

When the family alighted at the railway station in Morabadad, Parmod led them to the Mohan Brothers shop, which was half a mile from the station. Upon entering it, he complained (correctly) that the interior had been altered. When taken to the soda water machine, which had been disconnected in order to test him, he immediately explained what had to be done in order to get this quite complicated machine working again. He recognized a number of items which had belonged to Parmanand, and commented on changes which had been made in the family home since his death. When members of Parmanand's family appeared, he correctly recognized Parmanand's mother, wife, daughter, and two sons, as well as his brother, cousin, and nephew. And this recognition was by no means cool—Parmod wept, embraced them, and called them by name.

In addition, his behavior toward them was inappropriate to his new status as a five-year-old boy. For example, he would not allow Parmanand's sons to call him "Parmod." He insisted that they should call him "father," saying "I have only become small." His initial conversation with Parmanand's wife was equally bizarre. He said to her,

> "I have come but you have not fixed bindi." This remark referred to the round mark of red pigment worn on the forehead by wives in India, but not by widows. The remark would be a most unusual one for a small boy to make to a strange older woman, but entirely appropriate in the relationship of husband and wife. It indicates how firmly Parmod believed the lady was "his" wife. He also reproached her for wearing a white sari, as Hindu widows commonly do, instead of a colored one as wives do.[11]

Parmod's objections to her appearance as a widow were quite natural. After all, *he wasn't dead!*

The cases of Ravi Shankar, Robert, Corliss Chotkin, and Parmod are typical of those involving conscious, verifiable memories of a past existence. Dr. Ian Stevenson has personally investigated dozens of such cases, and he has already published thirty in detail. His investigations have been scrupulous, painstaking, and time-consuming. Every alternative explanation to that of reincarnation, such as deliberate fraud or errors of memory, has been carefully considered, assessed, and eventually rejected.

A favorite counter-explanation offered by skeptics has been "genetic memory"—the idea that the experiences of the former personality have somehow been genetically recorded and passed down to the second personality, who falsely experiences them as conscious memories of his own past life. However, in the vast majority of Stevenson's cases, there is no genetic relationship whatever between the two personalities.

We can make a few generalizations about the onset and duration of such memories. A child will typically begin to refer to past life experiences as soon as he begins to talk—between the ages of two and three years. The average duration of intense identification with the former personality is seven years, although the memories will probably fade between the ages of five and ten. As time passes, the memories may be totally forgotten, may persist in faded form, or may be clearly retained. In Stevenson's experience, these three possibilities are about equally common. But the most important conclusion to be drawn from Dr. Stevenson's work is more dramatic. *He has proven, beyond all reasonable doubt, that there are people alive today who once died.*

Unconscious memories of a past life

We don't really know how common conscious memories of a past life are, as there is plenty of reason for a family to conceal and repress them. In the East, such memories are usually felt by parents to be troublesome and embarrassing; they lead to fears that their child will leave them (as he frequently declares he wishes to), and they are often thought to indicate an early death. For all of these reasons, efforts are usually made to stop the child from talking about them. In the West, of course, such claims are regarded at best as highly fantastic, or at worst, as evidence of mental illness. But despite the high likelihood of widespread suppression of such memories by parents, it seems obvious that those who claim them are definitely in the minority. This, however, does not justify a complacent return to the notion that most of us "only live once"—*for evidence from regression hypnosis strongly indicates that subconscious memories of past lives are carried by us all!*

Experiments by psychologists have revealed that hypnosis can take people back in time. They need simply be told to "go back."

"Going back" means reliving past memories in vivid detail, sometimes in such detail that the present personality seems literally to become younger: at "age six" a hypnotized person may write his name just as he did in first grade; at "age four," he may produce a childlike, preliterate scrawl. And where such memories can be checked, they turn out to be astonishingly accurate, right down to the wallpaper-pattern over the crib of a two-week-old baby. Taken back into the womb, subjects report warmth and darkness; some assume the fetal position. Progression forward to birth produces some painful memories: people writhe, twist, gasp, are crushed, squeezed and strangled, emerge into blinding light soaking wet and freezing cold, complain of being held upside down, and mourn that their mothers are unconscious and unable to cuddle them. And when they are taken back *beyond* the womb, *they begin to report in detail on past lives.*

Of every ten people, nine can be hypnotized, and will report in detail on past existences. Nor can this "reporting" be dismissed as mere fantasy, for subjects typically display a highly accurate knowledge of even the most obscure details of remote times and places where they claim to have lived. Verifying such memories may require the help of scholars who specialize in the history of the society involved, as well as an examination of obscure publications not available in English. *And almost always, these memories are verified as correct.* Deliberate efforts on the part of the hypnotist to persuade the subject to "change his story" are generally unsuccessful. Regressed subjects seem to tell the truth!

And when the one of ten who "cannot" be hypnotized is given special treatment, we often discover that his subconscious mind has been saying "No!" for a very understandable reason. If he is reassured that he is safe and that the hypnotist will protect him from discomfort, pain, and danger during the regression, he *can* sometimes be hypnotized after all. *And if he is, it frequently turns out that he has recently died a very painful and traumatic death.*

In examining the work of regression hypnotists who believe in reincarnation, I have been struck by the fact that, often, they seem to have become involved in this strange research because of personal experiences which have led them to believe that they and others have lived before. Hypnotherapist Arnall Bloxham reached this conclusion while still a child. Dreams are known to tap the subconscious, and his most vivid dreams were of the past, of people and of places completely unknown to him during his waking life. And then one day, on a vacation trip in the Cotswolds, he found himself in a place he recognized. It was a road which he had seen before, many times—*in his dreams*; a steep, tree-lined road, yellow and dusty. Bloxham knew that if he followed that road he would come to a castle. And he did—he came to Sudeley Castle. Bloxham recognized it. He knew the interior so well that he didn't need a guide. For he had lived there before—in another life![12]

Bloxham began doing past-life regressions when a man who was a hypochondriac came to him for help. He was in a lamentable state, imagining that he suffered from a multitude of ailments. Bloxham hypnotized him several times and convinced him that these ailments were only in his mind. He was cured, yet one problem still remained. He was so terrified of dying that he hardly dared to fall asleep at night—he feared he might never wake up![13]

This presented a more difficult problem than relieving hypochondria. The man was certainly going to die, eventually, and Bloxham felt it would be unethical to try to convince him otherwise under hypnosis. Nonetheless, he came up with a solution. He hypnotized the man, regressed him to a past life, and showed him that, as he had lived before, he would live again. And it worked. The man completely lost his fear of death.[14]

In the twenty years which have elapsed since that first experiment with past-life regression, Bloxham has taperecorded the recall of over four hundred past lives.

Until 1965 Dr. Helen Wambach was a perfectly conventional clinical psychologist who practiced at the Monmouth Medical Center in Long Branch, New Jersey, and taught at the local community college. Her life had been entirely normal—her consciousness had remained steadfastly ordinary over the years and she had never had anything like a "psychic experience." But in 1966, a few moments spent in a Quaker memorial house in Mount Holly, New Jersey, changed all of that.

> When I first entered the house, I was just a Sunday tourist coming to visit an obscure memorial. As I mounted the stairs to the second floor, a feeling of being in another time and place came over me. As I entered the small library room, I saw myself going automatically to the shelf of books and taking one down. I seemed to "know" that this had been my book, and as I looked at the pages, a scene came before my inner eye. I was riding on a mule across a stubbled field, and this book was propped up on the saddle in front of me. The sun was hot on my back, and my clothes were scratchy. I could feel the horse moving under me while I sat in the saddle, deeply absorbed in reading the book propped before me. The book I was reading was a report of a minister's experience of the between-life state while he was in a coma. I seemed to know the book's contents before I turned the pages.[15]

In a few moments, Dr. Wambach returned to "normal." She was upset because she could not understand what had happened to her. Why had she suddenly felt that this was "her" book? And even more strange, why had she suddenly experienced herself in another body and another time? Although she was badly shaken by the vividness of the experience, it opened up a new and fascinating possibility. Perhaps it was just a fantasy. But perhaps, on the other hand, it was real—*a memory, buried in her subconscious, of a previous life!* And perhaps everyone carried such memories with them, and they could, in some way, be tapped. Dr. Wambach had been practicing psychotherapy since 1955. She now found that her strange experience gave her a new understanding of cases which had once puzzled her deeply. She particularly remembered Billy, who was brought into the clinic because of hyperactive behavior and an inability to relax or settle down in the classroom:

Billy spent no longer than ten seconds with each toy in the playroom, running from one to the other as though driven, so I took him to my office. He was too distractable to be able to perform well on the psychological tests, and I wanted to establish a rapport with him before I began testing him. At last, he was willing to sit on my lap and talk. To my complete astonishment, he began talking about his life as a rookie policeman. He talked about how he played basketball, and said he wished he [could] smoke. He said he liked smoking cigarettes before and didn't know why he couldn't now. It took me a while to realize that Billy was talking about a past life. At first, I thought he was relating some story he had seen on television, but the more he spoke about it, the more it seemed he was describing some experience he felt had been his own. I was curious about his policeman experiences, so I encouraged him to talk about them more. This surprised Billy, because he told me that only his three-year-old sister had ever listened to him when he talked about "the policeman."

When I asked Billy's mother whether he had ever discussed this past life with her, she reported that he had begun talking about it when he was about three. "I told him he shouldn't make up stories, and then he didn't talk about it much anymore," she reported. I worked with Billy ... for three months. His hyperactivity continued, though he was able to sit and relax when he discussed his life as a policeman with me. The subject seemed to obsess him.... One day his mother reported that a policeman had brought him home because he was out in the middle of the street trying to direct traffic ... he had told me about his traffic assignment in his life as a policeman.... Billy's behavior showed no signs of improvement [and] his mother ... withdrew [him] from treatment.... I have no idea what became of the bright-eyed little boy who remembered his past life.[16]

Dr. Wambach's experience, and other similarly puzzling cases that she had encountered in therapy, clinched it. *She had to find out whether this was fantasy, or a profound reality which she had never before suspected.* It took her ten years and the hypnotic regression of more than 1,000 people to some 1,100 purported past lives to discover the answer. Her analysis of the intricately consistent detail of this vast body of data led to one conclusion—that whether we like it or not, and whether or not we can deal with its staggering implications, reincarnation is a fact and *we have all lived before.*

Denys Kelsey is a British psychiatrist who sometimes uses hypnotherapy on his patients. When he began his practice, he had no interest whatsoever in reincarnation, and certainly no belief in it. But during his first ten years as a therapist, a series of cases came his way which forced him to a rather unorthodox conclusion: that reincarnation is not a theory but a fact. He was stunned by the discovery that phobias sometimes originated not in the present but in a *past* life. And he was profoundly impressed by the vividness of experience and the authenticity of detail that his patients reported when he regressed them hypnotically to a past existence. Fascinated, he finally had to try it for himself. And when he did, he got a good deal more than he bargained for.

> I was very doubtful of being able to recover anything, especially as hypnotists are notoriously difficult to hypnotise.... I fixed my gaze on [a candle] flame and gave myself suggestions of relaxation. The transition of a sceptical psychiatrist lying on his own couch to a man racing a chariot was instantaneous. On my left there was a barrier surrounding an island of spectators in the centre of the arena. On my right a chariot was overtaking me. I knew I should give way to it, but instead I forced my pair into the narrowing gap. There was a shuddering impact as our wheels interlocked. I was catapulted forwards and felt a wheel run over my chest. As the chariot overturned, it swung the horses against the barrier. The last thing I remembered was their screaming.
>
> At this point, Joan [his wife] brought me back to the present. But the terrible realization that through a desire to show off I had caused the destruction of a pair of beloved horses brought a

> degree of shame which in my current life I had never previously experienced. There was no possibility of dissociating myself from this event: that it had occurred two thousand years ago was entirely irrelevant. It was I who had done it; and it was happening now.[17]

This certainly sounds incredible. But it is my opinion, based on personal experience of hypnotic regression, that people who feel skeptical about such claims should not scoff too elaborately until they have tried hypnotic regression themselves. And when they have done so, they may discover, in a very direct way, *that some of their own past life memories are just as vivid.*

In addition, belief or disbelief in reincarnation has no effect on the results of hypnotic regression, as the following case will show. One evening a young man came to dinner at the Kelseys'. He confided his fear that he was becoming an alcoholic, and asked for help. This was a tall order, as he had to leave in forty-eight hours, but Dr. Kelsey agreed to try a preliminary diagnostic session, using hypnosis. The young man was highly intelligent and did not, the doctor discovered, believe in reincarnation.

> I thought he would be difficult to hypnotise, but he reached a deep level very rapidly, and immediately went into a curious spasm. I called for Joan, and by the time she arrived, in a couple of minutes, the spasms had turned to a violent writhing, which affected only his head and trunk. It seemed as though he was struggling to escape from bonds which were holding his arms in a spread-eagled position. He thrust his head back until his spine arched in an extremity of effort. He was making heart-rending noises, half groan, half cry. In a barely decipherable splutter he gasped, "They are cutting my tongue out … with a shiv [knife]."
>
> [We] could only get a sketchy outline of the background, as we were both fully occupied in keeping him from falling off the couch. The period was the Spanish Civil War … in 1938. He had been working for some kind of resistance movement, or else was

taking a message behind the enemy lines ... he had been caught, and was being tortured to reveal the names of people he was working with. He had been savagely beaten and kicked in a stone-built hut. The four men who were trying to extract information must have heard something which alarmed them; for they suddenly decided that they must make a fast getaway. They had already trussed his feet together, and they now tied his wrists to iron rings in opposite walls. Cutting out his tongue was an afterthought to make sure that as he would not give his secret away to them he would not be able to tell it to anyone. He died alone, many hours later, agonised not only by pain but by thirst ... the craving for water becoming more and more predominant.

It was very difficult to pull him back to the present day. When I first grasped his hand he identified me with one of his captors and became violent. Gradually I got him to obey such instructions as, "Grasp my hand: release it: grasp it again...." Slowly he reclaimed his present identity and recognised us and his surroundings. When I believed he was back in normal consciousness I told him to move from the couch to a chair. As he did so, he asked for a glass of water. I fetched him a large tumblerful, which he drained and then demanded a second and yet a third. I told him he had drunk as much water as was good for him, but he shouted, "Bring me a *jug!*"

At this point I realised that he was not completely back in the present, but was still suffering from the thirst in which he had died. I told him to sit on the edge of the couch while I counted slowly from twenty down to one; which brought him fully back into the present. He said, as though startled, "I am no longer in the least thirsty!"

He then told me, for the first time, that for as long as he could remember he had been subject to a compulsive thirst. Wherever he happened to be, he would be acutely anxious until he had assured himself that he would be able to get something to drink the moment he became thirsty. In a strange house, or in a classroom or cinema, he was ill at ease until he had found out

> where he could instantly get a glass of water. When he was older and had become introduced to alcohol this too often became the focus of his compulsive need.[18]

Bringing his last death to conscious awareness had a most interesting effect. His compulsive thirst immediately disappeared, as did his addiction to alcohol, which, from that day, he ceased to drink in any form.

Phobias with a past-life origin are commonly encountered in hypnotic regressions. But one of the more dramatic known to me was revealed not through hypnosis but through the direct perception of a gifted psychic, Joan Grant. One day Dr. Alec Kerr-Clarkson, a psychiatrist who had read her books, came to see her. His interest in reincarnation had originated when some of his hypnotized patients had begun talking about their past lives. He was invited by Joan and her husband Charles to stay for what proved to be an enjoyable weekend. When Dr. Kerr-Clarkson was about to leave, Charles gave him some pheasants.

> We were both surprised when instead of taking the birds, which were tied together by the neck with a loop of string, Alec looked very embarrassed and, backing away, asked that the birds should be wrapped securely in a parcel. Charles, mystified, explained that the birds would travel better unwrapped; at which Alec exclaimed, "But I can't touch feathers!"
>
> The words were hardly out of his mouth before I heard myself saying emphatically, "The reason you can't touch feathers is because you had a death which was very similar to one of mine. You were left among the dead on a battle field.... I don't know where or when ... but the ground is arid, pale sand and outcrops of grey rock. Vultures are watching you ... six vultures. You are very badly wounded, but you can still move your arms. Every time you move, the vultures hop a little further away. But then they hop closer again.... Now they are so close that you can smell them ... they are beginning to tear at your flesh.

> At this point Charles interrupted me; for Alec was clearly distressed. He had collapsed onto the sofa and was sweating profusely. He was obviously in no condition to travel and thankfully accepted our suggestion that he remain at least until the following day. He went up to his room, but soon called me. Although he had tried to stop his violent shivering by having a hot bath, and had put himself to bed, he was still in the grip of a spontaneous recall. He exhorted me to drive the vultures away, and waved his arm as though he could still see them hopping inexorably towards him.... "Why did they leave me to die alone ... why? ... why? Every other man had a friend to cut his throat.... why did they betray me ... Me!" His terror had been replaced by a rising fury of indignation.
>
> Suddenly I realised that it was this emotion which had caused him to become bound to his death by vultures. He felt that he had suffered not just a horrific death, but betrayal by his comrades, who had left him to die alone. .... I spent most of that night sitting on his bed, while he ... shivered and sweated as though suffering from ... malaria. But at last I was able to make the man he had been realise that he had not been deliberately abandoned, and he said with infinite relief, "They must have thought I was dead.... I am not angry any more.... I have no reason to hate them for leaving me to die among the dead...." Then he was Alec and no one else, and he went quietly to sleep.[19]

The psychiatrist slept deeply until noon the next day. When he awakened, he confessed that he had had an acute phobia about feathers since childhood. He had found it highly embarrassing, particularly when his children teased him because he was unable to rescue birds which had become entangled in the strawberry nets in his garden. He tried in vain to cure himself, and went, without success, to several of his colleagues. But when he left, he was carrying the pheasants by their necks. Later he wrote to thank Joan and her husband:

> I hope none of my fellow passengers knew I was a psychiatrist because they would have thought my behavior very odd.... I could not resist the temptation of taking the pheasants down from the rack and stroking them ... for I was so delighted to show myself that I now actually enjoy touching feathers![20]

A very, very strange story indeed. But it did happen. One psychic "flash," a little conversation, and a lifelong phobia is ended. Perhaps there's something to "reincarnation" after all, when a treatment based on it can get such rapid, dramatic, and permanent results!

The murder of Rebecca

Most of Arnall Bloxham's four hundred past-life tapes make pretty dull listening. They contain exactly the kind of thing you would expect them to if reincarnation really were true—the rather monotonous, uneventful, and obscure details of perfectly ordinary lives. Some, however, are quite dramatic and contain a wealth of historical detail, which usually turns out to be incredibly accurate. And sometimes, as in the following case, the regressed person makes a claim which historians don't believe—and is proven right!

Jane Evans, a perfectly normal Welsh housewife, has led an uneventful life—in the twentieth century. But when regressed to the twelfth, she relived her own murder so vividly that afterwards she walked out of Arnall Bloxham's consulting room and fainted.

Bloxham had directed the hypnotized woman to go "back, back in time," to the twelfth century. When asked the date, she replied that it was "the Christian year 1189," and she was living in York, England. Her name was Rebecca, and her husband was a wealthy Jewish moneylender named Joseph. This was a highly dangerous time to be a Jew in York, for the following year anti-Semitic riots, generated by Christian religious fervor prior to the Third Crusade, led to the ugly deaths of one hundred and fifty of York's Jewish inhabitants. From the beginning of her narrative, Rebecca was deeply concerned about the consequences of the anti-Jewish atmosphere for herself and her family, and talked bitterly of the humiliations they endured. Interestingly, her story makes no mention of the best-known features of this massacre, as they appear in history books; as she was not physically present at these events, she does not report them. She talks only of the personal fate of herself and her family.

The atmosphere of hatred becomes so intense that Rebecca and her family consider fleeing from York. But, unwilling to abandon their home and possessions, they postpone this drastic decision. And then one evening it is forced upon them. A mob attacks the Jewish quarter, murdering some of the inhabitants and burning homes. With the house next door in flames, the family flees—Rebecca and Joseph, their daughter Rachel, and their son. But the mob is at their heels. Joseph empties a sack of coins into the road. A wild scramble for the money delays their pursuers just long enough to enable them to escape. Exhausted and desperate, they seek refuge in a church. After tying up the priest, they hide themselves in the dark crypt beneath the floor. Hungry and thirsty, huddling in the cold, they know that if they are found they will be killed. But they must have food, and Joseph and his son go to find some. And now Rebecca's voice becomes filled with panic, for from their dark hiding-place she and Rachel can hear horses—coming nearer and nearer.

Bloxham: I expect your son and husband will be back soon?

Rebecca: Yes, they must be back, they must be back, we're worried, we're frightened—we can hear them [the mob] coming, we can hear the horses coming, we can hear the screaming and the shouting and the crying, "Burn the Jews, burn the Jews, burn the Jews." *(Pause)* Where is Joseph? Why doesn't he come back, why doesn't he come back? *(Pause, then almost screams.)* Oh, God—they're coming—they—they are coming—Rachel's crying—don't cry—don't cry—don't cry. (*Pause*) Aah, they've entered the church—we can hear them—they've entered the church—the priest is loose—the priest has got free—he has told them we are here—they're coming—they're coming down—the priest is free and they're coming down. *(Pause, and voice almost incoherent with terror.)* Oh, not—not not not Rachel! No, don't take her—don't—stop—they're going to kill her—they—don't—not Rachel, no, no, no, no—not Rachel—oh, don't take Rachel—no, don't take Rachel—no, no, no, no, no, don't take Rachel—no!

Bloxham *(shocked):* They're not going to take her, are they?

Rebecca *(grief-stricken voice):* They've taken Rachel—they've taken Rachel. ...

Bloxham: They are not going to harm you, are they? *(Silence)*

Bloxham: Are you all right? They have left you alone, have they?

Rebecca: Dark ... dark.[21]

Rebecca was dead.

Jane Evans walked out of Bloxham's office and fainted. Afterwards, she felt ill for days. Was this a fantasy? There is plenty of material available for fantasy in the twelfth century knights, crusaders, and castles. But watching your own eleven-year-old child murdered, and being murdered yourself in the dark crypt of a church? Jeffrey Iverson, who has written a book about the Bloxham tapes, gave the complete tape-recording of Rebecca's life and death to Barrie Dobson, a Professor of History at the University of York, who is an expert on this historical period. What was his reaction to the tape? After listening to it, he said that Rebecca's story was

> "true to what we know of the events and the times themselves." Much of the detail he found "impressively accurate," and some disputed points "could well have been true." A few aspects, he thought, would have been known only to professional historians.[22]

Professor Dobson is an expert on the topography of the medieval city of York. And the detail in Rebecca's narrative led him to the conclusion that there was only one church in York which could possibly have been the one in which Rebecca had hidden—St. Mary's, Castlegate. There was, however, a major difficulty with her account. *This church had no crypt.* In fact, none of York's medieval churches do, with the single exception of York Minster Cathedral, and she had insisted that she was not hiding there. If she could be completely wrong on such a major aspect of her story, then all of it—despite its amazing accuracy—must seem highly questionable. Somewhat disappointed, Iverson and Professor Dobson put "Rebecca" back on the shelf with the rest of Bloxham's tapes.

In the spring of 1975, workmen began turning St. Mary's Church, Castlegate, into a museum. And during the course of these renovations, one of them discovered something that was unknown to any living human being. *Beneath the altar lay a crypt.*

The gunner's mate

There is another aspect of the Bloxham tapes that is particularly interesting, and seems to be a standard feature of experiences under hypnotic regression—striking voice and character changes. Sometimes men and women who in their normal state are obviously well-educated and refined undergo the most remarkable transformations when regressed to a past life. Their speech becomes coarse and ungrammatical, and, in unrecognizable voices, they exhibit "a knowledge of slang and archaic terms and a general familiarity with life in the gutter of a bygone age that [is] simply astounding."[23] In one such case a well-educated Swansea man, regressed to the year 1800, suddenly began speaking in a coarse South of England accent. But it was *what this voice said* that was so gripping—a vivid account of the filth and degradation of life as a pressganged gunner aboard a British naval frigate. Earl Louis Mountbatten, former First Lord of the Admiralty, listened to the tape and was so fascinated that he asked Bloxham for a personal copy.

When Graham Huxtable met Arnall Bloxham in 1965, he was a cultivated, charming man with a soft, well-modulated voice, who did not believe in reincarnation. Agreeing to try a regression, he lay down in Bloxham's office and at the hypnotist's direction began to drift back in time. Suddenly, a remarkable transformation occurred. He began to speak in a voice utterly different from his own—a deep voice, with a strong country accent. And what the voice said was accented by coarse laughter and a hollow, tubercular cough. The "voice" claimed to be that of a gunner's mate in the British navy. It spoke archaic naval slang, some of it so obscure that it is incomprehensible to the modern ear and had to be translated by naval historians at the National Maritime Museum at Greenwich. Certain details on the tape enabled these historians to date the events described fairly precisely: they happened between 1803 and 1809.

The gunner's mate is on a British frigate, blockading French ports during the Napoleonic wars. Illiterate, dirty, and scarred from many battles, he wryly complains of navy life—of the stink of the ship, of weevils in the food and worms in the water tank. He had been captured by a press gang while still a lad, struck such a blow over the head that he complains of the pain of it still. It is before dawn, and the frigate waits off Calais, protected from the shore batteries by fog, so close in that he can hear the breakers. They wait for a French ship to try to run the blockade. It is growing light and the fog begins to lift. Huxtable's voice is tense. He ignores Bloxham's questions and shouts orders to his gun crew. And suddenly, as a French ship looms out of the thinning mist, his voice becomes a bellow.

Bloxham: Have you fired your cannon?
Huxtable: Waiting, waiting! Waiting for the order—steady, lads, steady—now hold it, hold it, hold it—wait for the order, wait for it … stand clear from behind—NOW, you fool. Now up, fool, now—NOW! *(Screams in exultation as the shot is fired.)* Well done, lads—run 'em up, run 'em up, get 'em up, get 'em up—get 'em up the front—*(shrieks)*—pull that man out, pull 'im out—send him in the cockpit—now get 'im back—get up there—get on the chocks there—run them up again! The shot in—ramrods—swab it, swab it, you fool, swab it first—the shot in, shot in—

> come on, number four, you should be up by now—shot in, ram it home—prime ... aye, aye, sir—ready! And again, lads—you had him then—hurry, men—by God, you bastard—got him that aim—that's the way to lay a gun. My Christ, they've got old Pearce, they've got Pearce—*(sudden terrible screaming)*—MY BLOODY LEG—*(screaming and moaning uncontrollably)*—MY LEG—MY LEG![24]

The cultivated, charming, soft-spoken Swansea man who did not believe in reincarnation was screaming in agony, his leg mangled or shot away by a nineteenth-century naval cannon-ball.

Bloxham was alarmed by Huxtable's anguish, but had difficulty bringing him out of the trance. He was forced to slap his face repeatedly to do so, reassuring him that his leg was all right. They were both so badly shaken that Bloxham never regressed him again.

Hypnotic regression and historical personalities

Memories of past lives may be conscious or unconscious, but the most convincing reports of either should contain the following features: First, they should involve a great deal of historical detail, which should, when researched, turn out to be correct. Secondly, it should be possible to prove that this historical detail was not already known to the present personality. If it were, then the regression could be a fantasy based on this knowledge and concocted under hypnosis. Thirdly, it is more convincing if the person whose life is described in the regression is completely obscure, and not someone so familiar to historians that books and articles have already been written about him. And finally, it should be possible to establish, through historical research, that this completely obscure personality from the past *actually did exist.*

In the case of *conscious* memories of past lives, all four criteria can often be met; a good deal of authentic detail about an obscure personality is often recalled. And the past personality can often be identified as well because only a few years have passed between the death of the first person and the birth of the second.

In the case of *unconscious* memories elicited by hypnosis, the first three criteria are almost always met—we are given historically authentic detail originating from an obscure personality. In fact, of some 1,500 past lives reported under hypnosis, nearly all concerned completely obscure individuals. But with the final criterion—proving that this obscure personality actually lived—we have a bit more trouble. In the case of hypnotically elicited memories, a lengthy period usually exists between the past death and the present birth. Although it can range from a few months to several centuries, it is, on the average, fifty-two years. Given the total obscurity of the personalities involved, historical records are usually too poor to permit identifications for periods seventy-five years or more in the past.

The case of Jonathan Powell

Despite these difficulties, however, hypnotist Loring Williams claims several tentative identifications. His best-documented case is that of Jonathan Powell. In 1965 Williams regressed a fifteen-year-old neighbor, George Field.

The boy, in a deep hypnotic trance, reported a life as an illiterate, reclusive farmer near a very small town called Jefferson, North Carolina. He claimed that he had been born in 1832 and was murdered in 1863 by renegade Civil War troops who wanted to buy his potatoes at an unreasonable price. Angry words were exchanged and they shot him in the stomach. Williams checked as many of the details of Jonathan's story as historical records permitted, and he turned out to know many highly obscure facts about the town and that part of the country during those times. Taken to Jefferson and hypnotized, the boy was questioned at length by a local historian. She was not disappointed. His knowledge of obscure local personalities of that time was astonishing. He knew about their financial status, their physical appearance, their children's names, and the location and appearance of their homes.

But no official record of Jonathan's existence could be found. Birth and death records were not kept in the area until 1912, half a century after Jonathan's death, and most property transfers of the time were not officially recorded. There was one clue, however. Jonathan had said that his grandmother was "Mary Powell," and Powell proved to be an uncommon name in the area. A property deed for 1803 showed that a Mary Powell had bought a parcel of land in that year. But that was the only scrap of information local records could yield, and on this intriguing but inconclusive note the effort to establish the existence of Jonathan Powell came to a dead end. Despite this, the case was an impressive one, and Williams wrote and published an article on it. [25]

Soon after the article appeared, George Field received a letter. It came from a woman whose maiden name had been Powell. She stated that she was a great-niece of Jonathan's and commented at length on details of Jonathan's life that had been passed down to her as part of her family's oral history. She wrote:

> Jonathan Powell was my great-uncle. He was killed by the Yankees.[26]

"Xenoglossy"

When people are hypnotically regressed, then, they talk about past lives which they claim to have lived. And sometimes they do more than just talk. They talk *in a foreign language which they do not speak in this life.* And it is not just a matter of the recitation, under hypnosis, of a few words or phrases they may have picked up. They can carry on a fluent conversation with speakers of that language. This phenomenon is technically known as "responsive xenoglossy."

Needless to say, the foreign language spoken perfectly fits the place in which the person claims to be living in his past life. It also fits the time—for in cases in which the language has been subjected to expert analysis, it turns out to be an *archaic* form. *It is being spoken as it was centuries ago.* It is remarkable enough suddenly to be able to speak a new language, but to speak an *archaic* form of it is more remarkable still. Additionally, these conversations often have a rather curious feature. The hypnotized person understands perfectly questions addressed to him in the language that he speaks in this life, and he can respond in this language. But he sometimes shows a *preference* for replying in the foreign tongue.

K.E., a Philadelphia doctor, occasionally made use of hypnosis in his general practice, and in 1955 began hypnotic experimentation with his thirty-seven-year-old wife, T.E. He discovered that she readily went into a deep trance and he began some age regression experiments with her. During one of these, she began speaking broken English in a deep masculine voice, and with what seemed a Scandinavian accent. This masculine personality identified himself as "Jensen Jacoby" and sometimes replied to questions in what sounded like a Scandinavian language. T.E. was regressed to this personality eight times, and at some of these sessions native speakers of Scandinavian languages were present, including Dr. Nils G. Sahlin, a native speaker of Swedish and former Director of the American Swedish Historical Museum in Philadelphia.

"Jensen" proved to understand modern Swedish, but himself spoke an archaic form of it. He described a life as a simple peasant farmer in Sweden centuries ago.

> He seemed to have little knowledge of his country beyond his own village and the trading center he visited. He had heard of English sailors landing.... He had heard of Russia and shared the common fear of Russians in Scandinavia. Apart from these scant references to international affairs, Jensen spoke only of the narrow round of life in his village, composed of hard work and simple sensuous diversions. According to Jensen's account of himself, he lived in a place called Mörby Hagar.... This seems to

> have been his name for the place where his house was, evidently a tiny village at most.... Some distance away—a day or two by horse—there was a town with a harbor called Haverö. Here Jensen took his produce for sale....
>
> Jensen ... venerated a "ruler" called Hansen. The latter may have been a local hero or chief. Several times Jensen described Hansen as "förste man" *(first man or chief).* In one session Jensen relived an incident occurring when he was sixty-two.... Engaged in some kind of fight with enemies, he waded into water (or was pushed into it) and then received a blow on the head which seems to have killed him.... Jensen showed an intense dislike of war. He delivered most of his answers to questions in a rather quiet voice.... But when an interpreter [interviewer who spoke Swedish] touched upon the subject of war, Jensen fairly shouted his disapproval.... Jensen also showed strong emotion in referring to his hero or chief, Hansen, the speaking of whose name he once accompanied by beating his own chest repeatedly and vigorously with both fists.[27]

During another session, Jensen was asked to open his eyes and look at a number of objects and pictures, some borrowed from the American Swedish Historical Museum in Philadelphia. He was asked to identify them. Dr. Sahlin comments:

> There were innumerable indications that Jensen was totally unacquainted with modern articles. On the other hand, he showed immediate familiarity with ... things dating back to and before the seventeenth century.... While Jensen ... understood modern Swedish ... without difficulty, he had no modern vocabulary, no words for things of exclusively modern date.[28]

Ten scholars of the Swedish language examined transcripts of the tape-recorded, Swedish-speaking sessions with Jensen.[29] *The consensus was that Jensen was a seventeenth-century Swedish peasant farmer who lived in southwestern Sweden near the Norwegian border.*

The Philadelphia housewife was speaking in a voice three hundred years old!

Could she have "faked" it? Could this be some kind of fraud? Dr. Ian Stevenson conducted a scrupulously careful investigation of T.E.'s background. It took him some six years to complete. And he proved conclusively that T.E. knew nothing whatever of any Scandinavian language, much less seventeenth-century peasant Swedish!

Large-scale research support for reincarnation

Dr. Ian Stevenson has proven that reincarnation *does happen*—that *there are people alive today who once died.* And the regressions of hypnotists like Arnall Bloxham and Loring Williams *suggest* that the Stevenson cases are more than mere oddities, and that many people—perhaps most—have in fact reincarnated and can remember past existences. But it is the data derived from Dr. Helen Wambach's regressions of over 1,000 people to some 1,100 past lives which proves, beyond any reasonable doubt, that we have all lived before.

One extremely consistent and very impressive finding emerges from the massive collection of data gathered by Dr. Wambach. In every respect, we get exactly what we should if people were actually recalling lives they had in fact lived in the past, rather than simply inventing fantasies based on normal sources of knowledge like books and movies. And as we are about to see, the detail in support of this statement is so intricate and so consistent that it simply cannot be explained away as mere fantasy.

Dr. Wambach reasoned that no matter how convincing an individual regression might be, it could not produce the most valid proof of reincarnation. One could not rule out the possibility that what the person produced was a fantasy-life based on normally-acquired knowledge of a particular time and place. But if, on the other hand, she were to regress hundreds of people into the past, and hundreds claimed, when regressed, to have had a life in a particular time and place, with all consistently reporting the same obscure details of daily life, then this result would indeed be difficult to explain away as a fantasy. How could 100 people possibly have the *same* fantasy?

Dr. Wambach therefore began experimenting with groups of people, hypnotizing them simultaneously, and, once that was done, sending them back to particular times and places. Two basic techniques were used, a temporal and a geographical one. She would offer her hypnotized subjects a choice of dates from the past, and ask them to choose the one for which they got the most vivid imagery. Or she would ask them to visualize a map of the earth and tell them that they would feel themselves especially drawn to a certain place. They would then be asked a series of questions about the particular life they were experiencing.

> I set up a series of questions that would help locate my subjects, and would also serve as a check on the validity of their recall. I asked them to see the color of their skin, whether their hair was curly or straight and what its color was, and I asked them about the landscape and climate they found themselves in. My purpose was to see if they were of the appropriate race for the place they had chosen, and whether the landscape and climate corresponded to what we know of the area.
>
> I wanted to get information of the kind I could check in archeological texts and historical records. I asked my subjects to visualize the food they were eating ... because there are many records of the kinds of foodstuffs eaten in each time period and place. I also asked them to see the eating utensil and other household objects they were using, because this too could be checked.
>
> I decided to ask my subjects to go to a market to get supplies and to describe the market and the supplies that they bought. Money is also a clue to a place and time in the past, so I asked them to visualize the money they might have exchanged for goods.
>
> Other areas that could be checked were the architecture they saw and the kind of clothing and footgear they wore. Not only

> could I see whether the clothing they described was accurate according to historical texts, but I could tell whether other subjects in the same time period and in the same place wore similar types of clothing.[30]

And this method succeeded beyond her wildest dreams.

No Caesars, and no Cleopatras

Most of the people who lived and died in the past have been obscure persons who led extremely humble lives. Critics of reincarnation have often claimed that people supposedly having memories of past lives are simply fantasizing about life as an historically prominent person. In fact, nothing could be further from the truth. In Dr. Wambach's 1,100 lives, we simply do not meet Caesar, Cleopatra, Henry the Eighth, George Washington, or, in fact, anybody of historical importance. That statement does have to be slightly qualified; there was *one.* A woman described a life in which she had been James Buchanan, fifteenth president of the United States, during the years 1857-61. In fact, she provided some exceedingly obscure details of his life which lent a good deal of authenticity to her claim. And there were a few people who claimed to have been kings or rulers who were not absolutely unknown to history, but they were obscure rulers in rather remote societies; not at all the sorts of people about whom historical romances are written.

But with the exception of this tiny handful of persons, the overwhelming majority of the lives reported from the past were those of simple peasants, who led lives of extreme hardship, filled with unremitting toil, and maintained by a diet of the utmost dullness. And, in fact, a good many of them commented afterwards on how hard and restricted these lives were; the contrast with the relative luxury and openness of their present lives was dramatic. Lovers of hamburgers and fries, rare roast beef, and pork chops smothered in mushroom gravy were more than a trifle astounded to have found themselves living in wretched huts and sustaining themselves on ground acorns and cereal grains mixed to a mush with water. This extremely rudimentary diet was reported to be enlivened by the occasional greasy rodent.

Dr. Wambach's subjects described very restricted lives, close to the soil and focused within small local groups. They usually had little or no knowledge of anything beyond their own communities, and the biggest event of their lives was the arrival of strangers. They also reported a great many deaths as infants, which is in fact exactly what did happen, though it is hardly the sort of life that one would be likely to fantasize. As Dr. Wambach put it:

> Among my subjects, I find that hardly anybody is anybody! I have discovered that the vast majority of people were in their past lives so unlettered and so out of touch with what is recorded in the history books that I couldn't even tell when they were alive unless I suggested a time period. If I regressed them to the year 1600, say, and determined that they were in England and asked who was king, they wouldn't have the faintest notion and couldn't care less. I generally found that if I attempted to find out who was pope or what great battles had taken place—great historical events and that sort of thing—these matters were of no concern to them. They lived in their own little circles and were indifferent to people or events that were beyond their ken.[31]

And further surprises were in store. Two of the most basic aspects of identity are one's sex and race. Research done on North Americans has shown that most people, if given a choice, would prefer to be white males. Therefore if reported "past lives" are the product of fantasy, we would expect lives as white males to predominate. But they don't. Although most of Dr. Wambach's subjects were white, *a great many reported past lives as members of races and sexes other than their own.* It is a biological fact that, throughout human history, approximately half of the population has been male, and half female.

Therefore, if regressions really do reflect historical reality, we would expect to get roughly a fifty-fifty split between male and female lives for any reasonably-sized sample of regressed subjects. And in fact exactly this has proven to be the case! Of 1,100 past lives reported, 49.4 percent were as women, and 50.6 percent as men.

Dr. Wambach's first sample group of regressed subjects was 78 percent female:

> *Regardless of the sex they had had in the current lifetime, when regressed to the past, my subjects split neatly and evenly into 50.3 percent male and 49.7 percent female lives.* When this finding emerged in my first sample group, I wanted very much to see if it would prove to be true in another sample group. It could be that 28 percent of my female subjects preferred to think of themselves as male, and that was why I had gotten the 50-50 ratio. So in my second sample group of three hundred cases, I had a much closer ratio of males to females in their here-and-now lives; 45 percent of my subjects were male in the second sample, and 55 percent female. But when I regressed them I once again found the virtual 50-50 split—this time, 50.9 percent male and 49.1 percent female. *This result, I feel, is the strongest objective evidence I have yet discovered that when people are hypnotized and taken to past lives, they are tapping some real knowledge of the past.*[32]

When hypnotized and regressed, people simply don't report the kinds of lives that make any sense at all as wish-fulfilling fantasies. For example, when Dr. Wambach began her regression research, she took her first few dozen subjects back to several past existences. "Betty" was a typical subject. Regressed to the 1400s, she reported a life as a male, a poor Pakistani native.

> Out hunting one day, [he] was attacked by a wild boar, which injured his leg and crippled him. Since his family was too poor to support a cripple, he became a beggar and died of starvation

> several years later. In this lifetime, Betty's ... facial expressions and bodily movements were quite striking. When she went to the time of the boar's attack she grimaced and pulled her leg up awkwardly. Throughout the rest of this regression, she held her leg in this painful, contorted position.

In a later life, Betty was a fifteen-year-old girl in England in the 1600s.

> She was despondent because she had just escaped from a fire that destroyed her home and that of many others.... Because all other members of her family died in the fire, she was apprenticed to a tavern keeper, and thereafter led a very difficult life as a barmaid. Although her personality as a feisty wench who fought for herself came through, she was repeatedly abused and mistreated, and eventually died, very painfully, after being raped and beaten by several drunken men.
>
> Betty experienced considerable emotion ... after she came out of the hypnotic session. "You know, I smelled the alcohol on those men," she said. "And I felt the same feeling that I've had in this life.... I've always been unusually afraid of people who are drinking. Now I feel I understand why. It's because I died at the hands of drunken men."

Regressed to 1902, Betty reported that she "saw trees."

> It turned out that she was a young infant strapped in a leather carrying basket, propped up next to a tree. However, when I progressed her to 1903, she was no longer alive. Realizing she had died, I took her to the death experience. I asked her to see a map that would pinpoint the place where she had lived that life. It was Florida that she saw, and she became aware that she had been born into a Seminole Indian tribe.[33]

In none of these three lives is there any evidence of wish-fulfilling fantasy—a crippled beggar who starves to death, a barmaid who is raped and beaten and dies painfully as a result, and an infant who dies after a very brief period of life. These lives bear the stamp of historical authenticity more than of fantasy.

If any theme comes through clearly in Dr. Wambach's regressions it is the absolute ordinariness of these lives and deaths. A young woman named Frances was regressed to the 1700s. To her great surprise, she found herself wearing obviously masculine boots.

> Then, when I looked at my clothes and my hands, I realized that I was a man. I seemed to be some kind of laborer, because there was mud on my boots and my clothing was rough. My hands were calloused and work-worn. I was standing in a plowed field, but could see a small hut in the distance. Apparently, this was where I lived, because I found myself eating my evening meal in this small dark hut. I ate with a wooden spoon from a wooden bowl.... [My] death ... was some kind of accident with horses.... it happened very fast, and I was out of my body before I seemed to know what had happened.... I was glad that that lifetime was over. It was a hard ... life. The date of my death flashed as 1721, and the place where I lived was around Arles, France.[34]

A young man named Peter, when regressed to the ninth century, found himself in Italy.

> It was northern Italy.... I saw some high mountains in the distance. I was working with a pitchfork in a countryside setting. I was short and stout, with stubby little hands. I died fairly young ... it was some kind of disease. Dying ... I seemed to leave my body ... and ... floated over this small dark hut, where my body lay.[35]

Two subjects, Janet and Lynn, were regressed to 1,000 B.C. Janet experienced herself as a woman, a member of a primitive Asian tribe.

> Her home was a kind of dugout on the side of a hill. In her mature life, she found herself scraping hides. She died in childbirth. "I certainly was glad to leave that lifetime," she said. "I can smell the hides even now … I would have thought primitive life would be fun, but that life was hard. I was … glad to die and leave it."[36]

Lynn, too, was a woman in Asia at that time.

> She lived on a flat plain near the sea: "There were a lot of buildings where I lived. They were flat-roofed and made of some sort of mud construction, like bricks. In my mature life I mostly seemed to cook some sort of grain and take care of my family. I died of old age."[37]

These lives don't sound like fantasy. What they sound like is reality.

The Wambach regressions are filled with the most striking agreements among subjects who went to the same time and place. A young woman was regressed to 25 A.D. and found herself a male in northern Italy close to the Adriatic Sea. She was a carpenter of some kind, working with wood and tools. She found herself purchasing supplies with a very odd coin:

> **Subject:** "[It] was dark gray and had a hole in the middle. It seemed to be shaped like a square with the corners pounded to try to make it look round. I've never seen anything like it!"
> **Dr. Wambach:** "Did it seem to be crude around the edges?"
> **Subject:** "Yes, as though it had been hammered rather than molded."
> **Dr. Wambach:** "I've had that coin described to me at least twenty times before. It was used around the Mediterranean Sea in the time period 500 B.C. to 25 A.D."[38]

This is certainly extraordinary. Twenty-one people, at different times and in different groups, went to the same place and time period and all found themselves using the same peculiar coin.

Five of her subjects, regressed in different groups and at different times, described lives between 2,000 and 1,000 B.C. in a region near the Caucasus Mountains north of Iran and toward Pakistan, in what is now Russia. All of them described it as mountainous and barren.

> [They] were apparently nomadic, and described tents and lean-tos rather than buildings ... all five expressed surprise when they looked down at their hands and found that their skin was white. Three described their hair as light brown, and two as blond. Three ... had written on their data sheets, "This doesn't seem right to me. I was surprised when the map flashed on [central] Asia ... I think I should have had tan skin and dark hair."
>
> All five ... described themselves as wearing some kind of leather pants. Trousers were unusual in the regressions in the earliest time periods; only in this region did my subjects see themselves wearing pants. I researched the costumes worn at that time, and found an illustration of Scythians and Parthians clad in leather trousers. Furthermore, the population of this region was made up of the original Caucasians, and did have white skin and fair hair. So in these instances in which my subjects felt that their data were wrong, according to their own view of history, research showed that their unconscious had presented them with a more accurate picture of life in the Caucasus Mountains in 2,000 B.C. than their conscious awareness.
>
> This was to happen again and again as I checked the data on individual cases, and to me, it was the most evidential of all the material I collected in my research. If past-life recall is fantasy, one would expect our conscious knowledge of history to provide the images. When the images contrast with what we believe to be true, and yet prove on careful study to be accurate, then we must look anew at the concept of past-life recall as fantasy.[39]

It would be difficult indeed to imagine a stronger validation of the claim that past-life recall under hypnosis is genuine. Consider the example of a woman who was regressed to 1200, and saw herself as a knight:

> "I thought to myself that this was really trite and must be a fantasy," she reported...."I looked down at my feet and saw a triangular toeplate. I thought to myself that it should be round, like the armor I had seen in museums."[40]

In that life the subject found herself in Italy, and experienced herself as dying in 1254. Some research on the history of armor turned up something of great interest: triangular toeplates had existed—but only in Italy and only until the year 1280!

Some of Dr. Wambach's subjects turned out to have had a previous life in the twentieth century, and to have died in bombing raids in World War II. Many of these claimed to have died, not directly from the explosion of the bomb, but from smoke inhalation. Trapped in the rubble, they were asphyxiated, they said, by smoke from the fire the bomb started. *The truth is that this claim corresponds exactly with known facts concerning World War II bombing casualties. And it is one of those significant details that seems highly unlikely to be the product of fantasy.*

Such striking agreement among subjects who claimed to be living at the same time and place characterized all of her data for the entire 4,000-year time span which she investigated—from 2,000 B.C. until the twentieth century. Dr. Wambach was careful to ask each subject several standardized questions concerning his style of life. These questions later enabled her to classify reported past lives as upper, middle, or lower class for each time period. Upper class lives were in a small minority in every time period, never exceeding 10 percent. Middle class lives varied in frequency, depending upon the general level of civilization, and lower class lives as slaves or peasants were always in the majority, ranging from a low of 60 to a high of 77 percent. The consistency of these social class levels was striking. Such statistics make it dramatically clear that an objective reality, and not a subjective fantasy, is being reported.

Don't population statistics disprove reincarnation?

Reincarnation requires human bodies. If these don't exist, then reincarnation quite obviously cannot occur. And hasn't the world's population increased enormously over the centuries? It certainly has. Scholars of human population trends estimate that the world's population doubled between the first century A.D. and 1500, doubled again by the nineteenth century, and has since quadrupled. Therefore, isn't reincarnation impossible?

This is certainly a very powerful argument against reincarnation. Since Dr. Wambach asked her 1,100 subjects to specify the time-period to which they were regressing, were any "population trends" apparent in their choices? Indeed they were. And these trends display precisely what we would expect to find if reincarnation actually does occur: Dr. Wambach's subjects chose to be born into different time periods with a frequency which precisely paralleled scholars' estimates of the size of the human population at those times. Their past-life choices double from the first century to 1500, double again by the nineteenth century, and quadruple from then until the twentieth. In other words, reincarnation is entirely dependent on the availability of human bodies, and if we were to regress individual human beings from the present back, generation by generation, to the first century, they would report many lives when the population was large and few when it was small.

Therefore, no contradiction of any kind exists between the regression data and world population statistics.

Who are you?

The regression data open up some stupendous possibilities, possibilities which will be profoundly shocking to most of us, who have been absolutely convinced by our experience in this life that we belong to one sex, one race, one social level, one nationality, and one ethnic group. For the regression data make it apparent that most of us have been, at different times, both men and women, black, white, yellow and brown, rich and poor, and a variety of nationalities and ethnicities. When individuals are regressed through a succession of lives (and this has been done with only a small sample), these lives are extremely varied with respect to sex, race, social level, and ethnic group. For example, Dr. Wambach says:

> Some were fairly wealthy in past lives, but the rich ones are not rich in their next lives. Often they are very poor. If they were important in one life, they didn't stay that way.[41]

One of her subjects, for instance, a woman in her present life, was in the 1400s a male athlete in Central America, who died at age 40; then a black male native of New Guinea in the 1500s who died young; a middle-class Venetian housewife who was born in 1540 and died in old age; a woman who lived in Normandy in the early eighteenth century and was a servant in a tavern or inn; a redheaded boy who lived in the eastern United States in the early nineteenth century and died at age eight of smallpox, and, between 1888 and 1916, a Norwegian seaman who died of an unspecified disease at the age of 28. No effort was made to make a complete inventory of her lives; these are probably only a few of them.

Another subject, a San Francisco businessman, spontaneously regressed to fourteen past lives. In 2,000 B.C. he was an Egyptian priest whose responsibilities were commercial—the administration of trade with neighboring peoples—rather than religious. His next reported life was in 1300 B.C. when he was again male, a lowly Egyptian cart driver. Drifting next to 400 B.C., he was again in Egypt, this time as a woman from a merchant family, who was involved in court intrigue. She was coldly materialistic and unsuccessful in her schemes to obtain great wealth, and committed suicide. He was after that a cheesemaker and trader in western Lebanon, and a Greek orphan in 100 A.D. who had a homosexual relationship with a Roman governor and died young of a disease. He did not spontaneously go to any lives between that one and his next in 1300 A.D., when he was a woman living in a primitive village in Central America, who died of a fever at twenty-eight. In 1450 he was again a woman living in modest circumstances in a Portuguese town; she too died young. In the 1500s he reported a cold and unsatisfying life as an Italian nobleman. From 1590 to 1618 he was a Welsh girl who died in childbirth; next, he was a male French peasant whose most treasured possession was a wooden spoon; an eighteenth-century English merchant who prospered trading in wool; and a nineteenth-century Egyptian cotton-mill supervisor who died of a heart attack at sixty in the year 1870. Within four months he was reborn as an urchin who hung around the London docks living by his wits. He was befriended by a sea captain and became a sailor on his vessel from the age of eleven. His next life was as a female who was born in Baltimore, Maryland in 1900 and died there in 1902. When asked why he had died so young, he said something of great interest which Dr. Wambach later followed up with systematic research:

> "I seemed to know after I'd been born that I'd chosen the wrong parents," he replied. "Apparently, I knew this wouldn't work out well, so I just left."[42]

In his present life, he was born in California in 1930.

What are we to make of such a bewilderingly varied life-experience? Was there a developmental process linking these lives? As we will shortly see, a process of some sort can be found. At the very least, we can see powerful evidence of a claim sometimes made by discarnate communicators that the purpose of human life is to "learn" by acquiring highly varied experiences in all kinds of times, societies, and bodies. And from this there emerges one clear revelation, a revelation which, were it taken seriously, would introduce some profoundly new dimensions into human relationships. Human identity, and human animosities, are based on fundamental distinctions—of sex, of class, of religion, of nationality, of ethnicity. But regressions make it clear that we ourselves have been, or will be, all of that which we now are not, and even that which we now despise and hate. What could be more profoundly educational than to express, in one life, hatred and contempt for others different from oneself, and to then return, in a later life, as a member of the despised group, to endure that same hatred and contempt? Such considerations bring us to the ancient doctrine of *karma*.

Past life research and the doctrine of karma

The doctrine of karma is a simple one. It holds that, through reincarnation, all human beings will eventually learn the "golden rule" the hard way: that injury and evil done to others will be atoned for by personal suffering in subsequent lives, while love and compassion shown to others will "return" as personal fulfillment.

The emphasis of this book has been empirical: it has concentrated upon actual human experiences which seem to illuminate the immense mysteries of life and death. Are there any human experiences, then, which are relevant to an assessment of the doctrine of karma? Some such research does exist, and it is enough to support the beginning of just such an assessment. It stems from three sources: the hypnotic regressions of Loring Williams and Dr. Helen Wambach, and the "life readings" of the remarkable American clairvoyant, Edgar Cayce.

Loring Williams

Williams, a hypnotist who has regressed many people, has some definite opinions about karma, based on those regressions. In a conversation with the writer Brad Steiger, he said:

> Karma is difficult to pin down unless you know a lot about your subject's background and you are able to obtain … a good many regressions from the same subject. In those cases where I have known something of my subject's history … and have been able

> to get good detail on several of his past lives, I have seen a definite pattern of Karma.[43]

Williams went on to illustrate his case by citing a regression which he had recently performed. A woman, regressed to 1800, claimed to be a governess in France.

> In that capacity she managed to meet and marry a wealthy older man. She was very selfish and obsessed by money, jewels, servants and power. She devoted many years to making her elderly husband just as miserable as possible, and she was delighted when he finally died and left her in control of the property and money.
>
> She was a tyrant in dealing with her servants, so much so, in fact, that she was finally murdered by one of her maids, who refused to be so thoroughly demeaned. This woman's present life has strongly borne out the Karma concept. The youngest of several girls, she was born into a very poor family. She was brought up with little money or luxuries. For some unexplainable reason, her mother and her sisters abused her. One of her sisters told me, "Poor Gloria spent her childhood crying. I don't know why, but we were always so mean to her. Even when she was a teenager there seemed to be an unspoken household conspiracy to give her the dirtiest jobs and to make her life miserable."
>
> It seems that this woman was receiving from everyone in this life the same treatment she had dealt to others in the previous life experience.

Was a person like Gloria, in his experience, doomed to persecution throughout all of a subsequent life? Not necessarily, it appears.

> When this girl grew up she was able to adjust emotionally and her family attitude changed. She is now … happily married … one seems to have the opportunity to overcome, or to adjust, to the conditions into which he is born. If he [does this success-

> fully] there will be a corresponding improvement in the conditions into which he is born next time. In some cases, like that of Gloria, one begins to reap the harvest of his adjustment in the present life.[44]

These are intriguing ideas: their implications are fascinating. Regrettably, Williams does not document them very thoroughly in his published work, although he clearly implies that they are based on much data which he does not reveal.

Edgar Cayce

Edgar Cayce was born in 1877 on a farm near Hopkinsville, Kentucky. Leaving school at the end of the ninth grade, he worked as a bookstore clerk and then as an insurance salesman. But an odd ailment brought his career as a salesman to an end. He lost his voice to laryngitis, and the condition proved impervious to medical treatment. Cayce had been mute for a year when a traveling hypnotist named Hart came to Hopkinsville. When Hart learned of Cayce's ailment, he offered to treat the young man hypnotically. Under hypnosis, Cayce's normal voice returned, only to disappear again when he resumed normal consciousness. At this point a local man named Layne, who had studied hypnosis, took an interest in the case, and made an unorthodox suggestion—that, under hypnosis, Cayce diagnose his own condition. The results were remarkable. The uneducated farm boy spoke, under hypnosis, like a professor of medicine.

> "Yes," he began, "We can see the body.... In the normal state, this body is unable to speak, because of a partial paralysis of the inferior muscles of the vocal cords, produced by nerve strain. This is a psychological condition producing a physical effect. It may be removed by increasing the circulation to the affected

> parts by suggestion while in the unconscious condition."
>
> Layne promptly suggested to Cayce that his circulation would increase to the affected parts and the condition would be alleviated. Gradually Cayce's upper chest and then his throat began to turn pink—then rose—then a violent red. After about twenty minutes the [hypnotized Cayce] cleared his throat and said: "It's all right now. The condition is removed. Make the suggestion that the circulation return to normal and that after that, the body awaken." Layne gave the suggestion as directed; Cayce awoke, and began to speak normally for the first time in more than a year. In the following months he experienced occasional relapses. Each time Layne made the same suggestion with regard to circulation, and each time the condition was removed.[45]

Cayce, of course, was overjoyed to have his voice back, and simply wished to resume his normal life. And he would have, had it not been for Layne. But the hypnotist realized that if Cayce could give himself such an extraordinary diagnosis and cure under hypnosis, he might be able to do the same for others. Reluctantly, Cayce agreed to try the experiment on Layne himself, who had been ill for some time with a stomach ailment. What happened was precisely what had happened before. Under hypnosis, Cayce diagnosed the illness and prescribed for Layne a rather unorthodox treatment of drugs, diet, and exercises. The diagnosis perfectly matched Layne's symptoms and what his doctors had told him, and the treatment did something which theirs had not—it worked. Within a few weeks, Layne was feeling better. Word of Cayce's unusual medical gifts spread, and finally he was diagnosing and treating, in hypnotic trance, the illnesses of hundreds of people, often those whom orthodox medicine had been unable to help. Although in his normal state he knew nothing whatever of medicine, in trance his diagnoses showed deep medical knowledge, and the treatments he prescribed were astonishingly effective:

> A Catholic priest in Canada was healed of epilepsy; a young high-school graduate of Dayton, Ohio, was relieved of a severe case of arthritis; a New York dentist was relieved in two weeks of a migraine headache that had been tormenting him for two years; a young woman musician of Kentucky, given up as a hopeless case by a famous Tennessee clinic, was cured in a year of the strange malady called scleroderma; a boy in Philadelphia, born with infant glaucoma (commonly regarded as incurable), gained normal eyesight under treatment from a doctor who followed the instructions given by Cayce.[46]

For over twenty years—from 1901 to 1923—Cayce dealt in trance with the medical problems of thousands. And then, one October afternoon in 1923, his clairvoyant powers were turned in a dramatically different direction. Arthur Lammers, a wealthy Ohio printer, was convinced that Cayce's clairvoyance could be directed to more significant matters than the functioning of the human body. Perhaps Cayce could also find the answers to some intriguing questions of a non-medical nature. Lammers had recently become interested in astrology. He wanted to know if there was anything in it. Would Cayce go into trance and give Lammers's horoscope? He agreed to try. The entranced Cayce declared, in response to Lammers's eager questions, that astrology, as currently practiced, did have some validity, and he went on to discuss it in a series of cryptic sentences. And then, almost at the end of this discussion, Edgar Cayce casually said something about Lammers. He said: "He was once a monk." Lammers was electrified by this statement. Was Cayce referring to reincarnation? Did he mean that that ancient theory was actually true? Subsequent trance interrogations made it crystal clear: the answer was "yes!"

According to Cayce, human embodiment was necessary for spiritual growth; eventually, sufficient growth was attained, through repeated incarnations, that a human body was no longer necessary to the developing soul and physical life on earth could come to an end.

At this point, higher possibilities awaited the soul in non-physical realms. Reincarnation, he said, was governed by the law of karma. Evil had to be expiated, and good returned in more richly fulfilling lives. And he sometimes implied that the larger "conscience" of the self had much to do with the operation of karma; in the between-lives period, the self could see what it must expiate, and would feel compelled to arrange appropriate penance for itself.

Lammers was enthralled by these revelations, and persuaded the reluctant Cayce to give him the first of a very different kind of reading which later became known as a "life" reading, to distinguish it from the original "physical" reading concerned with medical problems. "Life" readings focused upon the influence of past lives on the present one and discussed in detail the operation of karma as it applied to individual lives. When word about these exotic new readings got out, Cayce was deluged with requests for them. He gave 2,500 before his death in 1945. They contain many hundreds of examples of what Cayce claimed were karmic effects, or influences from past lives operating in the present one. Because most of those who came to Cayce were troubled people seeking help, we have many more examples of negative, expiatory karma in the life readings than of positive effects from the past.

Cayce claimed that he got much of his information on people's past lives from deeply-buried memories which lay in their subconscious minds: he was tapping the same source, in other words, as regression hypnosis!

But, he was asked, wouldn't a belief in karma lead to a fatalistic philosophy? If people "needed" to suffer for karmic reasons, then what justification was there for any effort to aid people in a less fortunate state than oneself? Cayce was quite explicit in his answer. He said that those who needed expiation through suffering for that which they had imposed on others would arrange to be born into a time and place where they would receive it. But, he added, their suffering was also an opportunity for the personal growth of others in more fortunate karmic circumstances. If the more karmically advantaged were foolish enough to abuse their positions by either ignoring or actively exploiting those in a less karmically favorable position, then they were doing something which would have to be paid for in later lives. Karmically determined misfortune and affliction thus offered opportunities both to those who appeared to be their victims and to those who were not. There was therefore no justification whatever, he said, for not trying to relieve human suffering.

Readers who are tempted to dismiss such statements as nonsense should remember that Cayce's clairvoyant powers on medical matters have been validated by all those who have investigated them. Perhaps, therefore, we should not too hastily dismiss his comments on other aspects of human existence!

Cayce also claimed that karma operated in various ways, and that its effects could be both physical and psychological. He implied that unwarranted negativity toward others—such as physical or psychological cruelty—must always be expiated. The cruelty of mockery and contemptuous disparagement of others, for example, was an ignoble form of self-assertion, for no selfhood is intrinsically superior to any other, and claims to the contrary must be "paid for." Consider the case of an eighteen-year-old girl who would have been attractive were it not for her gross obesity.

> Doctors diagnosed the condition as overactivity of the pituitary gland. The Cayce physical reading concurred in calling it a glandular condition, but ... the information is given that the glands themselves are focal points for the expression of the heredity of the psyche, or its karma ... this girl's glandular condition and her ... excess weight were karmic in origin.... Two lifetimes ago she had been an athlete ... [who] excelled both in beauty and in athletic prowess, but frequently ridiculed those who were less nimble than herself because of their heaviness of body.[47]

This prolonged mockery of others created a karmic condition whereby she had to endure herself what she had ridiculed in others.

In another example of a similar karmic process, a young man suffered from a marked homosexual urge which distressed him intensely and became the central problem of his life.

> The life reading taken on this young man at his request shows him to have been in a previous life a satirist and gossipmonger ... who took particular delight in exposing ... homosexual scandals ... with his cartoonist skill. "Condemn not, then," concludes the reading, "that you be not condemned. For indeed, with what measure you mete it shall be measured to you.... *And what you condemn in another, that you become in yourself.*"[48]

However peculiar such statements may seem, it must be admitted that, if they are true, it would be difficult to imagine a more dramatically effective form of education in equality and human compassion—you must become, and endure, what you yourself condemn and torment. Intolerance of others, it seems, is a karmically dangerous business.

Consider Cayce's reading for a young boy of eleven who had been a chronic bed-wetter from the age of two. Cayce's diagnosis and cure were as fascinating as they were bizarre. Nightly bed-wetting had led the parents to consult a psychiatrist when the boy was three, but in vain. The bed-wetting persisted, without a break, for the next five years. The boy was now eight, and psychiatric help was again sought, but again it failed to solve the problem.

> When the boy was eleven, the parents heard of the work of Edgar Cayce, and the father determined to obtain a reading on the peculiar case of his son. According to the boy's life reading, in the life previous to the present he had been a minister of the gospel in early Puritan days, at the time of the witchcraft trials; he had been active in punishing supposed witches by ducking them, on a stool, into a pond [a conventional punishment of the time for suspected witches].[49]

This provided the germ of a karmic explanation, but in addition, Cayce prescribed a cure. He instructed the parents, just before the boy went to sleep, to convey a certain message to him, based on the karmic nature of the case. That night the boy's mother put Cayce's prescription into effect. She waited at his bedside until he was almost asleep. And then, in a slow, calm voice, she began to repeat these words:

> "You are good and kind. You are going to make many people happy. You are going to help everyone with whom you come in contact.... You are good and kind...." The same idea was expressed in various forms for perhaps five or ten minutes to the now sleeping boy.
>
> That night, for the first time in almost nine years, the boy did not wet the bed. For several months the mother continued the suggestions, always in the same vein; not once, in that period, did the condition recur. Gradually she found it possible to give the suggestion only once a week; and finally not even that was necessary. The boy was completely cured.
>
> The suggestion which proved so efficacious mentioned nothing about not wetting the bed. It was not directed to the boy's physical consciousness at all, but rather to what might be called his spiritual consciousness ... to the consciousness of guilt which he carried over from his Salem incarnation, and which had been symbolically expressed ... [by] his own body. He once ducked others ... now he felt ... the need for retribution upon himself.
>
> Though in this life the child had not harmed anyone, a certain stratum of his mind still doubted his own kindness, his own social acceptability, because of the persistent memory of the cruel punishment he had once inflicted upon others. The suggestion reached that particular stratum, reassured him that his guilt ... could be expiated through social service and kindness, and ... erased the necessity for further symbolic retribution.[50]

And this fascinating karmic pattem had another aspect to it. By the time the boy was an adolescent, both parents had noted that one of his most marked personality traits was a great tolerance of others. For any character flaw pointed out in others, he would gently offer some justification, would say something redeeming of that person. The cruel righteousness of the Puritan clergyman had been completely transformed.

It would be no overstatement to say that the message of the Cayce readings is an immensely chastening one, and to add that, if it were to be taken seriously, its effect upon human conduct could scarcely be more profound.

Helen Wambach

Loring Williams gathered his evidence for karma by inference: past-life conduct reported by his subjects in a regression was later seen to be logically related, in an apparently karmic way, to their present life conditions. Edgar Cayce claimed to obtain his knowledge of karma from clairvoyant access to the subconscious minds of his subjects. Early in her research, Helen Wambach regressed a young man to a life in which he had died at the age of two. While he was still under hypnosis, she asked him why. His reply provided the idea for an entirely new aspect of regression research. He said he had realized he'd chosen the wrong parents, so he had just "left"—died.

This comment opened up some fascinating possibilities—could it be that people actually "chose" the life they were to lead, and that, in the deep levels of the subconscious, they retained the knowledge of how this choice had been made? Could it be that people actually carried with them the knowledge of why they were here on earth, and that this knowledge could be tapped in hypnosis? She decided to find out. She began hypnotizing subjects and asking them how they got into the particular body in which they found themselves. To her amazement, they answered her!

If people are asked, in their normal state of consciousness, why they were born and why they find themselves here on earth in a body, most will have no idea of the answer and many will find the question itself absurd. But when they are hypnotized and asked such questions, they respond in a dramatically different way. They give answers. They appear to "know"!

"Did you choose to be born?"
"*Yes, I chose.*"
"Did anyone help you choose?"
"Lots of beings helped, but ... I had to make the choice."
"How do you feel about the prospect of being born into another lifetime?"
"*I feel—sort of resigned.*"[51]

This is the voice of a regressed subject, who has been taken back in time to the period between his last death and his present birth. He's being asked to explain how he got into his present body. In a preliminary study, Dr. Wambach found that 38 percent of her subjects could not answer such questions. They "lost" her during the hypnosis and drifted into a sleep-like state, or they simply received no answers when such questions were put to them. She speculates that such subjects are similar to those who went "blank" and got nothing on past lives because they had suffered a recent, traumatic death. They receive no answers, she thinks, because their subconscious minds don't think they are "ready" for them. For those who are ready, however, karmic factors turn out to play a large role in their present lives.

Dr. Wambach talked to four hundred and two regressed and hypnotized subjects about the processes that had led to their current lives. And, like the well-disciplined scientist that she is, she condensed the results of those conversations into statistics. But these are not the usual cut-and-dried statistics of scientific research. They are statistics to make the head spin.

Did you choose to be born?

Five percent said that they had not, that they simply found themselves in a fetus, being born. The other 95 percent stated that they had "chosen" their current lifetime.

> The great majority ... said that they made their decision to be born on the basis of counseling by other entities during the between-life period. They were sometimes described as teachers, guides or gurus, but more often reported as friends and a group of kindred spirits. One ... reported: "There's a large group.... We're all working together.... Some of us will experience life in [physical embodiment]—about a third of us—while the others will not be born at this time."[52]

Did you want to be born?

While a majority—81 percent—felt they *needed* to be born in order to advance their personal development through the experiences of physical life, only 30 percent enjoyed physical life enough to really want it! One subject likened the decision to walking out onto the high board and trying to nerve yourself enough to dive off:

> It's like walking out on a high diving board, getting born. You know you want to do it to sharpen your skills, but when you get to the end of the board you want to turn around and go back and do it another day. But then it just seems as though there are people there who are coaching you and finally you just get pushed and—there you are. Born into life again.[53]

Others phrased their reluctance in various ways.

> I feel very reluctant.... I don't want to be so restricted. I would rather be ... in the between-life state ... than in that small,

> confined body, but it is ... something I have to do.[54]
>
> Actual tears were running down my cheeks as you asked us to come to the time of decision about being born. It isn't so much sadness.... I don't feel sad. [It's] just—well ... life in a body is rough.[55]

It was common for people who were regressed to the birth experience to say, immediately after birth:

> "I want to go back home!" By "home" they ... meant life outside ... a physical body.[56]

One expressed these feelings eloquently:

> The experience was ... one of deep compassion. I felt compassion not only for the infant who was me, but for my mother and indeed everyone in the delivery room.... I was leaving a beautiful ... place where many things were open to me, to come down into a very closed ... environment. It seemed as though I knew all of the troubles that lay ahead, and I felt that it was such a waste that we humans don't understand.... I know that sounds strange.... Don't ... understand *what?* Well ... under the hypnosis, it seemed so clear to me that to be alive in the body is to be isolated from our true selves and away from the ... knowledge that's available to us who are not in a body. I knew it was necessary to go through this experience.... Yet, it seemed such a tragedy that my mother, the doctor, and [the] others had no real understanding of what life is.[57]

But the 30 percent who looked forward to physical embodiment made much more optimistic comments, many of them seeing the life to come as an adventure. One said:

> It's like going on an expedition to a strange country. It's exciting.[58]

When did you join your body?

When asked this question, subjects answered, and the answers were rather startling. There was a general reluctance to join the fetus. Only 1 percent reported that they had entered it prior to the fourth month of pregnancy, and only 14 percent said they did between the fourth and eighth months. Thus, 85 percent joined their new bodies only after the eighth month of gestation! A large number (33 percent of the total) stated that they did not do so until just before the actual birth experience, and 15 percent, who particularly disliked becoming embodied again, said they did not join the fetus *until after birth had occurred!*

Why are you being born?

The answers received to this question were nothing less than fascinating. Eighty-five percent stated that they already knew their parents and other important people in their present lives from relationships they had had with them in past lives! But even more extraordinary, as these relationships carry over from life to life, they do not remain the same but undergo every conceivable sexual and relational alteration. Thus, the subject's parents or children in the present life had been something very different in the past: present mothers and fathers might have been past sisters, brothers, friends, lovers, or children; the subject's present children often turned out to have been his parents in a past life. Relational and sexual change was the rule! For example, one subject said:

> My mother had been my sister, my father and my child before.[59]

Another stated:

> My mother was my sister in a past life and my father was a lover. My first son had been a grandfather in one lifetime of mine, my second son had been a father, and my first daughter a friend. My second daughter I saw clearly as a mother of mine in a past life.[60]

New perceptions about these intricate relationships elicited some powerful feelings. Many parents found themselves with a totally new view of their relationships with their children, perceiving them for the first time as independent individuals tied to them in complex ways through repeated lives, although dependent upon them at this particular time in the present life:

> My daughter is an old friend of mine from another life. I sense ... that her unborn child will be another old friend.[61]

But what staggering learning prospects this opens! What conceivably better way to "know" someone than to have had a dozen different relationships with him—as parent, child, sibling, lover! In fact, precisely this, in karmic terms, was the stated purpose of these carry-overs. A majority of those who were aware of their purpose in choosing their present parents, and others with whom they would be closely involved, stated that this purpose was to work out karmic problems which had developed in past-life relationships, and, in particular, to learn to love them and to express love for them.

> I did see why I was born, why I chose my parents. It was to help them in ... their karmas.[62]

Another subject observed:

> This life seemed very burdensome. I came in with lots of burdens to clear up, especially ... [with] my mother. I have to learn to love them, to give to them, my whole family. Having to be dependent on my mother was one of my challenges.[63]

The decision to reincarnate in particular relationships was made, it was revealed, in consultation with spiritual "advisers" and/or in consultation with the other persons who were to be involved. *Thus karmic ties to others were the major single motivation for choosing to be born into a particular body.* But some subjects chose instead an environment which suited what they wished to achieve in the current life:

> A few chose on the basis of the opportunities their genetic, environmental and emotional situation in that childhood would provide for them. The people who reported this type of choice generally had a clearer notion of the purpose they wanted to achieve in this lifetime than those who chose their family to work out past karma.[64]

For example, one of these said:

> This life is a test, a challenge: I'm purposefully setting up a scenario for learning what I want to know.[65]

Another reported:

> I was reluctant to be born. I didn't want to go down and leave [the between-life state] … and feel cold and belittled. When I came through the birth canal … I felt afraid, vulnerable, alone. Lots of impersonal people and flashing light. My mother was asleep and no one held me or welcomed me and I felt that familiar longing for love. But when you asked the purpose … it was to go down and take some of that … peace and light [of the between-life state] and spread it around. To go into the confusion of this life, but at a time where my preoccupation didn't have to be survival. My purpose is to give out love as fully and freely as possible in whatever situation I get into.[66]

And some of these subjects who had chosen their present life primarily for its "environment," rather than for its karmic ties, stated that the time period selected—the last half of the twentieth century—had been chosen because it offered unprecedented possibilities for personal growth:

> I felt I needed to work out the female part of my entity. I chose this era because women will make great advances in my lifetime and I will help in that.[67]

As another put it:

> This will be my transcendent life, when I am able to know both physical and non-physical reality while still in the body.[68]

Is your life predetermined?

The idea that you "choose" your life in advance in order to accomplish certain things raises a deeply disquieting question. Does this mean that your life is predestined in all its particulars, a script, in effect, that has already been written for a cast of "robots"? If you "choose" all of this in advance, then is any element of choice present while living this life, or do you merely go through predetermined motions? Fortunately, the data gathered by Dr. Wambach are such that this disturbingly important question can be answered. For it is clear from the comments of her subjects that what they have "chosen" is not predetermined at all, but only a "situation" with a certain potential, with certain possibilities which the individual may or may not be able to realize!

Subjects frequently expressed grave doubt that they would be able to accomplish what they had chosen to achieve in their present life. They would report planning their current life, but it was common for them, when regressed to the period immediately after birth, to realize with a shock of dismay that they had underestimated the difficulties they would have to overcome if they were to achieve the goals they had set for themselves. Their courage would fail them, and they would yearn to go back to the between-life state. Again and again, they spoke of their chosen present lives as "challenges," as "tests" which they had to attempt, *clearly implying that failure was as probable an outcome of their efforts as success.*

> I have the stamina to do it ... I can accept the challenges. It is necessary to develop my strengths through being alive in a body. [69]
>
> They ["advisors" in the between-life state] said ... that I should wait till a better time, with a smaller family, more time for you.
>
> But I felt that it has to be now. Someone has to start first but I told my friends, "Don't wait too long."[70]

It is difficult to find words that can do justice to the revelations that have emerged from the research on which this chapter has been based. They are momentous, stunning, mind-blowing. And for those who are open enough to take them to heart, the world will never be the same.

CHAPTER EIGHT

BRIDGING THE WORLDS: ACCOUNTS FROM THE REALM BEYOND DEATH

That is a doubtful tale from Faery land
Hard for the non-elect to understand
– *John Keats,* Lamia

The Seventh state … baffles description. It is heart-breaking even to attempt to write of it.… the passage …. to the Seventh state means … flight from the material universe.… You dwell not only outside time but outside of the universe on this last plane of being.
– *Twenty-three years after his death, Frederic Myers, a founder of the British Society for Psychical Research, describes the highest plane of existence in the world beyond death.*

THE EVIDENCE presented in the preceding chapters has established, beyond all reasonable doubt, that you will survive the death of your body. And the evidence from 1,500 regressions shows that your present body will not be your last. After about fifty-two years, you'll get another. In the meantime, *you'll be dead.* And now at long last the time has come to talk about that: *what is it actually like to be dead?* Since we've all done it many times, we could ask *ourselves,* under hypnosis, what it's like. When this is done, however, the results are usually unsatisfactory. The hypnotized subject claims he is in a highly pleasurable realm of existence, and states that he will, only with the greatest reluctance, leave that realm to be reborn. But apart from these general expressions of pleasure and reluctance, details are not usually forthcoming. For reasons still unknown, the hypnotized cannot, as a rule, provide a lucid description of the after-death state. Possibly such knowledge, if remembered, would make the present life in the body too painful. But for whatever reason, this knowledge seems, usually, to be "blocked." That leaves us with only one source to whom we can turn for information: *those who are now dead.*

The existence of a special group of people, who claim the ability to communicate with the dead, has been extraordinarily widespread in human history. Such individuals, whether called shamans, seers, prophets, mediums or psychics, have appeared at all times and in virtually all places. They have only been studied, in a scientific spirit, in the last century. And the question which a century of research has put to them is simply this—*do the dead still live?*

Some claim to see the dead externalized in space, and to speak to them telepathically. (As one little psychic girl said, when asked how she "did" this—"we talk with our think.") Others see the dead in mental images, and are "spoken to" with graphic imagery created by the dead communicators. (This method apparently takes some practice on the part of the deceased, and is not without its comic side. Some psychics, for example, have described inexperienced communicators using this style as being reduced, on occasion, to spelling messages by creating and "holding up" single letters of the alphabet.) Others hear the dead speak. Some, in half-trance, receive communications through automatic writing or a ouija board, while others permit their bodies to be temporarily taken over by the dead, who then attempt, often it seems successfully, to speak directly to dwellers in the physical world in an eerie approximation of their own voices. But by whatever means these communications are effected—through thought, sight, or sound—those who receive them are convinced, by repeated experiences, that the answer to the question is "yes." *The dead still live.*

In fact, for some psychics, the dead may be all too much "alive" for comfort. People who have the ability to see the dead externalized in space do not always find it easy to distinguish them from the living, and a child with these capacities may comment innocently on the presence of a "dead" relative. More than one psychically sensitive child has received a paddled behind, bed without dinner, and indignant instructions to stop talking nonsense. Only after several such painful experiences does the child learn discretion and keep silent about those whom others cannot see.

Psychics may become unwilling mediums, forced to play host to the unknown and unwelcome dead, who, in their anguish to communicate, soon learn that certain human beings can perceive and converse with them. For this reason, most trance mediums urgently need a discarnate "doorkeeper," someone on the other side to protect them, for a psychic whose lines to the dead are "open"—such as one entranced—may draw a throng of the anxious and confused dead. And mediums who are aware of such entities in their ordinary state of consciousness must find ways to protect themselves by shutting out their unwelcome visitors much of the time. A number of those who have not succeeded have ended their days in mental institutions.

These, then, are people who talk with the dead, and we will now examine two such conversations. Though both are important, they are very different in nature. The first communicator is primarily interested in one of his legs. The second, who at one point remarks, "all … we imagined is not half wonderful enough for the truth,"[1] is concerned with the nature of human existence beyond the grave.

Hafsteinn Bjornsson and Runolfur Runolfsson

Hafsteinn Bjornsson lives in Reykjavik, Iceland, where he works for a radio station. He is not well known outside his own country; only a handful of scholars have ever heard of him. But some of these consider him one of the greatest mediums now living. From early childhood, he has been able to see the dead, and for the past forty years, they have spoken through him in trance. It was in the winter of 1937-38, when he was only twenty-three, that he first formalized his conversations with the dead, for in that year he began to conduct regular séances with an interested group in Reykjavik.

One of his first dead visitors was what students of séance phenomena call a "drop-in" communicator. "Drop-in" communicators appear "out of the blue." They are completely unknown to anyone present, and hence no effort has been made to contact them. They simply arrive uninvited, slip into the waiting body of the medium, and begin talking. This unknown communicator proved to be a rather bizarre personality. To begin with, he refused to identify himself. "What the hell does it matter to you what my name is?" he demanded. He was no more conventional when it came to explaining his purpose. When asked what he wanted, he said "I am looking for my leg."

Later he became more specific, and reduced the scope of his demands: it turned out he was only looking for one of his thigh bones. He appeared intermittently over the course of the next year, and his behavior was quite consistent. Never would he identify himself. And always, he demanded "his leg." This became not only irritating but boring.

There matters remained until January of 1939, when a newcomer, Ludvik Gudmundsson, joined the group. Gudmundsson owned a house in Sandgerdi, forty miles away. To his astonishment, their anonymous visitor was delighted to see him, because, he said, his missing leg was in the house at Sandgerdi! This completely senseless claim brought matters to a head. Their patience exhausted, the members of the séance circle soon gave the interloper an ultimatum: if he didn't tell them who he was at once, then they would not talk to him any further. Refusing to do so, he left, only to return a few weeks later in a conciliatory mood. And at last, not only did he reveal his identity, he told them how he had died and disclosed the reason for his strange request. "My name is Runolfur Runolfsson," he said. "And I was fifty-two years old when I died." In his story, he returned to the day of his death.

> [He] … had been drunk on that fateful day when he started for his home at Klappakot. The weather had been bad, and when he stopped at the house of friends they insisted that he must not leave in that condition unless somebody went with him. Ridiculous—especially to someone in an intoxicated condition—for home was only a fifteen-minute walk away. He became angry and said he would not go at all if he could not go alone. They let him go.
>
> Wet and tired, he set out. But he sat down on a rock when partway home, took out his bottle and drank some more. The tide came in. He was carried out to sea. When the tide washed his body back up on the shore, the dogs and ravens came and tore him to pieces. That was in October, and the year was 1879. The remains of his body were not discovered until January. They were buried in the Utskalar graveyard not far from Sandgerdi.
>
> It was never established that those who found the remains noticed that a thigh bone was missing, but Runki [Icelandic nickname for Runolfur] said it was. He said, "It was carried out to sea again, but later washed up at Sandgerdi. There it was passed around and now it is in Ludvik's house." He said proof of all this could be found in the Utskalar church book.

Intrigued, the members of the séance circle examined the church book, which now reposed in the National Archives in Reykjavik, and found the following note:

> On October 16, 1879, Runolfur Runolfsson, living in Klappakot, was missing on account of some accidental … occurrence on his way home … during a storm … in the middle of the night.… the sea carried him away … his bones were found dismembered much later.

A further note indicated that he had been buried on January 8, 1880, but said nothing about the missing thigh bone.

For Ludvik, this stirred some memories, and some inquiries. He remembered that when he had bought his Sandgerdi house, there had been some talk that it was haunted, and when he questioned elderly men in the village, some of them remembered that a human thigh bone had been found and passed around. But they did not know what had happened to it, although one thought that it had finally been interred in the north wall of Ludvik's house.

Ludvik persisted in his investigation. He succeeded in finding one of the carpenters who had actually built the house. Did he remember anything about a bone? He did. A human thigh bone had been washed up on the shore, and eventually they had put it to rest in a wall of the house. He remembered where. He pointed out the spot. The wall was opened. And, incredibly, there it was! It was very long, verifying Runki's statement that he had been an unusually tall man. Ludvik made a little coffin for it, and the thigh bone of the man who had died in the sea sixty years before was buried with solemn ceremony. A clergyman praised the long-dead man, a choir sang over the miniature coffin, and all of those who had attended this strange ritual retired to the clergyman's house for refreshment.

> Hafsteinn was not among those present, but he held a séance immediately following the burial service for the bone. Runki, naturally, made his presence known, expressed gratitude, and said that he had been present at the churchyard ceremony and the reception following. He described it all in … detail, even to the different kinds of cake served at the clergyman's house.[2]

Now that his long-lost thigh bone had at last been laid decently to rest, the truculent Runki began to mellow. He became gentler, and has for years now appeared at Hafsteinn's séances to help other, less experienced communicators.

Cases as convincing as this one are not rare in the recent history of mediumship. And it is certainly worthwhile to collect them, to prove that someone who once lived, and is now dead, yet survives. But we don't want to leave it at that. If they do survive, then there is surely more to be learned from them than the simple fact of their continued existence. *What we naturally want to know is what that existence is like.*

Frederic Myers

Frederic Myers was a professor of classics at Cambridge University in England. He was born in 1843 and he died in 1901. One overriding interest characterized this man: a passionate curiosity about the meaning of human life. He devoted most of his adult years to trying to satisfy this curiosity, but he did it in a rather unusual way. He did not pore over theological writings and philosophical speculation. He felt that if human life did have a purpose, then it could be discovered in only one way: through the study of actual human experiences. This conviction led him, in 1882, to found the first Society for Psychical Research with some of his Cambridge colleagues.

Myers and his associates devoted themselves to studying the kinds of experiences with which this book is concerned. In particular, they wanted to know if human beings survived bodily death. If they did, then life in a body must have a discoverable purpose. Myers was a man of enormous energy and great intellectual ability. After twenty years of intensive investigation, he concluded that he had answered this question. He wrote a book about what he had learned that became a classic—probably the most important work ever written in this strange field. It is called *Human Personality and Its Survival of Bodily Death.*

Myers had a strong interest in mediumship, and grappled until the end of his life with the problems involved in interpreting its results. The difficulties lay not with the limitations of the mediums' powers, but with their scope. When a medium became entranced, and a voice, remarkably like that of a dead person, issued forth from her mouth, claiming to be that person and showing an encyclopedic knowledge of that person's life, then it seemed to Myers that contact was being made with the dead. Or when a medium, in a half-trance, seemed to be talking to someone who had been in his grave for some time, and was able to answer detailed questions about his life, Myers at first reached the conclusion that the dead still live.

But his research, in the end, didn't turn out to be quite that simple. For he became aware of cases in which those attending a séance had been given such detail about a person they knew who claimed in the communication to be dead. Later, however, they would discover *that he was still alive!* And in a few cases, as an experiment, someone had gone to a medium and mentally concentrated on an entirely fictitious personality, only to receive "communications" from that "personality," claiming to come from beyond the grave! In other words, when mediums went into trance states, they could at times pick up accurate information about living or fictitious persons telepathically and deliver it as if it came from the dead. And this posed a problem, for if such information could be obtained from living minds about persons still alive, it could, in principle, be obtained from living minds about persons who were dead.

Mediums did not seem to do such things in a fraudulent spirit; they were sometimes unable to tell whether information came to them from the living or from the dead. *In other words, these bizarre abilities made it impossible to be certain that a communication came from a dead mind rather than a living one.* Maybe the dead did not live.

Myers never solved this problem during his life. What he did was even more impressive. *He solved it after he was dead!*

The cross-correspondences

Within a few weeks of Myers's death in 1901, some very strange communications began to be received by psychics in England, the United States, and India. They came through automatic writing, to a total of a dozen psychics, and continued for a period of thirty years. What was strangest about them was that they made no sense. Or perhaps they did—for they were so mysteriously worded that it almost seemed their meaning was being deliberately concealed. And most of them were signed "Myers."

But although the text of the messages seemed indecipherable, the "instructions" which often accompanied them were clear. These instructions repeated a number of themes. The "script" should be sent to a particular person (who would turn out to be one of the other psychics involved). Or it should be sent to the Society for Psychical Research. And that although its content might appear to be senseless, it was in reality anything but: it was an attempt by the deceased communicator to prove his continued existence. These instructions and explanations were, in fact, frequent and explicit: "Record the bits," wrote "Myers," "and when fitted they will make the whole." And again, "I will give the words between you neither alone can read but together they will give the clue."

It was some time, however, before the people involved fully realized what was happening. When they did, they gathered the fragments together and found that they had communications which were clear, coherent, and continuous. Most of these scripts consisted of references to and quotations from both classical and modern literature. Some were so obscure that only a scholar, and a specialized one at that, would recognize them.

> According to the scripts their intention was to make these fragments appear random and pointless to the individual [psychics] … in order to avoid giving clues to the train of thought behind them. They would only become meaningful and show evidence of design when pieced together by an independent investi-

> gator.... The interest lies in the question: Who selected them to convey a train of thought which could not be deduced from any one person's script?[3]

And the answer was: *the dead communicator.* Myers was trying to prove that the mind of the medium could not be the creator of the message: how could it be, when the message was only a fragment which made no sense unless linked with other, equally "meaningless" fragments? Myers was quite explicit about what he was doing. He was causing as many as a dozen psychics, in various widely separated parts of the world, not only to refer to the same topic—often a highly obscure one—but to do so in ways which were complementary. Like the parts of a jigsaw puzzle, these "pieces" did more than refer to the same theme; they did so in ways which were intricately intertwined. Those who studied and tried to interpret these "jigsaw puzzles" called them *cross-correspondences.*

The simplest cases involved the repetition of particular themes drawn from various languages and literary sources. On April 24th, 1907, while in trance in the United States, an American medium named Mrs. Piper three times uttered the word "Thanatos," a Greek word meaning "death," despite the fact that she had no knowledge of Greek. Such repetitions were often a signal that a cross-correspondence was about to begin. But it had begun already. A week earlier, in India, Mrs. Holland had done some automatic writing, and in that script the following enigmatic communication had appeared: "Mors [Latin for death]. And with that the shadow of death fell upon his limbs." On April 29th, in England, Mrs. Verrall, writing automatically, produced the words: "Warmed both hands before the fire of life. It fades and I am ready to depart." This is a quotation from a poem by a nineteenth-century English poet, Walter Savage Landor. Mrs. Verrall next drew a triangle. This could be delta, the fourth letter of the Greek alphabet. She had always considered it a symbol of death. She then wrote: "Manibus date lilia plenis" *(give lilies with full hands).* This is a quotation from Vergil's *Aeneid* in which an early death is foretold. This was followed by the statement: "Come away, come away, Pallida mors," (Latin for *pale death*), and, finally, an explicit comment from the communicator: "You have got the word plainly written all along in your writing. Look back." The "word," or "theme" was quite obvious when these fragments, given in the same month to three mediums thousands of miles apart, were put together and scrutinized. And in terms of the lifelong interests of the communicator, it was certainly an appropriate theme. *Death.*

This gives some indication of the complexity of even the simplest cross-correspondence. And most of those who have studied them have concluded that they were exactly what they claimed to be: an experiment conducted from beyond the grave to establish that Myers still lived.

Myers pursued this task with the diligence characteristic of him in life. From 1901 to 1932, more than three thousand scripts were communicated. Receiving and interpreting such a vast body of material was often burdensome to those involved. But for Myers, the whole enterprise was a source of anguish. He had survived physical death, as other men did. And now he was desperately eager to communicate this fact in a fashion which would convince his still living colleagues. But, because he had no body, he had to use the minds of others. He had to struggle to get "through." And in the scripts he sent, he refers again and again to the suffering that this cost him.

> "Oh, if I could only … leave you the proof … that I continue. Yet another attempt to run the blockade—to strive to get a message through—How can I make your hand docile enough—how can I convince them? … I am trying … amid unspeakable difficulties.… It is impossible for me to know how much of what I send reaches you.… I feel as if I had presented my credentials—reiterated the proofs of my identity in a wearisomely frequent manner.… Surely you sent them what I strove … to transmit.… The nearest simile I can find to express the difficulties of sending a message is that I appear to be standing behind a sheet of frosted glass—which blurs sight and deadens sound—dictating feebly—

> to a reluctant and somewhat obtuse secretary. A feeling of terrible impotence burdens me.... Oh it is a dark road.[4]

Myers, for all the grand scope of his interests, was a very modest man. And he was also a very systematic one. These two qualities perfectly explained the style and timing of his after-death communications. He had first to prove to his friends that he still lived. He devoted thirty years to that. But what was of course of even greater interest, once that was established, was *what was it like to be dead?* Myers, always the scholar, was not about to rush hastily into a discussion of such a momentous subject. He was very systematic and cautious about that too. *He had been dead for twenty-three years before, at last, he began to communicate on that most mysterious of all geographies—the world of the dead.*

Myers was not, of course, the first to describe life after death. Plenty of other communicators had done that in spiritualist séances. But, although their reports had at first been examined with fascinated anticipation, they were soon dismissed with snorts of derision.

For "heaven," the "afterlife," had always been something very special to man—a transcendent paradise where the pain and struggle of this world would be surmounted and the mysteries of human life and death at last revealed in the very abode of God himself. But what was reported was quite something else indeed. It seemed to most thoughtful people to be the height of inanity, the silliest, most pathetic self-delusion imaginable. For what the "communicators" described was nothing but an earth-life. It was terribly beautiful, and the dead were very happy, and active too. What exactly did they do there?—well, pretty much what they had always done. They played golf, for example, and drank Scotch. They had sexual adventures and they smoked cigars. They played cards, lived in houses like those they had occupied on earth, and even went to work! Now this, obviously, could not be heaven: it was clearly spiritualistic self-delusion. Myers, however, was to show that these communicators were right—at least in part. For it had never occurred to their critics that if men were going to transcend their earth-lives after death and move onward to a "divine" realm, then it would certainly be a kindness to them to start them off with something familiar—like the lives and surroundings they had known on earth.

The world of the dead

Hades

Hades, the underworld, the world of shadows, is the realm where the lowest states of consciousness possible after death occur. Myers did not have much to say about Hades, for it did not greatly interest him. But when the comments which he did make are put together with those of other investigators, a reasonably clear picture of this post-mortem world emerges. The dead who remain at this level have had their transition to the normal world of post-mortem existence aborted. In this realm dwell haunting ghosts and possessing spirits.

The lowest after-death state possible is complete unconsciousness, a comatose, sleep-like state. A brief period of unconsciousness often follows a tiring death and is recuperative and normal. But where it is prolonged, it usually results from a kind of "reverse faith"—a belief, or an intense hope, that only nothingness, complete personal extinction, follows death. This belief can produce a prolonged comatose state. When such spirits are brought by "helping" discarnates to the body of a medium engaged in "rescue" work for the dead, they typically produce instant loss of consciousness in the medium, and can be awakened and enlightened only with difficulty.

The next highest state involves consciousness without sensory input. Spirits in this state complain that they wander in darkness or dense mist. Should they come into the vicinity of a psychically sensitive person with a bright aura, they will be drawn to this "light" and may inadvertently "possess" the victim. Clearly, the immediate cause of this condition is a low state of consciousness. People at this level can perceive neither the normal post-mortem environment, nor even the normal physical one. The causes most often cited for this state are defects of character, such as extreme selfishness, but this seems to me to be merely speculation. At any rate, only a small minority of the dead will have to endure it.

One step above the state of "darkness" is the normal physical environment of the living. The dead who enter this condition find themselves "right here" with the physically embodied. The great majority of those who get involved in hauntings or possessions dwell at this level. The anger and vindictiveness so often displayed by such spirits is understandable, for they have to operate in the physical realm, with their old physical and earthly interests and desires, but without the body which would make their gratification possible, and often, as well, without even the realization that they are dead. This state can be prolonged; in fact, some communications with haunting ghosts during exorcisms show that it can last for centuries. A multitude of personality traits have been cited as causes for this condition—love, hatred, earthly desires, and so on. But the truth is we don't really know why some people end up like this after death. It may be that especially intense emotional attachments—of love, hatred, anguish—to embodied persons or earthly places or life-styles are responsible.

After death most of us, thankfully, will not have to endure unconsciousness, darkness, or bodiless frustration at the physical level. We will pass immediately to the first normal post-mortem plane—the "plane of illusion." Myers also called this realm the "lotus flower paradise." The two terms accurately suggest his feelings about it, which were deeply ambivalent. He had loved it, for it could be supremely beautiful. It was obvious that this paradise was the heaven for which men yearn, and of which their theologies had always told them. But he discovered that there was a realm beyond it. And once he had developed enough to dwell there, he defined this first paradise negatively: it now became "the plane of illusion."

The chain of being

Myers discovered more. In fact, although far from an immodest man, he claimed to have discovered nothing less than *the basic purpose of the universe.* Were he the only one ever to maintain that this particular intent underlay the existence of the physical universe, there would be less need to take him seriously than there is. For the truth is that identical explanations have been asserted by others, both disembodied and embodied.

Myers's theory links together perfectly all of the experiences reported in this book, and can be simply stated. Reality has two fundamental attributes—a psychic one and a physical one. The physical is represented by the universe of matter. The psychic constitutes another, complementary world. Each of us begins as an extremely rudimentary psychic entity, capable of only a very simple physical embodiment. Through repeated embodiments, the psyche grows steadily more complex and ascends the chain of matter. Reincarnation, then, doesn't just involve human bodies—it involves every kind of matter!

Hence, there are two fundamental kinds of "learning"—embodied or "physical," and disembodied or "psychic." Between each embodied life, there is a disembodied one. And to be a human being is not, according to Myers, anything like an ultimate state. One learns in a human body for a period of time, after which one passes beyond physical embodiment altogether. The ultimate existence conceivable to the mind of man is that of "God," and according to Myers, that is precisely where we are headed. We are "gods in training," and that training takes us through every form of existence—from mineral to plant, from plant to animal, from animal to human, from human to divine.

These stupendous conceptions endow a very odd poem with sense. Mystics have always claimed to have had direct experience of the nature of ultimate reality. And seven centuries ago, Rumi, a Persian mystic, wrote the following enigmatic lines:

I died a mineral and became a plant;
I died a plant and rose an animal.
I died an animal and I was man.

> Why should I fear? When was I less by dying?
> Yet once more I shall die as man, to soar
> With blessed angels; even from angelhood
> I must pass on....
> When I have sacrificed my angel soul,
> I shall become that which no mind conceived.[5]

Seven hundred years later we find the remarkable psychic Joan Grant reaffirming exactly those ideas, which she derived from her own paranormal experiences:

> I ... acquired sufficient empirical experience to see the broad outlines of the progress of an individual during the initial four phases of his evolution. He starts with only enough energy to organise a single molecule. As this energy increases, and his consciousness begins to expand, he requires more complex forms through which to express [it]. ...
>
> After growing too [complex] ... to be contained by the mineral phase of existence, he enters the [plant] ... kingdom, and then graduates, by a series of incarnations as various species of animal, to his first incarnation as a member of the [human] race.[6]

Myers states that human beings reincarnate from the plane of illusion, but that once they have learned enough from periodic existences in the confines of matter, they pass beyond that plane and need become embodied no longer.

An identical claim is made by "Seth," a discarnate teacher who communicates through the medium Jane Roberts. According to Seth, each individual consciousness must undergo a long period of training and learning through repeated physical embodiments. Being human is simply one "stage" in this process of development, and when, through repeated incarnations, this stage is finished, one passes onward to other planes of existence which offer more exalted opportunities for development. The most crucial "lesson" to be learned is karmic or ethical. Through repeated embodiments, the undeveloped individual treats others with cruelty and hatred, and, in accordance with the karmic process, is subjected to cruelty and hatred in return. The ultimate result of these hard lessons is spiritual development and a passage beyond physical embodiment, giving access to god-like creative powers once the entity is highly evolved enough to use these in a karmically responsible way. While he is still unevolved enough to use these powers to injure, control, exploit or destroy others, he does not have access to them.

In a series of trance communications, Seth had given Jane Roberts and her husband Rob a series of "lectures" on the nature of reality as he perceived it from a plane higher than the human. Jane writes:

> With all Seth ... told us about man's potentials ... we ... wondered ... why the race isn't more developed morally and spiritually.
>
> One night before our regular Wednesday session Rob and I were pretty upset over the state of the world in general. We sat talking and Rob wondered aloud why we behaved as we did. "What real sense or purpose is behind it all?" he said. "I don't know," I said. I felt as bad as he did.
>
> That was November 6, 1968, and ... on that ... evening ... Seth ... came through in [his] ... distinct clear voice. Among other things, Seth ... said: "The human race is a stage through which various forms of consciousness travel.... Before you can be allowed into systems of reality that are more extensive and open, you must first learn ... through physical [life].... As a child forms mud pies from dirt, so you form your civilizations....
>
> "When you leave the physical system after reincarnations, you have learned the lessons—and you are literally no longer a member of the human race, for you elect to leave it.... In more advanced systems, thoughts and emotions are automatically and immediately translated into ... whatever approximation of matter there exists. Therefore, the lessons must be taught and learned well.

> "The responsibility for creation must be clearly understood. [In physical life on earth] ... you are in a soundproof and isolated room. Hate creates destruction in that 'room,' and until the lessons are learned, destruction follows destruction ... the agonies ... are sorely felt.... you must be taught ... to create responsibly. [Earth life] ... is a training system for emerging consciousness.
>
> "If the sorrows and agonies within your system were not felt as real, the lessons would not be learned.... [It] ... is like an educational play."[7]

In other words, in these realms beyond the human, thought and emotion can immediately create a concrete, objectively real environment and situation; hence, entities cannot be allowed to enter these realms until they are highly developed enough to create "responsibly."

The idea that we have all been ascending, for uncounted centuries, an infinitely long evolutionary path, from the dim awareness of embodiment in inorganic molecules to the unimaginable heights of a god-like consciousness, is an enthralling conception. Not in my wildest dreams would I have expected to find evidence from living human beings to support such a staggering idea. And then I read Stanislav Grof's book, *Realms of the Human Unconscious: Observations from* LSD *Research.* Dr. Grof, a Czech-born psychiatrist now living in the United States, is the world's foremost expert on therapeutic procedures using the powerful drug LSD. I had already been struck by what research with hypnosis showed the subconscious mind to contain—not only an incredibly detailed and accurate record of present-life experiences, but a similar record for a whole set of *past existences.* But these, of course, were all lives in a *human* body. Non-human existences were not reported under hypnosis.

But as Dr. Grof's book makes clear, LSD can plumb the subconscious memory banks at levels even deeper than those possible with hypnosis. The results, and their implications, are astounding. If a patient is given a series of LSD treatments, his subconscious yields up its memories from progressively more remote points in time. First are memories from this life, vividly re-lived, including many from fetal life in the womb, and from the actual birth-experience. Once these memories have been retrieved and relived, they do not recur. The individual then begins to relive experiences from past human lives, including many which are of great karmic importance. Grof writes:

> The opening of the area of past-incarnation experiences in LSD sessions is sometimes preceded by complex instructions received through nonverbal means (i.e., on an intuitive level) that introduce the individual to the fact of reincarnation, make him recognize the responsibility for his past deeds, and present the law of karma as an important part of the cosmic order that is mandatory for all sentient beings.... According to the reports of LSD subjects ... the assignment of an individual spiritual entity to a particular physical body occurs ... according to its karmic past. [8]

Although this is extraordinary enough, the evidence from hypnotic regression will have prepared us for it. But with LSD regressions we find ourselves in an even more alien and dizzying realm, for LSD subjects not infrequently report, in addition, *experiences as animals, plants, and minerals!* And lest we be tempted, as of course we will be, to dismiss this at once as the most absurd fantasy imaginable, let me add that these experiences *are typically accompanied by an uncannily accurate knowledge of the nature of such creatures and structures.* With respect to animal experiences, Grof writes:

> Evolutionary memories have specific experiential characteristics that make them ... distinctly different from human experiences and often seem to transcend the scope and limits of human fantasy and imagination. The individual can have, for example, an illuminating insight into what it feels like when a snake is hungry, when a turtle is sexually excited, when a hummingbird is

feeding its young, or when a shark breathes through its gills. Subjects have reported that they have experienced the drive that sustains an eel or a … salmon on its heroic journey against a river's flow, the sensations of a spider spinning his web, or the mysterious process of metamorphosis from an egg through a caterpillar and chrysalis to a butterfly.…

It is not uncommon for subjects reporting … [these] experiences to manifest a detailed knowledge of the animals with whom they have identified—of their physical characteristics, habits, and behavior patterns—that far exceeds their education in the natural sciences.… subjects have accurately described courtship dances, complicated reproductive cycles, techniques of nest-building, patterns of aggression and defense, and many other zoological … facts about the animals they have experienced.… To illustrate this … we will use an example from an advanced LSD session.…

At one point in her session, Renata [the subject] had a sense of complete identification with a female of a species of large reptiles that became extinct millions of years ago. She felt sleepy and lazy as she rested on sand by a big lake and basked luxuriously in the sun. While experiencing this in the session, she opened her eyes and looked at the therapist [Dr. Grof], who seemed transformed into a good-looking male of the same species; her feelings of laziness immediately vanished, and she experienced a strong sexual arousal and attraction. According to her description, these feelings did not have anything to do with human erotic and sexual excitement; it was a quite unique and specific "reptilian" interest in and attraction to the opposite sex. Any notion of the mouth, genitals, or other parts of the body that might interest her in a human partner was completely missing. She was absolutely fascinated by scalelike facets that she visualized on the side of the therapist's head. One large field of this sort seemed to have a shape and color that she found irresistible; it appeared to be radiating powerful sexual vibrations.

Since certain characteristics of this experience were so

> unusual and concrete, I decided to consult a good friend of mine who was a paleontologist educated in zoology and well acquainted with animal behavior. As I expected, he did not have any information on the mating habits of antediluvian reptiles. However, he showed me passages in the zoological literature *indicating that in certain contemporary reptiles particular distinctly colored areas on the head play an important role as triggers of sexual arousal.*[9]

Such experiences offer a fascinating parallel to past-life memories under hypnosis: not only are the memories re-lived, they are found to be accurate in a way far exceeding the normal knowledge of the subject.

With respect to plant experiences, Grof has this to say:

> The instances of experiencing ... plant forms are ... less frequent than those concerning animal life. [The] individual ... has the unique feeling of ... participating in the basic physiological processes of plants. He can experience himself as a germinating seed, a leaf in the course of photosynthetic activity, or a root reaching out for ... nourishment.... a subject might ... become plankton in the ocean, and experience pollination or cellular divisions occurring during vegetable growth.
>
> The experiences of plant consciousness ... no matter how fantastic and absurd their content might seem to our common sense, [are] ... not easy to discard ... as mere fantasies. They occur independently in various individuals in advanced stages of treatment and have a very special experiential flavor that cannot be easily communicated.[10]

And these experiences of existence in forms simpler than the human are not confined to the world of biological life!

> They can include ... inorganic nature. Subjects have repeatedly reported that they experienced consciousness of the ocean....

> Many LSD subjects have also stated that they experienced consciousness of a particular material … [such as] diamond, granite, gold.… Similar experiences can reach even the microworld and depict the dynamic structure of the atoms, the nature of the electromagnetic forces involved, the world of inter-atomic bonds, or the Brownian dance of the molecules.[11]

After undergoing such experiences, Grof writes,

> LSD subjects often consider the possibility that consciousness is a basic cosmic phenomenon … and that it exists throughout the universe.… human consciousness appears to be only one of its many varieties.[12]

But let us return to Myers. His views closely parallel those cited, and are explicitly stated. He says that developing psychic entities

> must gather … numberless experiences, manifest and express themselves in uncountable forms before they attain to completion.… Once these are acquired, [these entities] … take on divine attributes. The reason, therefore, for the universe and … the purpose of existence … [is] the evolution of mind in matter.[13]

Of course the lower you go in the chain of matter, the greater the number of "forms" which exist. How can so many become so few? Myers replies:

> Place plants, insects, fish, birds and beasts into their several classes. These resemble the … [grades] in a … school. The … souls of plants, after dying, gather together in their myriads and … form … [larger psychic units]. These innumerable little beings ... go up one step … then, and … [as] one [psychic entity] ... enter the body of an insect. Myriads of insect lives again make one being which, in due course, enters the body of a fish or a bird. And so the process continues.[14]

> Finally … the embryonic souls of animals so … evolve that many, making one … [psychic entity], eventually become one human soul.[15]

In other words every material form, and every variety of life in the universe, is at a different stage in the same very long process of psychic evolution. More than "men" are "brothers"!

The plane of illusion

According to Myers, the first normal state of existence after death is the "lotus flower paradise," the "plane of illusion." He also called it the "third" plane, the first two being the physical world and a brief transitional state. Immediately after death, most of us can expect to enter this realm. Although extraordinary, this world will not seem strange, for our dreams and our earth life will have prepared us for it. Dreams, although manufactured mysteriously by our minds, seem completely real. The world of the third plane is similar, except that the "dreams" are *completely objectified.* The third plane, according to Myers, consists of a subtle form of matter which is *completely responsive to human emotion and thought.* And because human beings come there after years of mental and emotional immersion in earth life, the worlds their minds make there are based entirely on earth memories and desires.

In other words, the worlds of the third plane are created by thought, and the process may be either conscious or unconscious. In either case, what is created is based on one's deepest desires—for pleasure, for beauty, for the familiar. According to Myers, people who are close to one another, and who have similar life-tastes, come together in little communities where their entire worlds are mutually constructed. Those of a more solitary temperament may build their own worlds. Often, the real nature of these thought creations is completely unknown to their creators, who simply find themselves in a breathtakingly beautiful and extremely pleasant world where every desire is gratified by a thought. This world, then, is truly a literal depiction of the "heaven" or "paradise" of the ancient theologies.

Sometimes living persons have had a preview of this plane in out-of-the-body experiences. During surgical anaesthesia, Mrs. Geraldine Tuke found herself out of her body with her dead niece Eileen. Eileen, it turned out, was living in a home which perfectly suited her tastes because, she explained, she had made it with her mind, and, as long as she wanted it, it would continue to exist exactly as she wished. The contents of this house, however, were more variable, as she frequently "redecorated," mentally dissolving existing objects she no longer wanted and creating others. Mrs. Tuke was so fascinated by these astonishing revelations that she asked if *she* could "make" something. She could. All that the process required was that the creator develop a clear "thought-picture" of what was desired. Mrs. Tuke then visualized a vase of a lovely shape and color, and, instantly, it appeared in her hands.[16]

But because this "heaven" is based on earth desires, it is a far cry from the pallid and etherealized afterlife depicted in conventional religious prints. For example, a recently-dead alcoholic on the third plane might find himself surrounded by liquor in a favorite drinking environment, complete with congenial companions, who may be other dead alcoholics, or simply self-created thought-forms. Because such a person desires prolonged drunkenness, this is exactly what he will experience.

Thus the third plane is a paradise for voluptuaries. Those with intense sexual interests may have their every desire gratified, surrounded by orgiasts similarly committed to the pleasures of sexual adventure. Gourmands may dine in state, while ascetics are generously supplied—by their own minds—with bread and water.

The newly-dead are utterly enchanted by this paradise. They find themselves enthralled, fascinated. And because on this plane what is created depends entirely upon earthly tastes wedded to the scope and power of the creator's imagination, an almost infinite variety of different worlds can be effortlessly formed and dwelt within. And this of course explains the tremendous variety of post-mortem descriptions received through mediums; there can be as many afterlives as there are dead!

But there is a strange kind of limitation to this world. The effortless and instant satisfaction of any desire can enchant for a time, but eventually it begins to bore. A sense of dissatisfaction arises, a desire for some kind of effort or challenge in contrast to this dreamy lotusland. *And this, in fact, appears to be the major evolutionary purpose of the third plane—to partially exhaust the possibilities of creation and desire at the level of the world of earthly matter.* At this point the individual may choose to ascend to the fourth plane, and if he is highly enough developed, he may enter it.

The alternative is to choose to reincarnate again on earth. But before returning to earth, the individual undergoes a kind of karmic "review"—similar to, and yet in a crucial way different from, the "life review" he experienced immediately following death. The second review requires the addition of two crucial ingredients. The first is that as the individual relives the incidents of his previous life once again, he this time re-experiences the *emotions* he felt at the time. The second is that, simultaneously, he experiences *the emotions of the other persons who were involved.* In other words the torturer becomes, simultaneously, both torturer and victim. It would be difficult to imagine a more profoundly instructive, and chastening, experience than this. Speaking here of someone who had, in his earth life, been cruel to others, Myers writes:

> [The individual] is a spectator and perceives … the episodes in the past existence.… He becomes aware of all the emotions roused in his victims by his acts.… No pain, no anguish he has caused has perished. All has been registered.… his soul … becomes gradually purified through his identification with the sufferings of his victims.[17]

This experience appears to result in karmically-motivated decisions about the nature of the next earth life the individual will live.

> When a soul is born into a defective body it is due to the fact that in a previous existence it committed errors from the results of which it can only escape by submitting to this particular experience.
>
> The ... soul of an idiot, for instance, gathers certain lessons from its earth life. Actually, such men as tyrants and inquisitors often reincarnate as idiots or imbeciles. They have, on the other side of death, learned to sympathise with and understand the sufferings of their victims. These are sometimes of such an appalling character that their perpetrator's centre of imagination becomes disorganized and he is doomed to exist throughout his next incarnation in a state of mental dis-equilibrium.[18]

And, describing this "karmic" review, another communicator who had led a somewhat selfish life says:

> I have had the most disturbing experiences. I don't really know how I lived through them.... I have been shown the effects of all my acts upon other people.... It was the most humiliating and awful experience.... I have seen ... the emotional reactions to my own acts.... I am changed. I am a much softer person now.[19]

The higher planes

Beyond the third plane of reality lie others, but Myers finds it almost impossible to offer an adequate description of these. The reason for this is simple: they lie beyond human experience at the earthly level and therefore no vocabulary exists in which they can be portrayed. But he makes valiant, if somewhat despairing efforts.

The fourth plane he calls *the world of idealized form*, and when one attains this level, all desire for an earth existence is gone. Here one dwells in a realm from which no traveler returns to earth. Consciousness and existence are more intense and energized than anything we know. This is a world of magnificent, unimaginable beauty in which the mind learns the ultimate mastery of form. Using substances, light, and color unknown on earth, the mind, now god-like in its powers, learns to create an infinite variety of forms having beauty of an ultimate, unsurpassable quality. The beauty of the earth is but a dim and shadowy copy of some of them. The purpose of existence at this plane is to experience all of the possibilities of form so that the evolving soul may pass completely beyond all involvement with it.

Beyond the plane of form lies the plane of flame, in which the soul explores the physical universe beyond the earth, and thus completes its knowledge of matter. Beyond the plane of flame lies the plane of light. Souls who have attained this level have lived in every type of matter and wrought every variety of mentally-created form. They are therefore ready, after uncounted centuries of evolution, *to pass beyond matter and form.* Of such high souls Myers says:

> Souls who enter this last rich kingdom of experience … bear with them the wisdom of form, the incalculable secret wisdom, gathered only through limitation, harvested from numberless years, garnered from lives passed in myriad forms.… They are capable of living now without form, of existing as white light, as … pure thought.[20]

But one step now remains—the final passage to the ultimate plane of being, the achievement of the last goal on an infinitely long path of personal evolution. It is important to remember at this point that Myers was not a religious man. His lifelong commitment was to experience, and to the teachings of experience. When he communicated his account of the higher worlds beyond death, he had personally journeyed as far as the fourth plane. What he reports from beyond the grave he has either experienced himself, or been told of by those more highly evolved than he. Myers called this last goal the seventh plane, and he said that when one enters it, *he becomes a part of God.* He writes:

> The Seventh state … baffles description. It is heart-breaking even to attempt to write of it.… the passage … to the Seventh

> state means … flight from the material universe.… You dwell not only outside of time but outside of the universe on this last plane of being.… [It] might be described as the "passage from form into formlessness." But pray do not misunderstand the term "formlessness." I merely wish to indicate by it an existence that has no need to express itself in a shape, however tenuous, however fine. The soul who enters that Seventh state passes into the Beyond and becomes one with God.[21]

The orthodox medical and scientific view of death is an extremely simple and straightforward one. It holds that when your heart takes its last beat, when your lungs draw their last breath, when your blood pressure drops so low it is unreadable, when your body temperature begins to sink, when your pupils are fixed and dilated—that *you are dead.* By *you* is meant the *real you,* whatever it is that watches and listens, that is aware, that thinks and feels. As any physiologist will tell you, consciousness, personal existence, depend upon a body and a brain, upon a neurophysiology, and when those cease to exist, "you" are no more.

What could possibly dispute such an obvious truth? The answer is: the research reported in this book. And that research makes it perfectly clear that the orthodox medical and scientific view of death is completely wrong, *a gigantic mistake.* The real meaning of human embodiment and death is totally, staggeringly different.

To say, then, that we who now find ourselves on earth in human bodies have much before us would be something of an understatement—for when we have passed beyond the third plane, we will become what men once called gods.

NOTES

Notes Chapter 1

1. Nils O. Jacobson, M.D., *Life Without Death?,* (New York: Dell Publishing Co. Inc., 1974), pp. 129-130.
2. Edmund Gurney, F.W.H. Myers and Frank Podmore, *Phantasms of the Living,* Vol. 1, (London: Trubner and Co., 1886), pp. 532-534.
3. Celia Green and Charles McCreery, *Apparitions,* (London: Hamish Hamilton Ltd., 1975), p. 52.
4. Jacobson, *op. cit.,* pp. 137-139.
5. Andrew M. Greeley, *The Sociology of the Paranormal: A Reconnaissance,* Sage Research Papers in the Social Sciences (Studies in Religion and Ethnicity Series, No. 90-023), (Beverley Hills and London: Sage Publications, 1975).
6. Dr. E. Haraldsson, et al., "National Survey of Psychical Experiences and Attitudes Towards the Paranormal in Iceland," in: W.G. Roll, R.L. Morris and J.D. Morris, eds., *Research in Parapsychology 1976,* (Metuchen, New Jersey: Scarecrow Press, 1977).
7. Allen Spraggett, *The Case for Immortality,* (Scarborough, Ontario: New American Library of Canada Ltd., 1975), p. 58.
8. W. Dewi Rees, "The Hallucinations of Widowhood," *British Medical Journal,* Vol. 4, 1971, pp. 37-41.
9. Earl Dunn, M.D., and Janice Smith, "Ghosts: Their Appearance During Bereavement," *Canadian Family Physician,* October 1977, pp. 121-122. Also, Sidney Katz, "Seeing Ghosts of Loved Ones 'Normal' for Bereaved," *Toronto Daily Star,* December 20, 1977, p. D1.
10. P. Marris, *Widows and Their Families,* (London: Routledge and Kegan Paul Ltd., 1958).
11. Green, *op. cit.,* pp. 190-191.
12. Sir Ernest Bennett, *Apparitions and Haunted Houses: A Survey of Evidence,* (London: Faber and Faber Ltd., 1939). Republished by Gryphon Books, Ann Arbor, Michigan, 1971, pp. 135-136.
13. Andrew MacKenzie, *Apparitions and Ghosts: A Modern Study,* (London: Arthur Barker Ltd., 1971), pp. 26-27.
14. Green, *op. cit.,* pp. 82-83.
15. *Ibid.,* p. 154.

16. *Ibid.*, p. 163.
17. MacKenzie, *op. cit.*, pp. 38-39.
18. Green, *op. cit.*, p. 137.
19. Bennett, *op. cit.*, pp. 382-383.
20. *Ibid.*, p. 382.
21. William Brougham, *Life and Times of Henry, Lord Brougham,* 1871. Cited in Raynor C. Johnson, *The Imprisoned Splendour,* (A Quest Book, Wheaton, Illinois: Theosophical Publishing House, 1971), pp. 198-199.
22. Bennett, *op. cit.*, pp. 131-132.
23. MacKenzie, *op. cit.*, pp. 116-117.
24. *Ibid.*, pp. 94-95.
25. *Journal of the Society for Psychical Research,* Vol. 7. Cited in D. Scott Rogo, *An Experience of Phantoms,* (New York: Taplinger Publishing Co., Inc., 1974), pp. 16-17.
26. Spraggett, *op. cit.*, pp. 45-46.
27. MacKenzie, *op. cit.*, p. 21.
28. Green, *op. cit.*, p. 98.
29. *Ibid.*, p. 190.
30. *Ibid.*, p. 191.
31. *Ibid.*, pp. 188-189.
32. *Ibid.*, pp. 52-53.
33. *Fate,* April, 1972. Cited in Susy Smith, *Life Is Forever,* (New York: Dell Publishing Co. Inc., 1974), pp. 47-48.
34. MacKenzie, *op. cit.*, pp. 87-88.
35. Bennett, *op. cit.*, pp. 350-351.
36. Green, *op. cit.*, pp. 144-145.
37. G.N.M. Tyrrell, *Apparitions,* (New York: Collier Books, 1963), p. 23.
38. Green, *op. cit.*, pp. 123, 49-50, 135.
39. Tyrrell, *op. cit.*, p. 39.
40. Greeley, *op. cit.*
41. Bennett, *op. cit.*, pp. 156-158.
42. *Ibid.*, pp. 62-73.
43. Raymond Bayless, *Apparitions and Survival of Death,* (New Hyde Park, N.Y.: University Books Inc., 1973), pp. 27-38.
44. Bayless, *loc. cit.*, and Hornell Hart (with Ella B. Hart), "Visions and Apparitions Collectively and Reciprocally Perceived," *Proceedings of the Society for Psychical Research,* Vol. 41, 1933, p. 221.
45. MacKenzie, *op. cit.*, p. 56.
46. Isaac Kaufman Funk, *The Psychic Riddle,* (New York: Funk and Wagnalls, Inc., 1907). Cited in Hornell Hart, "Six Theories About

Apparitions," *Proceedings of the Society for Psychical Research,* Vol. 50, Part 185, May 1956, p. 176.

47. Hornell Hart, "Six Theories About Apparitions," *Proceedings of the Society for Psychical Research,* Vol. 50, Part 185, May 1956, pp. 153-239.

Notes Chapter 2

1. *Proceedings of the Society for Psychical Research,* Vol. 2, pp. 144 ff. Cited in Camille Flammarion, *Haunted Houses,* (London: T. Fisher Unwin, Ltd., 1924), p. 141.
2. *Ibid.,* pp. 141-142.
3. *Ibid.,* p. 143.
4. *Loc. cit.*
5. *Ibid.,* p. 144.
6. *Ibid.,* p. 145.
7. *Ibid.,* pp. 148-149.
8. Dr. Robert Morris, *Theta,* #33, #34, (1971-1972). Cited in D. Scott Rogo, *An Experience of Phantoms,* (New York: Taplinger Publishing Co., Inc., 1974), p. 50.
9. Edmund Gurney, *Proceedings of the Society for Psychical Research,* Vol. 3, pp. 126 ff. Cited in Flammarion, *op. cit.,* pp. 265-266.
10. *Ibid.,* p. 266.
11. *Ibid.,* pp. 267-268.
12. Andrew MacKenzie, *Apparitions and Ghosts: A Modern Study,* (London: Arthur Barker Ltd., 1971), pp. 43-44.
13. Hans Holzer, *Tomorrow,* Vol. 1, No. 3. Cited in Hans Holzer, *Ghost Hunter,* (New York: The Bobbs-Merrill Co., Inc., 1963), p. 218.
14. Flammarion, *op. cit.,* p. 210.
15. John Pearce-Higgins, "Poltergeists, Hauntings and Possession," chapter in Canon J.D. Pearce-Higgins and Rev. G. Stanley Whitby, eds., *Life, Death and Psychical Research,* (London: Rider & Co. Ltd., 1973), pp. 178-179.
16. Pearce-Higgins, *op. cit.,* pp. 168-169.
17. Sir William Barrett, "Poltergeists, Old and New," *Proceedings of the Society for Psychical Research,* Vol. 25, August 1911. Cited in A.R.G. Owen, *Can We Explain the Poltergeist?,* (New York: Garrett/Helix, 1964), p. 251.
18. Sir Ernest Bennett, *Apparitions and Haunted Houses: A Survey of Evidence,* (London: Faber and Faber Ltd., 1939). Republished by

Gryphon Books, Ann Arbor, Michigan, 1971, p. 86.
19. *Ibid.*, pp. 86-87.
20. *Ibid.*, pp. 87-88.
21. R.C. Morton, "Record of a Haunted House," *Proceedings of the Society for Psychical Research*, Vol. 8, pp. 311-332. Cited in Bennett, *op. cit.*, pp. 188-190.
22. *Ibid.* Cited in Bennett, *op. cit.*, pp. 191-192.
23. Nils O. Jacobson, M.D., *Life Without Death?*, (New York: Dell Publishing Co. Inc., 1974), pp. 128-129.
24. *Proceedings of the Society for Psychical Research*, Vol. 2, pp. 383 ff. Cited in Flammarion, *op. cit.*, p. 258.
25. Brian Lumley, *Yorkshire Evening Press*, October 10, 1953. Cited in Eric J. Dingwall and Trevor H. Hall, *Four Modern Ghosts*, (London: Gerald Duckworth & Co. Ltd., 1958), pp. 29-30.
26. W.H. Salter, *Ghosts and Apparitions*, (London: G. Bell and Sons Ltd., 1938), p. 105.
27. Andrew MacKenzie, *Frontiers of the Unknown*, (London: Arthur Barker Ltd., 1968). Cited in Susy Smith, *Life Is Forever*, (New York: Dell Publishing Co. Inc., 1977), pp. 48-50.
28. Denys Kelsey, M.D., and Joan Grant, *Many Lifetimes*, (New York: Doubleday & Co. Inc., 1967), pp. 221-224.
29. Celia Green and Charles McCreery, *Apparitions*, (London: Hamish Hamilton Ltd., 1975), p. 65.
30. *Ibid.*, p. 149.
31. Hans Holzer, *Ghost Hunter*, (New York: The Bobbs-Merrill Co., Inc., 1963), pp. 134-137.
32. *Ibid.*, p. 138.
33. *Ibid.*, pp. 138-141.
34. *Ibid.*, pp. 141-142.
35. *Ibid.*, pp. 224-229.
36. Eileen J. Garrett, *Adventures in the Supernormal*, (New York: Creative Age Press, 1949), pp. 207-210.
37. Pearce-Higgins, *op. cit.*, pp. 175-176.
38. *Ibid.*, pp. 177-178.
39. Garrett, *op. cit.*, pp. 115-116.
40. Eileen J. Garrett, *Many Voices*, (New York: G.P. Putnam's Sons, 1968), pp. 77-80.
41. Pearce-Higgins, *op. cit.*, p. 179.
42. Hans Holzer, *Ghosts I've Met*, (New York: The Bobbs-Merrill Co., Inc., 1965), pp. 52-56.

43. Pearce-Higgins, *op. cit.*, pp. 176-177.
44. Garrett, *Adventures in the Supernormal,* pp. 219-220.

Notes Chapter 3

1. Carl Jung, *Memories, Dreams, Reflections,* (New York: Vintage Books, 1963), p. 295.
2. "Psychiatrist says he has seen heaven," *Toronto Daily Star,* October 24, 1970; Allen Spraggett, "People who died, but lived to tell the tale," *Toronto Sunday Sun,* March 31, 1974; *Fate,* Vol. 23, No. 12, December, 1970. Cited in John Pearce-Higgins, "The Nature of Life After Death," Part 2, in Canon J.D. Pearce-Higgins and Rev. G. Stanley Whitby, eds., *Life, Death, and Psychical Research,* (London: Rider & Co. Ltd., 1973), pp. 229-231.
3. Dr. Eugene Osty, *Revue Métapsychique,* May-June, 1930. Cited in C.J. Ducasse, *A Critical Examination of the Belief in a Life After Death,* (Springfield, Illinois: Charles C. Thomas, Publisher, 1961), pp. 161-162.
4. Robert Crookall, "Out-of-the-Body Experiences and Survival," in Pearce-Higgins and Whitby, *op. cit.*, p. 73.
5. Sir Auckland Geddes, M.D., "A Voice from the Grandstand," *The Edinburgh Medical Journal,* N.S., (IVth), Vol. 44, 1937, p. 367.
6. Rosalind Heywood, "Attitudes to Death in the Light of Dreams and Other 'Out-of-the-Body' Experience," in Arnold Toynbee, et al., *Man's Concern With Death,* (London: Hodder & Stoughton, 1968), p. 191.
7. Herbert Greenhouse, *The Astral Journey,* (New York: Avon Books, 1976), pp. 15-16, 18, 179.
8. *Ibid.*, pp. 16-17, 24.
9. Heywood, *op. cit.*, p. 200.
10. *Loc. cit.*
11. Greenhouse, *op. cit.*, p. 330.
12. Crookall, *op. cit.*, p. 13.
13. Crookall, *The Study and Practice of Astral Projection,* (London: Aquarian Press, 1961). Cited in D. Scott Rogo, *The Welcoming Silence,* (Secaucus, New Jersey: University Books, Inc., 1973), p. 15.
14. Celia Green, *Out-of-the-Body Experiences,* (London: Hamish Hamilton Ltd., 1968), pp. 120, 122.
15. Sylvan Muldoon and Hereward Carrington, *The Phenomena of Astral Projection,* (New York: Samuel Weiser, 1970), pp. 186-187.
16. *Ibid.*, p. 177.

17. L. Landau, "An Unusual Out-of-the-Body Experience," *Journal of the Society for Psychical Research,* Vol. 42, 1963, pp. 126-128. Cited in D. Scott Rogo, *An Experience of Phantoms,* (New York: Taplinger Publishing Co., Inc., 1974), p. 120.
18. Greenhouse, *op. cit.,* p. 55.
19. Muldoon and Carrington, *op. cit.,* p. 79.
20. Oliver Fox, *Astral Projection: A Record of Out-of-the-Body Experiences,* (Secaucus, New Jersey: Citadel Press, 1975), pp. 57-59.
21. Sylvan Muldoon and Hereward Carrington, *The Projection of the Astral Body,* (New York: Samuel Weiser, 1970); Oliver Fox, (Hugh Callaway), *Astral Projection: A Record of Out-of-the-Body Experiences;* Yram (Marcel Louis Forhan), *Practical Astral Projection,* (New York: Samuel Weiser, 1967); Robert A. Monroe, *Journeys Out of the Body,* (New York: Doubleday & Co. Inc., 1971).
22. Charles T. Tart, "A Psychophysiological Study of Out-of-the-Body Experiences in a Selected Subject," *Journal of the American Society for Psychical Research,* Vol. 62, No. 1, January, 1968, p. 21.
23. Charles T. Tart, "A Second Psychophysiological Study of Out-of-the-Body Experiences in a Gifted Subject," *Parapsychology,* Vol. 9, December, 1967.
24. Dr. Karlis Osis, in "Proceedings of the First Canadian Conference on Psychokinesis," *New Horizons,* Vol. 1, Number 5, January, 1975, p. 231.
25. *Loc. cit.*
26. *Ibid.*, p. 232.
27. Greenhouse, *op. cit.,* p. 334.
28. David Black, *Ekstasy,* (New York: The Bobbs-Merrill Co., Inc., 1975), pp. 73, 75, 76, 80.
29. Greenhouse, *op. cit.,* pp. 279-292.
30. *Ibid.*, pp. 301-303; Black, *op. cit.*, p. 113.
31. Muldoon and Carrington, *The Phenomena of Astral Projection,* pp. 82-83.
32. Yram (Marcel Louis Forhan), *Practical Astral Projection,* (New York: Samuel Weiser, 1967), p. 58.
33. Green, *op. cit.*, p. 31.
34. *Loc. cit.*
35. *Loc. cit.*
36. *Ibid.,* p. 44.
37. *Ibid.,* pp. 85-86.
38. *Ibid.,* p. 30.
39. Landau, *op. cit.* Cited in Rogo, *op. cit.,* p. 120. (See note 17.)
40. Rogo, *op. cit.,* p. 163.

41. Green, *op. cit.,* p. 32.
42. Robert A. Monroe, *Journeys Out of the Body,* (New York: Doubleday & Co. Inc., 1971), p. 171.
43. Raymond Bayless, *Apparitions and Survival of Death,* (New Hyde Park, N.Y.: University Books, Inc., 1973), p. 153.
44. Green, *op. cit.,* p. 36.
45. Monroe, *op. cit.,* p. 170.
46. Fox, *op. cit.,* p. 129.
47. Douglas M. Baker, *The Techniques of Astral Projection,* printed and published by the author, not paginated, no date.
48. Monroe, *op. cit.*, p. 183.
49. F.W.H. Myers, *Human Personality,* Vol. 2, (London: Longmans, Green & Co., 1903), p. 316.
50. Green, *op. cit.,* p. 30.
51. Muldoon and Carrington, *The Projection of the Astral Body,* pp. 284-285.
52. Caroline D. Larsen, *My Travels in the Spirit World,* (Rutland, Vermont: Charles E. Tuttle Co., 1927). Cited in Muldoon and Carrington, *The Projection of the Astral Body,* pp. 308-309.
53. Fox, *op. cit.,* pp. 77-78.
54. Muldoon and Carrington, *The Phenomena of Astral Projection,* p. 80.
55. Cited in Muldoon and Carrington, *The Phenomena of Astral Projection.*
56. Muldoon and Carrington, *The Projection of the Astral Body,* p. 52.
57. Green, *op. cit.,* p. 69.
58. George H. Hepworth, *Brown Studies,* (no date or publisher given), pp. 243-279. Cited in Muldoon and Carrington, *The Phenomena of Astral Projection,* p. 178.
59. Muldoon and Carrington, *The Phenomena of Astral Projection,* p. 115.
60. Muldoon and Carrington, *The Projection of the Astral Body,* pp. 290-291.
61. Monroe, *op. cit.,* p. 63.
62. *Ibid.*, p. 172.
63. Fox, *op. cit.,* pp. 83-84.
64. Muldoon and Carrington, *The Phenomena of Astral Projection,* p. 151.
65. Green, *op. cit.,* p. 89.
66. *Ibid.,* p. 116.
67. Robert Crookall, *Out-of-the-Body Experiences: A Fourth Analysis,* (New York: University Books, Inc., 1970), p. 120.
68. D. Scott Rogo, *The Welcoming Silence,* (Secaucus, New Jersey: University Books, Inc., 1973), p. 45.
69. Monroe, *op. cit.,* pp. 108-111.
70. Raymond Bayless, *The Other Side of Death,* (New Hyde Park, N.Y.:

University Books, Inc., 1971), pp. 108-120.
71. Muldoon and Carrington, *The Phenomena of Astral Projection,* p. 215.
72. *Ibid.,* pp. 119-120.
73. George P. Hare, *Revue des Etudes Psychiques,* 1902. Cited in Muldoon and Carrington, *The Phenomena of Astral Projection,* pp. 168-169.
74. Muldoon and Carrington, *The Phenomena of Astral Projection,* p. 125.
75. Monroe, *op. cit.*, pp 160-161.
76. James H. Hyslop, *Journal of the American Society for Psychical Research,* August, 1919. Cited in Rogo, *The Welcoming Silence,* p. 44.
77. Brad Steiger, *In My Soul I Am Free,* (New York: Lancer Books, 1968).
78. Monroe, *op. cit.,* p. 189.
79. *Ibid.,* p. 83.

Notes Chapter 4

1. Wilma S. Ashby, "My Personal Miracle," *Fate,* June, 1972, p. 102.
2. Dr. Karlis Osis and Dr. Erlendur Haraldsson, *At the Hour of Death,* (New York: Avon Books, 1977), p. 99.
3. Sir William Barrett, *Death-Bed Visions,* (London: Methuen & Co Ltd., 1926), p. 28.
4. Osis and Haraldsson, *op. cit.,* p. 169.
5. *Ibid.,* p. 164.
6. Osis and Haraldsson, *op. cit.,* p. 127.
7. Francis Power Cobbe, "The Peak in Darien: The Riddle of Death," *Littell's Living Age and New Quarterly Review,* Vol. 134, 1877, pp. 374-379; Dr. James H. Hyslop, *Psychical Research and the Resurrection,* Chapter 4: "Visions of the Dying," (Boston: Small, Maynard & Co., 1908); Sir William Barrett, *Death-Bed Visions;* Dr. Karlis Osis, *Deathbed Observations by Physicians and Nurses,* (New York: Parapsychology Foundation, 1961); Dr. Karlis Osis and Dr. Erlendur Haraldsson, "Deathbed Observations by Physicians and Nurses: A Cross-Cultural Survey," *Journal of the American Society for Psychical Research,* Vol. 71, No. 3, July, 1977, pp. 237-259; Osis and Haraldsson, *At the Hour of Death.*
8. E.H. Clarke, *Visions, A Study of False Sight,* (Boston: Houghton, Osgood and Co., The Riverside Press, Cambridge, 1878), p. 277.
9. Dr. E.H. Pratt, *Journal of the American Society for Psychical Research,* 1918, Vol. 12, p. 623. Cited in Barrett, *op. cit.,* pp. 67-69.
10. Dr. James H. Hyslop, *Psychical Research and the Resurrection,* (Boston: Small, Maynard & Co., 1908), pp. 97-98.

11. Osis and Haraldsson, *At the Hour of Death,* p. 34.
12. M. Pelusi, *Luce e Ombra,* 1920, 20. Cited in Barrett, *op. cit.,* pp. 75-76.
13. Osis and Haraldsson, *At the Hour of Death,* pp. 66-67.
14. *Journal of the Society for Psychical Research,* February, 1904, pp. 185-187.
15. *Proceedings of the Society for Psychical Research,* Vol. 6, p. 20.
16. Dr. Walter Franklin Prince, *Noted Witnesses for Psychic Occurrences,* (Boston: Boston Society for Psychical Research, 1928), pp. 144-150.
17. Susy Smith, *Life Is Forever,* (New York: Dell Publishing Co., Inc., 1974), pp. 67-68.
18. Dr. Minot J. Savage, *Psychic Facts and Theories.* Cited in Hyslop, *op. cit.,* pp. 88-89.
19. Barrett, *op. cit.,* p. 14.
20. Smith, *op. cit.,* p. 74.
21. R. DeWitt Miller, *You DO Take It With You,* (New York: Citadel Press, 1955), p. 193.
22. Dr. Karlis Osis, *Deathbed Observations by Physicians and Nurses,* (New York: Parapsychology Foundation, 1961), p. 44.
23. Osis and Haraldsson, *At the Hour of Death,* p. 185.
24. J. Palmer and M. Dennis, "A Community Mail Survey of Psychic Experiences," in W.G. Roll, R.L. Morris, and J.D. Morris, eds., *Research in Parapsychology 1974,* (Metuchen, New Jersey: Scarecrow Press, Inc., 1975), pp. 130-133; H. Sidgwick, et al., "Report on the Census of Hallucinations," *Proceedings of the Society for Psychical Research,* Vol. 10, 1894, pp. 25-422; D.J. West, "A Mass Observation Questionnaire on Hallucinations," *Journal of the Society for Psychical Research,* Vol. 34, 1948, pp. 187-196.
25. Osis, *op. cit.,* p. 37.
26. Osis and Haraldsson, *At the Hour of Death,* pp. 64-65.
27. *Ibid.,* p. 109.
28. *Ibid.,* p. 91.
29. Osis, *op. cit.,* p. 84.
30. Osis and Haraldsson, *At the Hour of Death,* p. 162.
31. *Loc. cit.*
32. *Ibid.,* pp. 162-163.
33. *Ibid.,* p. 165.
34. *Ibid.,* p. 169.
35. Joy Snell, *The Ministry of Angels,* (London: G. Bell and Sons Ltd., 1918). Cited in Barrett, *op. cit.,* pp. 109-110.
36. Research on psychic experiences shows that they come from a realm beyond the five senses with which the body is equipped. Hence when

they are "translated" into visual images, these images may be only reflections or symbolizations of the underlying reality they represent (see Osis and Haraldsson, *At the Hour of Death,* p. 54). Hence, although the dying psychically perceive "heaven" as beautiful, this beauty is conveyed to them in a *variety* of visual images.

The third deathbed phenomenon, a sudden rise in mood to serenity or exaltation shortly before death, can also be readily explained as psychic in origin. Research on ESP shows that knowledge which is acquired by psychic sensitivity may not reach the receiver's consciousness, but it can influence his emotions (see Osis and Haraldsson, p. 139). Thus, subconscious awareness of tragedy can cause dramatically strong anxiety and depression, while the same awareness of happy events can cause exhilaration. (So, for example, a mother whose son has just been killed in some distant place may feel deeply depressed *before* she is told of his death.) Hence the apparently inexplicable exhilaration and serenity of the dying is caused by their subconscious awareness of the beautiful after-death world which they are about to enter.

37. Osis, *op. cit., p.* 84.
38. *Ibid.*, p. 48; Osis and Haraldsson, *At the Hour of Death,* pp. 71, 187.
39. Osis, *op. cit.*, p. 48; Osis and Haraldsson, *At the Hour of Death,* p. 71.
40. Osis and Haraldsson, *op. cit.,* pp. 72, 171.
41. Osis, *op. cit.*, p. 53; Osis and Haraldsson, *At the Hour of Death,* pp. 73, 134.
42. By "afterlife" visions I mean three types of experience which suggest there may be life after death: apparitions of close dead relatives or religious figures who are there to take the dying person away; landscape visions of unearthly beauty; and medically inexplicable mood elevations just before death.
43. Osis and Haraldsson, *At the Hour of Death,* p. 188.
44. *Ibid.*, pp. 85, 174.
45. *Ibid.*, p. 174.
46. *Ibid.*, pp. 86-87.
47. *Ibid.*, pp. 75, 123.
48. *Ibid.*, p. 170.
49. *Ibid.*, pp. 94, 173-174.
50. *Ibid.*, p. 173.
51. *Ibid.*, pp. 117, 193.
52. *Ibid.*, pp. 189-190.

Notes Chapter 5

1. Raymond A. Moody, Jr., *Life After Life,* (Atlanta: Mockingbird Books, 1975), p. 65.
2. Robert Crookall, *The Supreme Adventure,* (London: James Clarke & Co. Ltd., 1961), pp. 8-9.
3. Moody, *op. cit.,* p. 17.
4. Caresse Crosby, *The Passionate Years,* (New York: The Dial Press, 1953), pp. 18-19. Cited in Russell Noyes, Jr., "The Experience of Dying," Psychiatry, Vol. 35, May, 1972, pp. 176-177.
5. Russell Noyes, Jr., and Roy Kletti, "Depersonalization in the Face of Life-Threatening Danger: An Interpretation," *Omega*, Vol. 7(2), 1976, pp. 105-106.
6. David R. Wheeler, *Journey to the Other Side*, (New York: Ace Books, 1977), pp. 54-56.
7. *Ibid.,* pp. 97-98.
8. *Ibid.,* pp. 94-106.
9. Tom Harpur, "I floated away from my body, says man who 'died' in hospital," *The Toronto Star,* April 2, 1977, pp. A1, A4.
10. Wheeler, *op. cit.,* p. 42.
11. Dr. B. Kirkwood, *Light*, Vol. 55, 1935, p. 226. Cited in Crookall, *op. cit.,* p. 108.
12. Moody, *op. cit.,* p. 29.
13. *Ibid.,* p. 31.
14. *Ibid.,* p. 32.
15. *Ibid.,* p. 34.
16. *Loc. cit.*
17. Kenneth L. Woodward, "There Is Life After Death," *McCall's,* August, 1976, p. 134.
18. Moody, *op. cit.,* pp. 35-36.
19. *Ibid.,* p. 37.
20. *Loc. cit.*
21. Woodward, *op. cit.*, p. 136.
22. Moody, *op. cit.,* p. 41.
23. Wheeler, *op. cit.,* pp. 150-151.
24. Moody, *op. cit.,* p. 44.
25. Wheeler, *op. cit.*, p. 42.
26. Moody, *op. cit.,* p. 45.

27. More accurately, many but not all of the dying report this experience. In some cases, it seems reasonable to conclude that this being was present,

but not fully visible. For example, Arthur Sanders said of his encounter with death, "I seemed to be led on by a kind of shining mist that hovered near."

28. Moody, *op. cit.*, p. 46.
29. *Ibid.*, p. 48.
30. *Ibid.*, pp. 48-49.
31. Dr. Crookall is a distinguished English geologist who has written numerous books in the field of psychical research. Professor Heim, an eminent Swiss scholar and also a geologist, and Father Thurston, a Roman Catholic priest with a scholarly interest in psychical research, have both published papers on the phenomenon of "life review" at death. Dr. Hunter, a psychiatrist, published a case-study of a death-experience involving a life review.

    See Moody, *op. cit.*, pp. 49-54; Russell Noyes, Jr., "Dying and Mystical Consciousness," *Journal of Thanatology*, Vol. 1, January-February, 1971, pp. 25-41; Noyes, "The Experience of Dying," *Psychiatry*, Vol. 35, May, 1972, pp. 174-184; Noyes, and Roy Kletti, "Depersonalization in the Face of Life-Threatening Danger: A Description," *Psychiatry*, Vol. 39, February, 1976, pp. 19-27; Noyes and Kletti, "Depersonalization in the Face of life-Threatening Danger: An Interpretation," *Omega*, Vol. 7(2), 1976, pp. 103-114; Crookall, *The Supreme Adventure*, pp. 86-91, 166-167; Albert Heim, "Remarks on Fatal Falls," *Yearbook of the Swiss Alpine Club*, Vol. 27, 1892, pp. 327-337, translated by Noyes and Kletti in "The Experience of Dying From Falls," *Omega*, Vol. 3, 1972, pp. 45-52; R.C.A. Hunter, "On the Experience of Nearly Dying," *American Journal of Psychiatry*, 124:1, July 1967, pp. 84-88; Father Herbert Thurston, S.J., "Memory at Death," *The Month*, Vol. 165, 1935, pp. 49-60.
32. Moody, *op. cit.*, pp. 50-51.
33. *Ibid.*, pp. 52-53.
34. Noyes and Kletti interviewed fifty-nine people who found themselves in this situation. Among their findings were that 54 percent had out-of-the-body experiences, 47 percent underwent the "life review," and 37 percent felt themselves to be in the presence or under the control of an outside force (Noyes and Kletti, "Depersonalization in the Face of Life-Threatening Danger: A Description," p. 20). That this "force" is probably the "being of light" is suggested by the comments of some of those who have encountered it.
35. Father John Gerard, *The Month*, 1913, p. 126. Cited in Crookall, *The Supreme Adventure*, p. 89.
36. Oscar Pfister, "Shockdenken und Shock – Phantasien bei Höchster

Todesgefahr," *Internat. Z. Psychoanal.*, Vol. 16, 1930, p. 434. Cited in Noyes, "The Experience of Dying," p. 175; Albert Heim, *op. cit.*, p. 50.

37. Father Herbert Thurston, S.J., "Memory at Death," *The Month*, Vol. 165, 1935. Cited in Crookall, *The Supreme Adventure*, pp. 89-90.
38. Moody, *op. cit.*, pp. 49-54.
39. Personal interview.
40. Crosby, *op. cit.*, pp. 18-19.
41. Harpur, *op. cit.*, p. A1.
42. Noyes and Kletti, "Depersonalization in the Face of Life-Threatening Danger: An Interpretation," p. 112.
43. *Ibid.*, pp. 108, 111.
44. *Ibid.*, p. 111.
45. Oliver Fox, *Astral Projection: A Record of Out-of-the-Body Experiences*, p. 144; Muldoon and Carrington, *The Phenomena of Astral Projection*, pp. 178, 218; Muldoon and Carrington, *The Projection of the Astral Body*, pp. 28-29, 233; Monroe, *Journeys Out-of-the-Body*, pp. 123-125; Yram, *Practical Astral Projection*, pp. 49-50, 63, 84-85, 119; Janet Bord, *Astral Projection*, (New York: Samuel Weiser, 1973), p. 47; Nils O. Jacobson, M.D., *Life Without Death?* (New York: Dell Publishing Co. Inc., 1974), pp. 115, 121, 122; Crookall, *Out-of-the-Body Experiences: A Fourth Analysis*, pp. 13, 124; Celia Green, *Out-of-the-Body Experiences*, (London: Hamish Hamilton Ltd., 1968), pp. 83, 87.
46. Celia Green, *Out-of-the-Body Experiences*, (London: Hamish Hamilton, 1968), p. 87.
47. Moody, *op. cit.*, p. 61.
48. *Ibid.*, pp. 69-70.
49. *Ibid.*, p. 127.
50. *Ibid.*, p. 98.
51. Crookall, *The Supreme Adventure.*
52. Moody, *op. cit.*, p. 76.

Notes Chapter 6

1. Alan Vaughan, "Phantoms Stalked the Room...," in Martin Ebon, ed., *The Satan Trap: Dangers of the Occult*, (Garden City, N.Y.: Doubleday & Co. Inc., 1976), pp. 155-156.
2. *Ibid.*, pp. 158-159.
3. *Ibid.*, p. 160.
4. Dr. James H. Hyslop, *Contact With the Other World*, (New York: The

Century Company, 1919), p. 204.

5. *Ibid.,* p. 226.
6. Joy Snell, *The Ministry of Angels,* Greater World Association, p. 97. Cited in Cynthia Pettiward, *The Case for Possession,* (Bucks, England: Colin Smythe Ltd., 1975), pp. 77-78.
7. Raymond A. Moody, Jr., M.D., *Reflections On Life After Life,* (New York: Bantam/Mockingbird Books, 1977), pp. 19-21.
8. *Ibid.,* p. 21.
9. *Ibid.,* pp. 21-22.
10. Carl A. Wickland, M.D., *Thirty Years Among the Dead,* (London: Spiritualist Press, first published in 1924, this edition 1971); Dr. Walter Franklin Prince, "The Cure of Two Cases of Paranoia," *Bulletin 6,* 1927, Boston Society for Psychical Research; Dr. James H. Hyslop, *Contact With the Other World* ,Chapter 14: Robert Swain Gifford, and Chapter 24: Obsession; Dr. Wilson Van Dusen, "The Presence of Spirits in Madness," *New Philosophy,* 70, 1967, pp. 461-477 and Chapter 10: "Hallucinations," in *The Natural Depth in Man,* (New York: Harper and Row, Publishers, Inc., 1972), pp. 136-153; Dr. Inacio Ferreira, *Novos Rumos à Medicina, [New Pathways in Medicine],* A Flama, Brazil, Vol. 1, 1946, Vol. 2, 1949, cited in Pettiward, *op. cit.;* John Pearce-Higgins, "Poltergeists, Hauntings and Possession," in Canon J.D. Pearce-Higgins and Rev. G. Stanley Whitby, eds., *Life, Death and Psychical Research,* (London: Rider and Co., 1973), pp. 164-192, and John Pearce-Higgins, "Just Don't Call Me an Exorcist!" in Martin Ebon, *The Devil's Bride: Exorcism: Past and Present,* (New York: Harper and Row, Publishers, Inc., 1974), pp. 200-218; Paul Beard, "How to Guard Against Obsession," in Ebon, *The Satan Trap: Dangers of the Occult,* (Garden City, N.Y.: Doubleday & Co. Inc., 1976), pp. 187-190, (originally appeared under the title "How to Guard Against 'Possession,'" in *Spiritual Frontiers,* Autumn, 1970.)
11. Wickland, *op. cit.*
12. In "automatic writing" an individual tries to relax as completely as possible while loosely holding a pen, pencil, or planchette (a small board on castors with pencil attached) over a sheet of paper. As a rule, there is, for some time, no result, but if sufficient patience is employed, the pencil seems almost to begin writing of its own accord. Psychiatrists attribute the resulting "messages" to the subconscious mind, while spiritualists claim that they emanate from the dead. Both are probably correct. People who have had considerable experience with this phenomenon seem to agree that it is *potentially extremely dangerous*: as we will later see, it frequently leads to possession. On the other hand, it

must also be said that some apparently authentic and extremely interesting scripts have been received from deceased persons by this method. Perhaps the most interesting are extensive accounts of the nature of post-mortem existence.

13. Wickland, *op. cit.*, pp. 43-47.
14. *Ibid.*, pp. 95-101.
15. *Ibid.*, pp. 102-103.
16. *Ibid.*, pp. 39-40.
17. Cyril Scott, ed., *The Boy Who Saw True,* (London: Neville Spearman), pp. 42-44. Cited in Cynthia Pettiward, *The Case for Possession,* (Bucks, England: Colin Smythe Ltd., 1975), pp. 75-76.
18. Dr. Walter Franklin Prince, "The Cure of Two Cases of Paranoia," *Bulletin 6,* 1927, Boston Society for Psychical Research. Cited in Nils O. Jacobson, M.D., *Life Without Death?,* (New York: Dell Publishing Co. Inc., 1974), pp. 184-187.
19. Alan Gauld, "A Series of 'Drop In' Communicators," *Proceedings of the Society for Psychical Research,* Vol. 55, Part 204, July, 1971, pp. 306-309.
20. *Mediale Schriften,* (Therese Krauss Publishers, 1968). Cited in *Light,* Spring, 1972, p. 31. Cited in Pettiward, *op. cit.,* pp. 47-48. (Adler was an Austrian psychiatrist and pupil of Freud.)
21. A guide is a discarnate connected with a living human being for benevolent purposes. In the case of mediums such as Miss Cummins, one of the chief functions of a guide is the protection of the medium from discarnates who may attempt to harm her.
22. Raymond Bayless, *The Other Side of Death,* (New Hyde Park, N.Y.: University Books, Inc., 1971), pp. 161-162.
23. Robert H. Ashby, "The Guru Syndrome," in Martin Ebon, ed., *The Satan Trap: Dangers of the Occult,* (Garden City, N.Y.: Doubleday & Co. Inc., 1976), pp. 38-39.
24. Paul Beard, "How to Guard Against Obsession," in Ebon, *op. cit.,* pp. 187-189; originally appeared under the title "How to Guard Against 'Possession'" in *Spiritual Frontiers,* Autumn 1970.
25. *Ibid.,* p. 190.
26. Dr. Grof, who was born and educated in Czechoslovakia, is almost certainly the world's foremost expert on LSD and "psychedelic" therapy, which employs these powerful drugs in a therapeutic setting in order to release repressed material and permit the patient to plumb the subconscious mind. The incident was described in a presentation which he made on "psychedelic therapy" at a conference on "Consciousness and Healing" held at the University of Toronto in October of 1976. As I

recount Grof's experience from memory, my version may be inaccurate in minor details.

Notes Chapter 7

1. Joan Grant, *Far Memory,* (New York: Harper & Row, Publishers, Inc., 1956), p. 155.
2. Helen Wambach, PH.D., *Reliving Past Lives: The Evidence Under Hypnosis,* (New York: Harper & Row, Publishers, Inc., 1978), pp. 43-44. (As this pagination is taken from pre-publication galley proofs, it may not correspond with that of the published manuscript.)
3. Ian Stevenson, M.D., *Twenty Cases Suggestive of Reincarnation,* Second Edition, (Charlottesville: University Press of Virginia, 1974), pp. 91, 103. For further examples of this type of case, see also Stevenson, *Cases of the Reincarnation Type, Volume I, Ten Cases in India,* (Charlottesville: University Press of Virginia, 1975).
4. *Ibid.,* p. 101.
5. Nils O. Jacobson, M.D., *Life Without Death?,* (New York: Dell Publishing Co. Inc., 1974), pp. 209-210.
6. *Ibid.,* pp. 207-209.
7. Grant, *op. cit.,* pp. 154-155.
8. Stevenson, *op. cit.,* p. 260.
9. *Ibid.,* p. 261.
10. *Ibid.,* p. 262.
11. *Ibid.,* p. 117.
12. Jeffrey Iverson, *More Lives Than One? The Evidence of the Remarkable Bloxham Tapes,* (New York: Warner Books, Inc., 1977), p. 18.
13. *Ibid.,* p. 23.
14. *Loc. cit.*
15. Wambach, *op. cit.,* p. 2.
16. *Ibid.,* pp. 9-10.
17. Denys-Kelsey, M.D., and Joan Grant, *Many Lifetimes,* (New York: Doubleday & Co. Inc.), pp. 157-158.
18. *Ibid.,* pp. 100-102.
19. *Ibid.,* pp. 72-74.
20. *Ibid.,* pp. 74-75.
21. Iverson, *op. cit.,* pp. 66-67.
22. *Ibid.,* p. 75.
23. *Ibid.,* p. 39.

24. *Ibid.*, pp. 202-203.
25. Loring G. Williams, "Reincarnation of a Civil War Victim," *Fate,* December, 1966. Cited in Brad Steiger and Loring G. Williams, *Other Lives,* (New York: Award Books, 1969), p. 7.
26. Brad Steiger and Loring G. Williams, *Other Lives,* (New York: Award Books, 1969), pp. 52-53.
27. Ian Stevenson, M.D., *Xenoglossy: A Review and Report of a Case,* (Charlottesville: University Press of Virginia, 1974), pp. 27-28.
28. *Ibid.*, p. 32.
29. *Ibid.*, p. v-vi.
30. Wambach, *op. cit.,* pp. 89-90.
31. James Crenshaw, "Hang-ups from Past Lives," *Fate*, April, 1978, pp. 57-58.
32. Wambach, *op. cit.,* p. 125.
33. *Ibid.*, pp. 68-69.
34. *Ibid.*, p. 101.
35. *Ibid.*, p. 107.
36. *Ibid.*, p. 108.
37. *Loc. cit.*
38. *Ibid.*, p. 104.
39. *Ibid.*, p. 115.
40. *Ibid.*, p. 192.
41. Crenshaw, *op. cit.,* p. 58.
42. Wambach, *op. cit.,* p. 80.
43. Steiger and Williams, *op. cit.,* p. 127.
44. *Ibid.*, p. 140-141.
45. Gina Cerminara, PH.D., *Many Mansions,* (New York: New American Library, 1967), pp. 20-21.
46. *Ibid.*, p. 26.
47. *Ibid.*, pp. 58-59.
48. *Ibid.*, p. 59.
49. *Ibid.*, p. 51.
50. *Ibid.*, p. 52.
51. Helen Wambach, PH.D., "Life Before Life," *Psychic,* January/February, 1977, Vol. 7, No. 6, p. 10.
52. *Ibid.*, p. 11.
53. *Loc. cit.*
54. *Loc. cit.*
55. Helen Wambach, PH.D., *Life Before Life: Choosing To Be Born,* Chapter 9, p. 20. (This quotation is from a pre-publication manuscript, courtesy

of the author.)
56. Wambach, "Life Before Life," p. 11.
57. Wambach, *Life Before Life: Choosing To Be Born*, Chapter 9, pp. 19-20.
58. Wambach, "Life Before Life," p. 11.
59. Wambach, *Life Before Life: Choosing To Be Born*, Chapter 5, p. 22.
60. *Ibid.*, Chapter 5, pp. 22-23.
61. Wambach, "Life Before Life," p. 12.
62. *Ibid.*, p. 13.
63. *Loc. cit.*
64. *Ibid.*, p. 11.
65. *Loc. cit.*
66. *Ibid.*, p. 13.
67. *Loc. cit.*
68. *Loc. cit.*
69. *Ibid.*, pp. 11-12.
70. *Ibid.*, p. 12.

Notes Chapter 8

1. Geraldine Cummins, *Mind in Life and Death*, (London: The Aquarian Press, 1956), p. 163.
2. Naomi A. Hintze and J. Gaither Pratt, PH.D., *The Psychic Realm: What Can You Believe?*, (New York: Random House, 1975), pp. 211-214.
3. Rosalind Heywood, *Beyond the Reach of Sense*, (New York: E.P. Dutton, 1961), pp. 71, 74, 79.
4. *Ibid.*, pp. 84-85.
5. Jalaluddin Rumi, *The Mathnawi*, R.A. Nicholson, translator, (London: Cambridge University Press, 1926). Cited in Nils O. Jacobson, M.D., *Life Without Death?* (New York: Dell Publishing Co. Inc., 1974), p. 334.
6. Denys Kelsey, M.D., and Joan Grant, *Many Lifetimes*, (Garden City, N.Y.: Doubleday & Co. Inc., 1967), p. 2.
7. Jane Roberts, *The Seth Material*, (Englewood Cliffs, N.J.: Prentice-Hall Inc., 1970), pp. 275-277.
8. Stanislav Grof, M.D., *Realms of the Human Unconscious: Observations from LSD Research*, (New York: E.P. Dutton, 1976), p. 176.
9. *Ibid.*, pp. 171-173.
10. *Ibid.*, pp. 181-182.
11. *Ibid.*, p. 184.
12. *Loc. cit.*

13. Geraldine Cummins, *The Road To Immortality,* (London: Psychic Press, originally published 1932, this edition 1967), pp. 31-32.
14. *Ibid.,* p. 189.
15. Geraldine Cummins, *Beyond Human Personality,* (London: Ivor Nicholson & Watson, 1935), p. 67.
16. *Quarterly Review of the Churches' Fellowship for Psychical and Spiritual Studies,* Autumn, 1972. Cited in Allen Spraggett, *The Case for Immortality,* (New York: New American Library, 1974), pp. 91-92.
17. Geraldine Cummins, *Beyond Human Personality,* p. 29, and Geraldine Cummins, *The Road To Immortality,* p. 47.
18. Geraldine Cummins, *Beyond Human Personality,* p. 79.
19. *Light,* Vol. 55, 1935, p. 100. Cited in Robert Crookall, *The Supreme Adventure,* (London: James Clarke & Co. Ltd., 1961), p. 45.
20. Cummins, *The Road To Immortality,* p. 71.
21. *Ibid.,* pp. 72-73.

Acknowledgments

The Author wishes to thank the following for permission to reprint material included in this book: *Fate Magazine* for excerpts from "My Personal Miracle" by Wilma S. Ashby. University Books, Inc., 120 Enterprise Avenue, Secaucus, New Jersey 07094 for excerpts from *Apparitions And Survival Of Death* and *The Other Side Of Death,* by Raymond Bayless and *Astral Projection: A Record Of Out-Of-The-Body Experiences* by Oliver Fox. Sir Frederic Bennett for excerpts from *Apparitions and Haunted Houses: A Survey of Evidence* by Sir Ernest Bennett. William Morrow & Company for excerpts from *Many Mansions* by Gina Cerminara. Copyright © 1950 by Gina Cerminara. Psychic Press Limited for excerpts from *The Road To Immortality* by Geraldine Cummins. *Fate Magazine* for excerpts from "Hang-ups From Past Lives" by James Crenshaw. James Clarke & Co. Ltd. for excerpts from *The Supreme Adventure* by Robert Crookall. Citadel Press for excerpts from *You DO Take It With You* by R. DeWitt Miller. Charles C. Thomas, Publisher, Springfield, Illinois for excerpts from *A Critical Examination Of The Belief In A Life After Death* by C.J. Ducasse published in 1961. The Society for Psychical Research for excerpts from *Proceedings, July 1971,* "A Series Of 'Drop In' Communicators," by Alan Gauld. *Scottish Medical Journal* for excerpts from "A Voice from the Grandstand" by Sir Auckland Geddes. Institute of Psychophysical Research, Oxford, for excerpts from *Out-of-the-Body Experiences* by Celia Green. *The Toronto Star* for excerpts from "I Floated

Away From My Body" by Tom Harpur, and for excerpts from "Psychiatrist Says He Has Seen Heaven." Chatto and Windus Ltd. for excerpts from *Beyond the Reach of Sense* by Rosalind Heywood. Random House, Inc. for excerpts from *The Psychic Realm: What Can You Believe?* by Naomi Hintze and J. Gaither Pratt, PH.D. Hans Holzer for excerpts from *Ghost Hunter.* Copyright © 1963 by Hans Holzer. Hans Holzer for excerpts from *Ghosts I've Met.* Copyright © 1965 by Hans Holzer. Hodder & Stoughton Limited for excerpts from *The Imprisoned Splendour* by Raynor C. Johnson. Doubleday & Company, Inc. for excerpts from *Many Lifetimes* by Denys Kelsey, M.D. and Joan Grant. Copyright © 1967 by Denys Kelsey and Joan Grant. The Society for Psychical Research for excerpts from *Journal, 1963,* "An Unusual Out-Of-The-Body Experience" by L. Landau. The *Yorkshire Evening Press* for excerpts by Brian Lumley. A.M. Heath & Company Ltd. for excerpts from *Apparitions and Ghosts: A Modern Study* and *Frontiers of the Unknown* by Andrew MacKenzie. Doubleday & Company, Inc. for excerpts from *Journeys Out of The Body* by Robert A. Monroe. Copyright © 1971 by Robert A. Monroe. Mockingbird Books Inc. for excerpts from *Life After Life and Reflections On Life After Life* by Dr. Raymond Moody. Samuel Weiser, Inc., New York, for excerpts from *The Phenomena Of Astral Projection* and *The Projection Of The Astral Body* by Sylvan Muldoon and Hereward Carrington. Delacorte Press /Seymour Lawrence for excerpts from *Life Without Death?: On Parapsychology, Mysticism, and the Question of Survival* by Nils-Olof Jacobson. Translated by Sheila LaFarge. Translation Copyright © 1974 by Dell Publishing Co., Inc. Avon Books, New York for excerpts from *At The Hour Of Death* by Karlis Osis, PH.D. and Erlendur Haraldsson, PH.D. Copyright © 1977 by Dr. Karlis Osis and Dr. Erlendur Haraldsson. The College of Psychic Studies, 16 Queensbury Place, London SW7, for excerpts from an article by Wyatt Rawson in *Light.* Prentice-Hall, Inc. for excerpts from *The Seth Material* by Jane Roberts. Copyright © 1970 by Jane Roberts. Cambridge University Press for excerpts from *The Mathnawi* by Jalaluddin Rumi, translated by R.A. Nicholson. Neville Spearman Ltd. for excerpts from *The Boy Who Saw True,* edited by Cyril Scott. *Toronto Sun* for excerpts from "People Who Died But Lived To Tell The Tale" by Allen Spraggett. Hawthorn Books, Inc. for excerpts from *Other Lives* by Brad Steiger and Loring G. Williams. *New Realities Magazine,* 680 Beach Street, San Francisco, Ca. 94109 for excerpts from "Life Before Life" by Helen Wambach, PH.D. Grosset & Dunlap, Inc. for excerpts from *Journey to the Other Side* by David R. Wheeler. Copyright © 1976 by David R. Wheeler. Spiritualist Press for excerpts from *Thirty Years Among The Dead* by Dr. Carl A. Wickland.